CONQUERING
DEPRESSION AND ANXIETY
THROUGH
EXERCISE

"In this meticulously researched and elegantly written book, Keith Johnsgard convincingly demonstrates that exercise is good for body *and soul*. Required reading for anyone looking for a safe, effective, inexpensive way to manage moods, assuage anxiety, and enhance mental health."

—Carol Krucoff
Founding Editor, *Washington Post* Health Section

"We are not just a nation growing fatter; we are also a nation growing evermore anxious, depressed, and stressed out. Fortunately, Keith Johnsgard's exceptional new book has a solution to all these ills—exercise. It's simple, it's research based, and it works. What are your waiting for?"

—Amby Burfoot
Executive Editor, *Runner's World*

"This gem of a book contains a wealth of information. [. . .]Reading *Conquering Depression and Anxiety Through Exercise* is a personal treat for readers who seek research-based insight into the psychological beneficence of physical activity!"

—Bonnie G. Berger, EdD
Professor and Director,
School of Human Movement, Sport, and Leisure Studies at Bowling Green
State University
Fellow and Certified Consultant,
Association for the Advancement of Applied Sport Psychology

"The critical role that exercise plays in our negotiation of the depression and anxiety which permeate too many lives cannot be overemphasized. Johnsgard has been one of the global leaders in the exposition. This book is the latest update of his lifelong exploration of the topic."

—Walter M. Bortz, MD
Stanford School of Medicine
Board Chair, Fifty-Plus Lifelong Fitness

"[E]xcellent. [. . .]His personal background, clinical experience, and up-to-date knowledge of the research situation makes him the expert you want to consult. Johnsgard is wise, caring, enthusiastic about how we can change our lives. [. . .] Johnsgard's book may help change the lives of many people who suffer from depression and anxiety."

—Gunnar Breivik
Rector of Norwegian University of Sport and Physical Education

"This book shows how the demons of anxiety and depression can be reduced or overcome by making exercise a staple in one's life. It connects the clinical world of exercise research and the actual experience of 'feeling good' when you exercise and is valuable reading for skeptics."

—Jim Woollett
Past President, Fifty-Plus Lifelong Fitness

KEITH JOHNSGARD

CONQUERING
DEPRESSION AND ANXIETY
THROUGH
EXERCISE

Prometheus Books

59 John Glenn Drive
Amherst, New York 14228-2119

ALSO BY THE AUTHOR

The Exercise Prescription for Depression and Anxiety

DEDICATION

For my kids, Paula, Mark, and Kris
Each one a source of great pride
Each one a hero in my eyes

And for all coyotes, everywhere

Published 2004 by Prometheus Books

Inquiries should be addressed to
Prometheus Books
59 John Glenn Drive
Amherst, New York 14228–2119
VOICE: 716–691–0133, ext. 210
FAX: 716–691–0137
WWW.PROMETHEUSBOOKS.COM

12   5 4 3

Library of Congress Cataloging-in-Publication Data

Johnsgard, Keith W.
    Conquering depression and anxiety through exercise / Keith Johnsgard.
        p. cm.
    Includes bibliographical references.
    ISBN 978–1–59102–192–6 (pbk. : alk. paper)
    1. Depression, Mental—Treatment. 2. Exercise—Health aspects. I. Title.
RC537.J638 2004
616.85'2706—dc22

                                                        2004003898

Printed in the United States on acid-free paper

Man is a fraction of the animal world. Our history is an afterthought, no more, tacked to an infinite calendar. We are not as unique as we should like to believe. And if man in a time of need seeks deeper knowledge concerning himself, then he must explore those animal horizons from which we have made our quick little march.

—Robert Ardrey, *African Genesis*

CONTENTS

FOREWORD

What does it mean to conquer something? Typically, we think of a battle, the use of force, overcoming an enemy. Those are indeed all definitions of "conquer"; however, if you look more thoroughly, you will discover that there are other meanings, ones that may be more subtle but equally powerful: to gain, acquire, seek, or obtain *by effort*.

Does it matter how one goes about conquering something of importance? I would suggest that it does. Perhaps a personal example will illustrate this difference. When I first started running, I tackled the whole process with force, with gusto—and with very little knowledge. Much to my surprise, I had discovered that I loved the process and the outcome of a run, both the clarity of mind that occurred in motion and the sense of well-being that followed. Living in rural New Hampshire at the time, I encountered many hills early on. One in particular was long and steeply pitched—not impossible but formidable. How to reach the crest? I applied the force of physics to the process: If I got a running start as I went down the incline, perhaps the momentum would carry me along farther as I made my way uphill. It was a battle mentality: me versus the hill.

I finally recognized that using this method meant that all that happened was that I fought the hill rather than used the power that existed within my body. I shifted gears; I began approaching the hill from a different perspective.

Running up the hill became an opportunity to put in effort to see how far my legs would carry me. Each time that I could measure off another telephone pole length, another few steps beyond the distinctive crack in the pavement, I had a sense of triumph, of victory. I was conquering this hill through effort rather than force.

That is the sense, I think, in which Dr. Keith Johnsgard is speaking of conquering depression and anxiety—and a host of other ills and potential ills—through exercise. As he comments in this excellent book, the word for "running" among a California Indian tribe translates as "the Big Medicine." Exercise has the capacity both to prevent problems and to assist in curing them. Because of our compartmentalized lives, we often think of exercise as something that we *should* do, something that we need to add to our overly crowded, overly stressed lives. When exercise becomes an obligation, we shift into thinking of it as the enemy we need to vanquish. We lose sight of the fact that, as Dr. Johnsgard wisely points out, exercise is natural; our sedentary, twenty-first century lives are unnatural.

The word "conquer" originally meant that a person was "seeking something out." Mental or physical action is implied: the words "question," "inquire," and "require" are derived from the same root. Choosing to exercise means that we are seeking something out. We are addressing the essence of ourselves: our mental and physical health.

In a world where so much of the time we feel helpless to change and to take charge of our lives, deciding to take that first step—and then the second—means that we are taking action. Exercise is truly a lifestyle choice. We take those steps, perhaps tentatively at first and then with increasing confidence and vigor. It may be for prevention or treatment of depression, cancer, or anxiety; for immune system functioning; for self-esteem issues; for weight problems; for diabetes . . . One could go on and on. The list is powerful—and that's just looking at each of these issues singly. As we know, the interaction between mind and body means that actions that affect one system affect others as well. Movement, Dr. Johnsgard suggests, *is* medicine. It is medicine for body, mind, and soul.

Exercise is for everyone. Babies and children continually exercise—at least until we teach some of them that exercise exists only when they're playing organized sports, while we shove others to the sidelines as spectators! Some of us have seen the light early on, finding the benefits of physical activity in our youth and just continuing to this day. But many of us come to this recognition later in life. I tuned in to the value and pleasure of regular exercise as a vital aspect of my daily life in my thirties; Keith

Johnsgard, in his fifties. We know that it is never too late: some of the most powerful effects of exercise occur among the elderly.

We can make use of what we already know about ourselves and our likes and dislikes, our preferences and aversions. For every person, there is at least one form of physical activity that will give such satisfaction that you will *want* to maintain this activity. You have the opportunity to *seek* and to find it.

So lace up your sneakers and come out for a walk or a jog; dust off that bike helmet and go for a spin; stretch, hold, and breathe; or put on your bathing suit and come on in—the water's fine! You'll gain a sense of well-being; your physical health will improve; you'll discover creativity you'd forgotten was there. Your mood will improve—indeed, you will conquer and triumph.

Kate F. Hays, PhD, clinical psychology
Past President, American Psychological Association,
Division of Exercise and Sport Psychology
author of *Move Your Body, Tone Your Mood*
The Performing Edge, Toronto

ACKNOWLEDGMENTS

I learned a great deal when Linda Regan edited my first book on this topic a dozen years ago: a sobering lesson in tough love. Now, once again Linda has been my editor. Armed with lessons learned and given remarkably free reins, I explored the landscape of this new book, from the mountains of science to the sometimes-dark caverns of personal experience. I want to thank Linda for encouraging me to undertake this second book, for her trust in extending me such free reins, and for her kind, good-humored, and unfailing support of and enthusiasm for virtually everything I chose to write. Thanks also to copy editor Heather Ammermuller, another good-humored and supportive professional who consistently invited and welcomed my editorial suggestions.

PROLOGUE
SAM AND THE COYOTE

Sam's decision to commit suicide was not a hasty one, nor was it without ample cause. Both his physical and mental health were in dire straits. His internist had for years warned him that with his increasingly compromised arteries and elevated blood pressure, even a minor stress could put him at high risk for a fatal heart attack or stroke. He had been further warned throughout the steady increase in his blood sugar levels that he was on a collision course with diabetes, which would have all manner of serious consequences. Sam was a clear candidate for an early death.

Like the majority of Americans, Sam was a victim of two of those ancient seven deadly sins, gluttony and sloth, and he had long since crossed over the boundary that separated being overweight from being obese. He avoided any sort of exercise, since even modest physical activity quickly elevated his respiratory rate, pulse rate, and blood pressure. These signals in turn activated his anxiety about a heart attack or stroke and precipitated a rapid retreat to rest. His physician had often assured him that he could dramatically reduce his mortality risks by changing his lifestyle: dietary changes, weight loss, and a supervised program of physical activity.

But, like so many of us, Sam just couldn't make himself stop eating or start exercising. And like so many of us, he took pills instead, pills to suppress his appetite, lower his cholesterol, reduce his hypertension, and compensate for his bad dietary choices.

Sam also took pills for sleep, for anxiety, and for a long-standing depression. Despite years of psychotherapy and a variety of antidepressant drugs, his depression steadily worsened, and his friends had gradually drifted away, unwilling to shoulder the weight of his depression. Now middle-aged, single, and living alone in an apartment, he had a history of failed romances, friendships, and jobs. It seemed like nothing gave him any pleasure anymore. Weary and without hope, he privately decided that there was no reason to go on living.

Not wanting to embarrass his parents or compromise their life insurance benefits by an obvious suicide, after weeks of thought he came up with what seemed like a workable plan to end his life. Sam lived only a short drive from a county park that had hiking trails leading up into the hills and coastal mountains. His plan was to dress in sweats (like a legitimate athlete), get to the park well before sunrise the next day—when he assumed the trails would be empty—and then run as fast as he could up Coyote Hill. He figured that he would almost certainly die of a heart attack early on that steep two-mile climb.

Sam put his plan into action well before sunrise the next morning, and sure enough, a mile up the hill, his world suddenly turned utterly black, and he slammed down onto the trail. When he slowly regained consciousness, he found himself lying beneath a canopy of redwood trees beside a murmuring creek. Darkness was giving way to light, and a few yards away a coyote sat silently observing him.

His first thoughts were, "I'm not dead," "I've failed yet again," and finally, "Why is that coyote smiling at me?" He had desperately driven himself, stumbling dizzily up the trail, his cardiovascular system redlined, and he gasped for oxygen while lactic acid seared his cramping legs. Then a fail-safe mechanism took charge and laid him down before he died. Eventually, he struggled to his feet and semistaggered down to the parking lot.

But Sam was a determined man, so the next morning, in excruciating muscle and joint pain, he once again set off before dawn. The story played out much the same as the first day, except he made it a little farther up the trail. Same thing the next day, and the next.

On his way down the hill after his fifth failed attempt, Sam came to the surprising realization that *he no longer wanted to die.*

Over the course of the next few days, Sam's life seemed to be vaguely on hold. An unsettling restlessness pervaded his being. He gradually became aware of the fact that his body, in spite of the punishment he had inflicted upon it, somehow wasn't finished with Coyote Hill. It seemed like both the hill and his abused body were calling to him, and the message was clearly stronger than a simple invitation. It wasn't a challenge. It was more like a quiet, but insistent, command. And so he began to take his body for a walk up Coyote Hill each morning. After a week or so it was clear that even brisk walking wasn't filling the bill.

Having decided to live, and wanting information about a nonlethal exercise program, Sam turned, as usual, to his handy PC. But as he logged online, he had a sense that this habitual act didn't *feel* quite right. Very strange stuff for a linear man who had never paid attention to or acted upon such irrational messages. The music of movement had never been allowed to so much as even whisper in his soul. Much less sing or shout.

Sam turned off the computer, put on his sneakers, and walked a couple of miles that evening to the county library. There he found books with the answers to all of his questions about nonlethal exercise and more. He checked out five books and headed home.

During that solitary walk, Sam sensed that he had begun a private quest. Well down the line, he would look back and realize that it was at that point that he had importantly become his own primary care provider. He devoured book after book, and, without fanfare, entered a world that he never knew existed. A pilgrim, he learned about moderation and how to monitor his pulse rate while walking and jogging so that he could safely begin to get in shape without pushing himself to a cardiac catastrophe.

The next morning, he and Coyote Hill rekindled their affair. His adventures in the vacuous isolation of cyberspace had lost their appeal: his marriage to the computer was on the rocks. He was now being seduced by an interplay of his body's own internal commands and the invitations of the mountain.

One of the unexpected discoveries Sam made early on concerned his experiences with other runners on the trail. To his surprise, he found that a number of people arrived at the park regularly around sunrise to take a run before going to work. Sam had feared that these experienced runners would certainly look with disdain on his plodding jog, intermittent walking, and fatness. He was amazed to discover that, even on those first awful suicidal days, runners almost always spoke to him as they passed on the trail, typically with a "Good morning," "What a day!" or "How're you doing?" Often he received clearly supportive greetings like "Looking good," or "Keep it up." He gradually began to sense that *by virtue of simply showing up* and running each dawn he was accepted as a member of a tribe that he never even knew existed.

Over the weeks he began to talk with other walkers and runners in the parking area, getting all sorts of useful advice and eventually invitations to run with others who intended to run at about the same pace and distance. Before long he was invited to join a local running club, and after his first Saturday morning club run, he tagged along with them for their usual postrun breakfast.

That meal felt much like a family gathering, even including the waiters who were obviously well acquainted with the tribe (they already had a half dozen tables joined together and reserved when the group arrived). Having personally run farther and faster that morning than ever before, he figured he would reward himself, and ordered the "Working Man's Special" of sausage, eggs, and hash browns. He was quietly embarrassed when orders were delivered. Almost without exception the other club members had ordered fruit, pancakes, granola, French toast, cereal, and the like. Another new tribal lifestyle dimension was revealed. This was a clearly a clan of carbohydrate critters with eating habits that bordered on being un-American. The waitresses delivered a single check for the twenty-some runners at the long table. Members checked the menu for prices, figured tax, added a generous tip and passed money to add to the pile at the table center. How about that.

One day Sam came to the realization that he had yet to meet a depressed runner. He would later learn that, like the rest of us, members of the tribe sometimes went through periods of stress and mild depression that they typically treated with running. One member, who suffered from bipolar disorder, managed to remain functional and on the job during depressed phases with the help of club members who got him up and out onto the trail each morning. Still later Sam would learn that long-standing tribal wisdom, matter-of-factly stated, that no depression could withstand a ten-mile run.

Early one chilly morning, Sam stood well back from the starting line of his first foot race: a challenging 10K (6.2-mile) event. Entering the race was an act of courage. He was worried about finishing last. But the feeling on the starting line that morning was like nothing he had every known, and he quickly lost his concerns. Here were hundreds people, who, for most of their waking hours on the job, mixed with others whose lifestyles and priorities were dramatically different than their own. These scattered tribal members quietly and privately lived lives that approximated the ways of their hunter-gatherer forebears. They followed this ancestral path because it felt right, and they lived this way strictly for themselves, having no wish to convert others. The air that morning was simply electric with camaraderie and energy: it was clearly a gathering of the tribe, an affirmation of a way of life, and a celebration of life itself.

The race was an eye-opener. After mile one, Sam realized that he didn't have to worry about finishing dead last, and he began to relax and enjoy himself. He found there were all kinds of people running. Some elite runners who had stood at the front of the other five thousand on the starting line were clearly competing, some were challenging themselves for a new personal best, and others were not competing at all but were just being carried along with the joy of participating. He found people who ran at his pace here and there. He chatted with a seven-year-old girl for a mile or so before she said good-bye and zoomed off to catch her mom. As the miles passed, he was very surprised to find himself sometimes silently dueling with other runners. He sometimes won these duels and forged ahead, but he was also passed by runners who were even fatter than himself, and others who ran like members of Monty Python's British Ministry of Silly Walks. About a block before the finish line, after a friendly conversational duel that lasted for five minutes or so, he was left behind by a grinning young woman who zipped ahead in her wheelchair.

Many times, when he was running alone on the trails, Sam's thoughts predictably returned to that first dawn on that redwood trail when he awoke from the unconsciousness that had saved his life. Those images were forever seared into his brain: the murmuring creek, the cool redwood canopy, and the smiling coyote. Finally, curiosity got the best of him, and he walked to the library to check out coyotes. Almost all the sources led him to American Indian tribal legends. It turns out that most Indian tribes had considerably more regard for the coyote than contemporary Americans: The coyote was seen as a respected brother instead of a varmint to be eliminated. That afternoon, while sitting in the sun in the library atrium, he read that in one tribal legend the coyote played a central role in the creation of man. On reading that, he grinned and looked out at the mountains through eyes that were tearing, feeling a brotherhood with the coyote that had sat quietly smiling on him as darkness gave way to light that morning.

One day Sam called his Internet server. After listening to a pleasant recorded female voice lead him through the predictable series of menu choices, and after punching in all the appropriate numbers, a second equally pleasant recorded voice warmly informed him that his call was really important to her and that she would connect him to the next available living human. When the Muzak stopped, Gloria inquired as to how she could help. Sam said he was calling to close his account. Gloria wondered if he was really sure he wanted to take such a serious step, and when reassured that he was, she was quite insistent about hearing his reasons for doing so.

Sam received a negative reply when he inquired as to whether her "Reasons Checklist" had a space titled "philosophical" and another similar reply when he inquired about a choice titled "health concerns." Gloria then remained silent, so Sam went on to tell her that the more time he spent in cyberspace, the more isolated, and more depressed, and fatter he got—not to mention those backaches and headaches. Added to that, he explained, was his growing philosophical concern that technology got in the way of his experiencing the world, other people, and himself. He told Gloria that he had concluded that the Internet was hazardous to his health. Gloria was getting weary of listening and began to suspect that she was talking to a semiweirdo, so they mutually agreed to end Sam's lonely journey through cyberspace.

Then one day Sam visited his internist to hear about the results of his annual examination. His blood work revealed that his carbohydrate metabolism was normalizing (in all probability early enough to veer him away from his collision course with diabetes), his blood pressure had dropped, and his resting pulse rate was now about twenty beats per minute below normal. His total cholesterol count was now in the normal risk range, and, more importantly, his HDL fraction had moved into the very low risk category. He'd lost fifty pounds and was still losing. He'd also stopped taking pills of all kinds.

His internist was dumbfounded. He was nonetheless very supportive, congratulating Sam for taking control of his own well-being and telling him that he wished he had more patients like him. When it was time to leave, Sam thanked his doc and said that he'd see him in a year. Then he turned at the door and mentioned that in the meantime he would rely on his two other new docs. Puzzled by this, his internist asked who they might be. Sam smiled and answered, "My left foot and my right foot."

Now that we've heard Sam's story, let's discuss what his story suggests and what kinds of questions it raises.

For starters, the story strongly suggests that running has a powerful antidepressant effect, not only for Sam but for many of his fellow runners as well. Would regular running have a similar effect on others of us who are suffering from depression? Do scientific studies demonstrate that aerobic training actually reduces depression, and, if so, how does exercise therapy compare to the traditional treatments: psychotherapy and antidepressant drugs? Is it as effective, as fast, as durable? Are there circumstances in which exercise by itself is an appropriate or inappropriate intervention? And what about the most severely depressed hospitalized patients—can we even get them to exercise?

Sam, the hero of our story, was suffering a major depressive episode and was suicidal. Would exercise help those of us who are less depressed: people who are dealing with common stressors, such as family problems, relationship problems, work-related problems, divorce, or grief? And what about the effects of exercise on moods other than depression? What about anxiety, frustration, or anger?

If running does reduce depression, do we have to keep doing it for the rest of our lives to continue to feel good? Is running the only form of exercise that works, or will other forms of aerobic exercise, such as lap-swimming or cross country skiing, work as well? If so, what kinds of exercise, how frequent and intense should it be, and how long must each session be? Will a single bout of exercise provide temporary relief from our depression, and will weeks or months of regular exercise offer a more long-lasting effect? And what about anaerobic exercise? Will weight training or less vigorous activities, such as meditation, stretching, yoga, or relaxation training, also reduce depression?

There's also the question of just how exercise works to reduce symptoms. What are the cognitive and biochemical factors that may be involved? Is exercising simply a distraction? Does it elevate feelings of self-esteem? Might vigorous physical exercise produce neurochemical changes that are similar to those produced by anxiolytic or antidepressant drugs? Could exercise-induced neurochemical changes substitute for those produced by dependency-producing stimulants, opiates, and alcohol? Should exercise have a role in "detox" and in subsequently in staying clean?

What about those of us with other clinical mental disorders? Can exercise help those of us with bipolar disorder, substance-use disorders, anxiety disorders, or psychotic disorders?

With regard to Sam's physical health, did his lifestyle changes genuinely cut the risks of chronic disease and premature death? Does exercise positively affect our immune systems? And what do we know about the role of exercise in weight loss and control? What's the best type of exercise program to shed pounds and keep them off?

The issue of safety also must be considered. We're much more likely to incur a fatal heart attack while exercising or shortly thereafter than at times when we are inactive. Yet those of us who are aerobically fit are far less at risk to suffer such an exercise-induced fatal heart attack than those of us who are unfit. A big-time catch-22: How do we get fit without killing ourselves in the process? And there's also the issue of exercise abuse and dependency. Is exercise a "positive addiction," or does it carry the same hazards as dependency-producing drugs?

Finally, the question of motivation must be dealt with. If there is a central message in Sam's story, it is that such significant positive lifestyle changes are clearly possible but often require enormous motivation. Is there any hope for the rest of us who want to change our ways but may not be so urgently motivated? Does it have to be a life-or-death matter for us to take action? What does research tell us about the best strategies to get started and keeping going?

These are some of the basic questions that this book will address. And while it is based on solid science, it is my hope that it touches your life, that it causes you to pause and consider how you are living, and that it helps to get you moving.

PART 1:
TROUBLE IN PARADISE

1.
HUNTER-GATHERERS LOST IN CYBERSPACE

We Americans are living longer, but many of us are enjoying it less. For decades, our average life expectancies have steadily increased with each succeeding generation, while at the same time rates of depression have escalated. What's more, we're making some very bad choices about how we live, adopting self-destructive habits in ever-increasing numbers. We inhabit hunter-gatherer bodies: physiological systems fine-tuned over nearly two and a half million years of human evolution to function optimally within the parameters of the hunter-gatherer lifestyle. We now have to make special efforts even to approximate those ways of living. Most of us don't.

Because of unwise lifestyle choices, about one of every two of us now dies a premature preventable death.[1] Rates of some of our most common mental disorders have skyrocketed. By 1990, substance abuse and dependencies had become our most widespread mental disorders. There appears to be trouble in paradise.

In order to understand how our highly envied and much-emulated Western lifestyle is hazardous to our mental and physical health, we need to become familiar with the ancient lifestyle within which our hunter-gatherer bodies function best.

OUT OF AFRICA

We Homo sapiens have a short history but a long past. Until recently, the only clues to our origins were the bones of our ancestors unearthed in East Africa and thereabouts. Now genetic surveys of mitochondrial DNA in women and Y chromosome segment DNA in men (both of which escape the shuffling that occurs in the reproductive process) supplement archaeological findings to provide a more accurate picture of how we came to be what we are today. DNA hybridization and melting analysis techniques also allow molecular biologists to compute the percentage of common DNA structure between species. Factoring in mutation rates allows biologists to make reasonable estimates of how long ago different species shared a common ancestor.

It turns out that chimpanzees are our closest relatives and that the "Garden of Eden" was in Africa. The chimps and we split from a common ancestor more than seven million years ago, and we share more than 98 percent common DNA structure. Chimpanzees are more closely related to us than they are to any other primate, including the gorilla.

Skeletal remains discovered in Chad recently by French anthropologist Michel Brunet suggest that an almost-seven-million-year-old erect-walking hominid, about as tall as a chimpanzee and nicknamed Toumai (child of the dry season), may have had a role in our ancestral line.[2] So too might recent specimens unearthed in Kenya (*Orrorin tugenensis*) and Ethiopia (*Ardipithecus ramidus*) that appear to be about six million years old. Then there was a succession of evolving Australopithecines (southern apes) that appeared in Africa about four million years ago.

Physical anthropology is an unending and exciting detective story. Just when we're ready to close the book, a new ancestral lineage plot unfolds. If you should ever decide to visit your roots, check out the tiny museum on the rim of the Olduvai Gorge in Tanzania where you'll find a plaster cast of the footprints of an adult and a child walking along together. They look very much like our own, but they were left by our Australopithecine ancestors 3.75 million years ago.

Homo Habilis, named "handy man" because he was the earliest stone toolmaker, was the first of the genus Homo, or man. *Habilis* showed up some 2.4 million years ago. *Homo Erectus*, who arrived about a half-million years later, had a skeleton that resembles our own, but his brain was no bigger than that of a one-year-old today. Nevertheless, it was brain power enough to take him out of Africa to places as distant as China and

Java. While you're checking out your roots in Africa, have a look at a 1.75-million-year-old skeleton of a *Homo Erectus* youth in the National Museum in Nairobi. It could pass for the kid next door.

"Anatomically correct" modern humans evolved only about one hundred thousand years ago. They looked like us, but they were a work in progress, requiring some fine-tuning before they would leave Africa to populate the world. Recent DNA genetic surveys of dozens of ethnic groups from all over the world reveal that while we humans may look superficially different, because of adaptations to where and how we choose to live, we all have the same parents.

There was no single Adam or Eve, but all living humans can trace their ancestry back to a group of about two thousand men and women who lived in Africa about fifty thousand years ago.[3] These "behaviorally modern" humans emigrated out of Africa, following the beaches across the south of Asia, then on to Australia.[4] Our ancestors would later leave Southern Asia and move westward up into Europe, and others would travel to the northwest through Mongolia and across the Bering land bridge to the Americas.[5]

They were called behaviorally modern man because they had language, sophisticated stone tools, and the skills to build rafts or boats. They arrived in Australia not long after they left Africa. At that time, ocean levels were lower, due to the formation of widespread Ice Age glaciers. Nonetheless, Australia remained separated from the southernmost reaches of Asia by about one hundred and fifty miles of ocean, and our ancestors had to have developed primitive sea-going craft of some kind in order to make that journey, whether the result of purpose or accident.

HOMO SAPIENS SAPIENS

Exactly when our American ancestors arrived in what is now the United States remains a mystery still under investigation. Although the most recent Ice Age glaciers were receding, as little as twelve thousand years ago most of what is now Canada was still buried under a two-mile-deep sheet of ice, forming a barrier between Washington state and Alaska, where our ancestors had lived in a coastal area spared from nearby glaciers for at least seventeen thousand years. Did we emigrate south ten thousand to twelve thousand years ago, when glacial melting opened an ice-free corridor down to Washington state? Or did we somehow arrive earlier, before that corridor opened? "Clovis" stone spear points found with the bones of mammoths during the

1930s in New Mexico have been dated at about 11,200 years. But there is recent evidence that our ancestors were butchering mammoths in Wisconsin, Nebraska, and Virginia between thirteen thousand five hundred and eighteen thousand years ago.[6]

There is also evidence that early Americans were painting figures on cave walls along the Amazon at about the same time as the Clovis People appeared, and there is compelling evidence that the village of Monte Verde in Southern Chile existed at least twelve thousand five hundred years ago in Peru.[7] Linguist Johanna Nichols at the University of California–Berkeley is an expert on the diversification of language. She suggests that the first wave of American Indian immigrants may have arrived thirty thousand to forty thousand years ago, followed by a second wave about fourteen thousand years ago.[8] Just when and how we got here remains a fascinating archaeological adventure.

Perhaps we arrived by boat, following a greenbelt of coastline southward, sustained by fish, seals, clams, and the like. Ocean levels were much lower at that time, so evidence of our passage would now be mostly under coastal waters.

However we arrived, we early Americans were *Homo sapiens sapiens*, "man the wise," the selected survivors of a long series of evolutionary experiments that had begun nearly four million years earlier, when our distant ancestors first began leaving footprints across central Africa. About thirty-five thousand years ago our distant cousins, the Neanderthals, abruptly vanished from Europe, leaving us alone, the last of the Homo line. Our ancestors who, by torch light, used sticks to paint bison on cave walls in France were virtually the same as those of us who today spray paint graffiti on subway walls. Our customs, language, and tools have changed, but we are the same.

Our time is brief, a passing squall in the immense evolutionary rainstorm that has spawned life on this planet for hundreds of millions of years. But we modern humans have a clear genetic legacy, and it is becoming increasingly apparent that if we stray too far from the lifestyle we lived during our last tens of thousands of years, we put ourselves at serious risk.

In pursuit of consciousness and civilized ways, we have left much of ourselves behind, disrespected and disowned. We have relinquished our spiritual bonds with, and our respect for, the plants and animals with which we must cooperate and coexist if life on earth is to continue. We have stopped listening to the voices that sing within our souls, and we have stopped respecting and attending to our dreams. Prisoners of distressingly narrow and irrelevant skills in an increasingly complex world, we are less and less able to do for ourselves.

And we have become sedentary. The original High Plains Drifters, we had foraged and hunted across the sky-swept savannahs, the pursued and the pursuers, forever on our feet, and always on the move. With spear in hand we flowed with the passing millennia on a seemingly endless journey into the slow dawn of civilization.

Up until only about ten thousand years ago, our human ancestors roamed the earth in small kin-clan hunter-gatherer groups, each numbering perhaps fewer than about two hundred individuals. Our ancestors were polygamous and xenophobic, suspicious of and aggressive toward others who looked or behaved differently than themselves. There were no villages, territories, or nations. What we owned, we carried.

By five thousand years ago, when average life expectancy was about seventeen years, some of our ancestors here in America and abroad had turned to farming, and in the Near East the first forms of writing appeared. Prehistory was about to end. As little as two thousand years ago, about half of us still remained hunter-gatherers, but half had stepped off our ancient lifestyle path to become farmers and herders.

As time went on, our ways became increasingly divergent from how we had lived when we evolved as the sole survivors of that long line of man-apes. But even as recently as a century ago here in America, most of our lives involved long hours of hard physical labor and diets reasonably similar to those of our forebears. The lifestyle of the late 1800s still fell within the basic parameters of our ancient ways. Our Cro-Magnon physiological systems with their interdependent functions and feedback mechanisms still worked. We toiled hard and we ate simple foods. But the 1900s would bring previously undreamed-of lifestyle changes, and the consequences were both wondrous and disastrous.

Civilization and morality are very recent inventions that constitute a very thin and tenuous veneer separating us from our fundamental animal nature. Predictably, when our security is threatened, when our lives are on the line, when we don't have sufficient food, or when law and order are suspended, we revert to our primitive xenophobic, amoral animal ways. It's tough being a moral animal.

It's even tougher for us to incorporate the health-essential basics of a hunter-gatherer lifestyle in present-day America. Before examining the dramatic lifestyle changes that occurred in America during the last century, it's important that we get a grasp on how our forebears lived.

THE SHANGRI-LA VILLAGERS

There are probably no true hunter-gatherers around today. Even Kalahari Bushmen, some of whom now survive by leading tourists on authentic hunts, carrying their tiny bows and poison-tipped arrows, often do so while wearing Hard Rock Cafe T-shirts and Michael Jordan sneakers. The more predictable food supplies offered by agriculture and herding have largely prevailed. But not so long ago, remote cultures that were relatively uninfluenced by Western living offered clues as to our more immediate ancestral lifestyle.

Spurred on by stories told by returning World War II veterans, who spoke of very remote Himalayan mountain villages where men and women were said to live to be very old, University of Minnesota scientist Alexander Leaf decided to visit these so-called Shangri-la villages.

Shangri-la refers to a mythical valley in the Himalayas where people lived forever (according to a circa 1930s black-and-white movie in which actor Ronald Coleman's airplane crash-landed in Shangri-la). Fifteen years ago I was surprised to discover that a place called Shangri-la actually does exist. "La" is the Tibetan word for mountain pass, and Shangri-la (the pass above the summer yak pastures named Shangri) is a treacherous eighteen-thousand-foot Himalayan mountain pass that shares a portion of common trail (on the Everest side) with a less formidable, and far safer, pass called Chugyima La.

One November afternoon I sat exhausted, drinking steaming hot tea with my companions in our just-erected tent camp. We had left the Gokyo Valley at sunrise that morning and spent most of the day climbing, traversing, and descending from Chugyima La, conditioning ourselves for a climb up north. We were joined for tea by a young American couple and their single Sherpa porter. They were traveling the opposite direction and were intent on traversing Chugyima La into the Gokyo Valley before sunset. In spite of the lateness of the hour, we were unable to dissuade them. A few days later word reached us that they had taken a wrong turn and perished on Shangri-la. So much for eternal life and Hollywood.

Alexander Leaf managed to visit a group of remote "Shangri-la" villages located very high in the Caucasus, Karakoram, and Andes Mountains. And, as the returning World War II veterans had reported, he found what appeared to be very healthy and active villagers who claimed to be very old indeed.[9] He also discovered that even though these communities were separated by vast distances and language, their ways of living were unusually similar. The lifestyle "common denominators" of their robust health and longevity were

1. diets low in calories, fat, and protein
2. daily vigorous physical activity
3. no use, or moderate use, of tobacco or alcohol
4. the absence of retirement (everyone worked the fields and remained active in village life)

These disparate remote communities shared a common lifestyle that reflected the transition from hunter-gatherer to agrarian. In my own high-altitude wanderings, I've also noticed striking lifestyle similarities between the Sherpas, who kept yaks and grew tiny potatoes and barley at thirteen thousand to fourteen thousand feet in remote Himalayan valleys, and Bolivian Indians, who kept llamas and grew potatoes at similar elevations in the Andes. Apart from these similarities, their stature and even the ear-flap helmet caps they knitted from yak and llama wool were virtually identical.

Unfortunately, the villagers Leaf studied a half century ago did not keep accurate birth records, so there was a growing suspicion that Shangri-la villagers began to increasingly exaggerate their ages with each succeeding wave of Western anthropologists.

The issue was at least partially laid to rest in 1997, when a study was done in a remote county in southern China, where a simple rural lifestyle has remained unchanged for centuries. Commonly referred to by the Chinese as "the home of longevity," the province called Bama has maintained accurate birth records and is the home of dozens of centenarians (people over the age of one hundred) and hundreds of people in their nineties. Of Bama's 260,000 residents, seventy-nine were found to be centenarians. In contrast, the 1990 census found Beijing's population of eleven million to include fifty-six. These figures reveal that the per capita rate of centenarians in Bama, whose highly active farmers have not strayed far from the lifestyle path of their ancestors, is an astounding sixty times greater than those who live in Beijing.

In Bama, men as old as 112 awake with the sun, walk barefoot up into the rocky hills to work their fields, eat a diet of corn, rice, and vegetables (almost no meat), don't smoke or drink alcohol, and go to bed at sundown. They aren't simply alive; they are alive, well, and productive. One 105-year-old Bama farmer related, "When I'm working, I have nothing to worry about."[10]

Those of us who are struggling with a decision about which of the many diet fads is right for us, and are further concerned about which has the most favorable long-term health outcomes, should pay special attention to the diets of the Shangri-la and Bama centenarians: low calories, low fat, and low protein. These active, healthy, and long-lived people don't overeat and are carbohydrate fueled.

OLD-FASHIONED AMERICANS

Here in America there are subcultures of people who, because of religious conviction, have, at least in part, resisted the monumental lifestyle changes that have occurred over just the past century. Some basic aspects of their lifestyles are similar to the long-lived people of Bama. For example, University of Minnesota epidemiologist David Snowden studied a group of twenty-six thousand California Seventh-Day Adventists from 1960 to 1980.[11] This church urges members not to use alcohol, tobacco, and caffeine. It further encourages members to follow a vegetarian diet (which may include dairy products and eggs). However, about half of the Adventists Snowden studied were "adherents" (strict vegetarians). Snowden found that the Adventists as a group lived an average of seven years longer than Americans in general. The more strictly adherent members lived an astounding average of twelve years longer. As in the case of the long-lived Bama farmers, this group of long-lived contemporary Americans were fueled largely by carbohydrates.

Like Leaf, Snowden found that physical activity played a role in longevity. Regular exercise appeared to protect Adventists against fatal coronary heart disease. Its effect was greatest among former smokers and among those who included meat in their diets. It appeared to play a compensatory role for those two groups, as it added little benefit for vegetarians and those who had never smoked.

James Enstrom studied mortality rates of ten thousand Mormon high priests and their wives.[12] The Mormon Church also proscribes alcohol, tobacco, and caffeine and makes recommendations for a healthy diet. Enstrom found significantly lower cardiovascular and cancer death rates among the priests and their wives than among American men and women in general. The Mormon priests and their wives did die of heart attacks and cancer but at far later ages than typical Americans.

In 1960 epidemiologist Lester Breslow of UCLA began to study a group of men and women who weren't affiliated with any particular religious group. He followed the lives and the deaths of seven thousand adults in Alameda County, California, for thirty years. In 1993 he reported that those men and women who had engaged in what he called "anti-life habits" (the main culprits being tobacco, obesity, alcohol, and physical inactivity) had twice the chance of dying prematurely as compared to those Alameda dwellers in his study group who lived less dangerously. What's more, they were twice as likely to be disabled for ten or more years before their premature deaths, one of the early findings that linked disability to lifestyle.[13]

These and other similar investigations consistently suggest that special groups of Americans who, for whatever reasons, have resisted dangerous and seductive aspects of our "good life" and have lived lives more similar to those of our forebears are likely to live longer and suffer less disability in later years.

THE TWENTIETH CENTURY: THE GOOD, THE BAD, AND THE UGLY

Our lifestyle here in America has changed more in the past one hundred years or so than during the entire 2.4 million years of human evolution. It was during the twentieth century that industrial and technological revolutions made it possible for us Americans to lapse into habits that would be our undoing. Around mid-century we settled into a dangerous, immediate-gratification binge.

We sat around stuffing too much of the wrong sorts of things into our mouths—trading immediate relief for potential addiction, future disability, and premature death. We gave our children to television and our games to professionals. We no longer had to provide our own mediocre heroics or, for that matter, even participate in physical play. We bought recliners and TV sets. We became a nation of increasingly nonheroic, overweight observers.

Those were the years of the good life. In the 1950s the big war was over, and we had emerged as a world power. Most of us had jobs, and families could get along fine with only Dad working. Veterans could buy decent houses for $5,000, with nothing down and a 3.25 percent GI loan. The GI bill made college possible for people who never dreamed of higher education. After years of rationing, hard times, and doing without, we could now afford at least one car in every garage, at least one TV, T-bones on the barbecue, tickets for the ball games, incredible food selection the year around, all the twenty-five-cents-a-pack cigarettes we could smoke, and all the beer we could drink. Laborsaving home appliances and power equipment made sweating something we did only beside the pool on our chaise lounges.

As time went on, while we may have looked like a herd of contented cows, our bodies were in crisis. Designed to run on physical activity and fifty thousand-year-old menus, we asked them to deal with substances that weren't around and factored into the selective process of our evolution. We coughed, vomited, spit up blood, staggered, and sometimes drugged ourselves into unconsciousness. And those were only the immediate acute reactions to some of the twentieth-century substances we asked our bodies to ingest. The lethal chronic effects came later.

It's not hard to understand why we all dipped so deeply into the punch bowl of the good life. It was marvelously seductive, and the bleak effects of the habits that would disable and prematurely kill us were insidious and unhurried. The slow but steady increases in blood pressure and heart rate whispered only softly through arteries that were slowly occluding. We didn't notice. We forgot that there had been distant mornings when we awoke without coughing and times we climbed stairs without being left breathless. We were surprised when we felt those first sharp and unfamiliar chest pains that signaled a cardiac problem. We couldn't believe the chest x-rays that spoke of lung cancer. Even our seemingly indestructible and larger-than-life hero, John Wayne, paid the price.

The habits that will plug our arteries, scar our livers, and turn our lungs into uneasy tar pits are often laid down in youth: a time when we most strongly feel the urge to follow the crowd and mimic adults, a time when we just can't wait for time to pass so that we can get on with things. As kids, it seems we will live forever. Perhaps we carry this myth with us into adulthood, the myth that we are somehow special, and that the odds and rules that apply to other people don't have much to do with us. Perhaps that is why we go right on doing the things that will kill other people.

Medical historians are going to look back and marvel at the twentieth century. Besides the near doubling of life expectancy, there was this curious twist in the nature of what killed us. When the century began, we were victims of other killers, but by mid-century we were busy killing ourselves.

In 1900 most of us died of acute infectious diseases. Heart disease had just replaced tuberculosis as the leading cause of death. Typhoid fever was number three, with rates nearly as high as tuberculosis. Today hardly anyone dies of tuberculosis, typhoid fever, smallpox, measles, whooping cough, and the other major infectious killers of a century ago. Only influenza and pneumonia remain uncontrolled, and deaths from these illnesses occur almost without exception among the very old or people who are already seriously ill.[14]

It is of significance that the sparing of millions of lives and the dramatic increase in average life expectancies during that century were almost completely the result of improvements in hygiene, diet, and preventive medical care.

Today, nearly all of us will die from slow-developing chronic diseases. Vascular diseases, which result in heart attacks and strokes, are the number one and number three killers. Cancer comes in second, and diseases such as diabetes, cirrhosis, emphysema, and the consequences of osteoporosis take up a large part of the remaining slack.

You're probably figuring that this makes sense—that with acute diseases licked, we now live long enough to develop the slow-developing chronic diseases that naturally come with aging. There certainly is some truth to that line of thought. Arteries don't occlude overnight, and our lungs put up a long and brave fight against the carcinogens we inhale. But epidemiologists James Fries and Lawrence Crapo of the Stanford University Center for the Study of Disease Prevention point out that chronic diseases are not simply the *natural consequence of aging*. They also appear, to a considerable extent, to be the consequence of an *unnatural lifestyle*.[15]

OPTIONAL PREMATURE DEATH IN AMERICA

In the November 1994 issue of the *Journal of the American Medical Association* (JAMA), government researchers published a unique benchmark study of death in America that lent strong empirical support to the assertions of Fries and Crapo. The investigators examined 2.15 million deaths that had occurred in this country during 1990. Heart disease and cancer remained America's leading killers, but *the purpose of this study was to uncover the actual causes*: what caused the heart disease and what caused the cancer.

The researchers discovered that nearly half of those 2.15 million deaths could have been prevented. About one million of the deaths were the result of self-destructive lifestyle choices: tobacco (four hundred thousand deaths), obesity (three hundred thousand), and alcohol (one hundred thousand) were the major root causes, accounting for 80 percent of all preventable deaths. It's interesting that we spend countless billions at home and abroad in our war on illegal drugs, when 80 percent of all preventable deaths (eight hundred thousand) were the result of using legal substances (tobacco, alcohol, and food). Only 2 percent (twenty thousand deaths) were the result of using illegal drugs during that year.[16]

For more than a half century, evidence that cigarettes will kill us has steadily mounted, and many of us have managed to stop—no small task, as nicotine is deadly addictive. The percentage of Americans who smoke has dropped substantially over the past half century and now fluctuates in the low twenties. But on the other hand, two-thirds of adults have now become overweight or obese. In 1980, 15 percent of us were obese, and by 1994 the figure had risen to 23 percent. In 2000, 31 percent of us were obese. More than half of non-Hispanic black women over the age of forty are now obese, and 80 percent are overweight. Nearly 5 percent of Americans suffer from extreme obesity (body mass index greater than forty), and the escalation of obesity rates shows no sign of slowing.[17] Here in the San Francisco Bay area, two prominent hospitals have just announced that they are now offering stomach stapling for dangerously obese children—unheard of a generation ago.

Experts at the Centers for Disease Control have been quite astounded at these figures and now refer to the spread of obesity as an epidemic, since its characteristics so much resemble the spread of an infectious disease. Obesity is sweeping across America and will soon replace tobacco as the leading cause of preventable death. The rock-bottom indisputable causes of our national obesity epidemic are too many calories and too little exercise.

Clearly our national goal should not be self-esteem workshops for those of us who are overweight or obese. Instead, government dollars should be spent on programs to help promote weight loss and, more importantly, on prevention programs especially aimed at young people. About 93 percent of the money spent on health care in America targets the sick, half of them people who have lived unwisely. A fraction of the remainder is spent on prevention.[18]

Amazingly, the authors of the "Actual Causes" study estimated that a sedentary lifestyle *by itself* is responsible for *nearly one-fourth of all deaths from chronic diseases* in this country.

HIGH-RISK SPORTS

The astounding figures on preventable deaths give me pause. Many years ago I spent nearly a decade of my academic life researching the personalities of race car drivers and sport parachutists: people engaged in high-risk sports, where a single misjudgment or just plain bad luck could result in death. Those sorts of deaths are spectacular—race cars crashing and burning at extreme speeds or parachutists smashing into the ground after their chutes failed. Such deaths make great television drama and always receive a great deal of press.

Public opinion at that time was that these "daredevils" were either (1) stupid, (2) crazy, or (3) possessed by some sort of Freudian death wish. My studies of nearly a thousand such people convincingly revealed that none of these perceptions were true. The drivers are far brighter than most of us, and they are definitely not crazy. Would you, as a sponsor, put millions of dollars into a racing program and fit a stupid, crazy man with an unconscious death wish into the cockpit?

Elite race car drivers, parachutists, jet fighter pilots, and the like score far lower than the general population on measures of neuroticism. What's more, they weren't impulsive daredevils: the risk-taking being incidental to what centrally motivated them to pursue their chosen sports or professions. They did, in fact, do everything possible to minimize their risks.[19]

While pursuing my studies of "risk-takers," I noted that only a small handful of race drivers and parachutists died each year. Now smoking and obesity kill seven hundred thousand of us annually. It seems appropriate to reorganize our thinking at this point. Looks to me like *smoking*, *sitting*, and *eating* are the actual high-risk behaviors for the great majority of Americans.

Of course, a TV series titled *Behind Closed Doors: America's Most Risky Activities* showing scene after scene of obese people sitting in front of their TV sets and engaging in gluttony would be a hard sell. For starters, this is the age of sensitivity. What's more, in a commercial television industry, supported in part by fast-food advertisements, who would commercially support such a series? Finally, who would watch? No one wants to be reminded that they are engaging in essentially suicidal behavior.

It may also be time we rename *preventable* deaths as *optional* deaths. Preventable death has a kind of impersonal group statistic ring to it, allowing us to think that we're reading about other people. Optional death is more personal. Optional suggests individual choice, which may help move us away from professing to being victims of one thing or another (genes, slow metabolism, bad parents) toward taking responsibility for our personal high-risk habits. Perhaps we have options about what we put in our mouths.

THE BIRTH OF THE BLUES

There is consistent evidence that our physical health has been negatively impacted by our radical new lifestyle, and now it appears that our mental health has also been affected. Distinguished psychologist and past president of the American Psychological Association Martin Seligman suggests that our new Western lifestyle has resulted in alarmingly higher rates of depression, and depression is striking us at much earlier ages. In an invited address at the 1988 American Psychological Association Meetings, he discussed two surveys that revealed tenfold to twentyfold increases in depression in America during the last century. One investigation found that people born after 1945 were ten times more likely to suffer depression than those born during the preceding fifty years, and a follow-up investigation revealed depression rates twenty times higher in people born after 1950 than in those born prior to 1910.[20]

Seligman believes that modernization of cultures results in greater passivity and feelings of helplessness, hopelessness, despair, and low self-esteem. He points out that other, less westernized cultures show no such consistent trends as have been revealed in America, and suicide and depression are completely unknown in some contemporary cultures that have remained relatively primitive.[21]

I would add that Americans have become unnaturally sedentary during the past century.

Rates of major depression, America's most common mental disorder, reveal very interesting trends over the course of the past century. The benchmark Epidemiological Catchment Area Study was based on administering excellent diagnostic interviews to a large sample of Americans during the years 1980–1982.[22] Five to six percent of those twenty to twenty-five years old (born around 1960) had had at least a single major depressive episode during their lifetimes. Those who were twenty-five to forty-four years old (having a longer period of risk) had slightly higher percentages, with 8–9 percent of them suffering such an episode. But then a strange statistical event occurred. Those born around 1925, with a far longer period to suffer a major depressive episode, had rates of only 4 percent. Even stranger was the finding that those born around World War I had rates of only 1 percent, despite the fact that they had had seventy years to suffer the disorder.

An excellent epidemiological study conducted in the early 1990s showed that lifetime rates of major depression had risen to more than 17 percent in

America. Thus, rates elevated from perhaps as low as 1 percent to 17 percent over the course of the last century.[23] It sounds like the American Dream, for many, has turned into the American Nightmare.

Two other investigations shed light on how where (urban versus rural) as well as how we live may to be related to rates of depression. The first was a 1987 study of the Amish people in Pennsylvania. This group of farmers had largely managed to cling to a mid-nineteenth century way of life in which electricity, automobiles, and other laborsaving devices have no place. Physical activity was a central aspect of their lifestyle.

In the Amish community, rates of bipolar depression, which has an unusually strong genetic predisposition, were the same as in other areas of America. But Amish rates of major depression (which is less genetically influenced and is more sensitive to social forces) were only one-fifth to one-tenth the rates seen in other survey areas.[24]

A summary of studies that have targeted the role of genetic predisposition in depressive disorders has revealed that bipolar disorder concordance rates (the percentage of twins who both have the disorder) are 14 percent for fraternal twins and 72 percent for identical twins. The respective concordance rates for unipolar major depression are 11 and 40 percent.[25] These figures suggest that the Amish lifestyle has a protective effect with regard to the odds of suffering (less genetically predisposed) major depression.

Besides the Amish, there are other rural areas that also resisted the rapid urbanization that characterized the mid–twentieth century. One study on lifestyle and rates of anxiety and depression was conducted in Stirling County (a pseudonym) in Canada. This county was essentially rural at mid-century and had moved only very slowly toward small-scale urbanization in the ensuing twenty years. It was the site of large-scale mental health surveys in 1952 and again in 1970. Rates of depression and anxiety disorders showed no change during that time span in a large representative sample of more than two thousand men and women in that area.[26]

The highly regarded 1994 National Comorbidity Survey found a trend for rural residents to suffer lower overall mental disorder rates than urban residents. It also revealed that when the United States was divided into four large geographical areas, the Northeast had higher rates of anxiety disorders, and the West had higher rates of substance abuse, antisocial disorders, and comorbidity rates (two or more disorders suffered by the same individual). The South had the lowest rates of virtually all mental disorders.[27]

THE DARK SIDE OF AMERICANIZATION

A series of studies has now consistently revealed that immigrants who have come to the United States to find a better life have done so at considerable risk. It appears that the more time immigrants spend in America, the greater their risks of physical and mental disease.

A 314-page Federal Report titled, "From Generation to Generation: The Health and Well-Being of Children in Immigrant Families," which addressed these studies, was made public in September of 1998. It reported that second-generation children of immigrants across the nation had higher rates of physical illnesses such as obesity and asthma, higher rates of delinquent and violent acts, higher rates of drug abuse, and higher rates of learning difficulties than did first-generation immigrant children.

The report did not examine specific causes, but it speculated that the breakdown of extended families, drug abuse, physical inactivity, and fatty foods may have all contributed to the greater risks of mental and physical disorders (such as obesity, heart disease, and cancer) among immigrants of all ages who remain in the United States for many years.[28]

William Vega, a professor of health at the University of California at Berkeley, in 1998 reported research on a large group of Mexican-Americans in nearby Fresno County. He found that the lifetime mental disorder rate of the Mexican-Americans born in this country was 48 percent, precisely the same as our national rate. However, he found that recent immigrants had lifetime rates of only 24.9 percent. With regard to rates of our most common mental disorder, major depression, immigrants who had been here less than thirteen years had rates of 3.2 percent, those here for more than thirteen years had rates of 7.9 percent, and first-generation U.S.-born had rates of 14.4 percent.[29]

As westernization spreads across the world, the nature of what kills and disables people internationally will shift. Movies, satellite television, and the Internet have now made it possible for us to export our crippling ways of life to other developing countries. Those who are drawn to the seductive glitter dome of westernization pay a substantial price in both physical and mental health, and life in the dome will cost their succeeding generations even more.

THE SILICON ZOO

From around 1850 to the present time, the lifestyle of humans has changed more than in the entire 2.4 million years of our evolution. The industrial revolution, electricity, telephones, automobiles, telecommunication, a myriad of timesaving and laborsaving devices, and readily available food are some of the factors that have contributed to that change. Little more than a century ago, nearly our entire national product was produced by muscle power: today, almost none.

While at San Jose State University, I taught a course that focused on the interplay between lifestyle and health. I talked to my students about the parallels between the lions in the San Francisco Zoo and us humans in the Silicon Valley, making the case that our once lovely semirural and orchard-filled valley had, in fact, been transformed into a human zoo.

In the case of both lions and humans, we observe overweight, sedentary, highly stressed, and often depressed animals inhabiting cages, cubicles, or offices during most of their waking hours: animals designed for highly active lives in vast spaces. The lions, of course, have no choice in the matter, and as much as they pace endlessly back and forth in their cages, they soon learn that a zoo is not the Serengeti. They give up and retreat to a life of eating and sleeping. But we human animals have chosen to live and work in an overcrowded urban cage, enduring road rage and intrusive neighbors, earning a living with our heads instead of our bodies, staying awake with the help of caffeine, remaining functional with the help of pills, and pacifying ourselves with cigarettes, alcohol, sugar, and cholesterol.

I suggested that both the lions and Silicon Valley humans were *living unnatural lives in unnatural environments*, and both species were paying a heavy price in mental and physical health.

CHOICES

If you've ever left your cell phone at home and gone backpacking or paddling in the wilderness for a week or two with a few kin or clan members, you may have experienced the true meaning of the word "recreation." For those quiet days, away from the masses and laborsaving devices, preparing and eating simple foods, using your body instead of your head, bonded with your companions, experiencing the fact that the forces of nature were in charge, and feeling *a part of* instead of *apart from* nature, you may have at some point sensed that "This is who I am," or "This is what I am made for." This is recreation (to re-create or rediscover one's fundamental self) in its purest form.

Even a long, solitary walk in the wild, apart from the urban stresses, may give you this fundamental sense of yourself and sense of where you belong. Make no mistake, you are a hunter-gatherer, and these sorts of scattered reminders should make you stop and evaluate just who you are and how you are living. You have choices.

This, of course, is not to suggest that we all totally abandon our present lives, don loincloths, and disappear into the wilderness. The essential message here is that we consider making peace with our hunter-gatherer bodies; show them some respect. A long and healthy life must be a cooperative enterprise. We can order our bodies around for only so long before they refuse to cooperate, cause us serious problems, or simply quit on us. First comes disability, and then, much too soon, the big silence.

We can fulfill our hunter-gatherer limited warranties by avoiding tobacco, not overdoing alcohol, adopting a diet more like that of our forebears, and making regular physical activity a part of our lives. We don't have to become marathoners, and we don't have to live on a diet of corn and beans supplemented once a month with a scrawny chicken. We can gradually bring exercise back into our lives and move toward adopting the simple, widely accepted FDA food pyramid guidelines for a healthy diet. We can limit our visits to the fast-food emporiums to those occasional days when we feel calorically suicidal and overwhelmed by a need to mainline cholesterol.

2.
PART-TIME CONTEMPORARY PRIMITIVES

It was a few minutes before eight o'clock on a cold and misty March morning on a silent and still-slumbering Stanford University campus. In the shadow of the towering football stadium, a few hundred men and women wearing running shorts and T-shirts stood shivering in the dampness. Ranging in age from fifty to the mid-nineties, they were eagerly awaiting the sound of the starter's gun that would send them off on their annual footrace around the campus.

I was the current president of the sponsoring group, the Fifty-Plus Runner's Association, and had decided to observe rather than race that day. I stood about ten yards down course from the starting line. As the countdown progressed, a woman who was standing on the edge of the starting line increasingly puzzled me. She was wearing a wool overcoat that came down to her ankles. I figured she was a spectator, there to watch a friend who was participating, but had drifted over onto the starting line. But when the countdown reached ten seconds she peeled off her coat and handed it off. She was wearing pedal pushers, a flowered blouse, gray socks, tennis shoes, and a bibnumber. I realized that she was intending to run the race. And so she did. That morning she set a world record eight-kilometer (five-mile) time for eighty-three-year-old women.

When I interviewed her later, it turned out that she was a visitor from

Illinois. She was in the Bay Area seeing her sixty-something son who had registered for the race. She related that she had quietly and independently challenged herself to take up running only two years earlier, setting a goal to be able to first briskly walk and then eventually jog for an entire mile within one year. She had been tempted to run the race with her son that morning but was undecided, so she registered, pinned her number on her semi–street clothes, and kept her coat on until she made her decision a few seconds before the gun. The race was her first.

This Illinois great-grandmother and the other men and women who celebrated life and raced that day certainly weren't your typical Americans, but they did demonstrate that it's never too late to become physically active. They also demonstrated that possessing aerobic fitness and health similar to men and women decades younger than themselves is a viable alternative to that of being hunched over, playing shuffle board and bridge in a retirement community, where taking a daily handful of pills is necessary to stay functional and alive and where memorial services are common social events.

Typical Americans don't exercise. Typical Americans *don't have to exercise*. Exercise is no longer necessary in order to feed and shelter ourselves. Food is as far away as the refrigerator and freezer. Typical American women and men now weigh an average of 153 and 189 pounds, respectively, and are sedentary. They sit in front of the tube and watch other people being physically active.

On crisp fall Sundays, which almost beg us to get outdoors, smell the air, and be physically active, television offers endless mind-numbing golf, baseball, and football. There are three professional football games. On the West Coast, they begin at nine in the morning and end at ten that night. Eleven hours of couch time: three hours of actual playing time, and the remaining eight hours are mostly repetitive commercials that encourage us to eat fast food, drink beer, and drive fast. Professional baseball and basketball, with their endless periods of inactivity, constitute commercial heaven for sponsors. Even the once-marvelous flow of hockey games has been ruined by television: play is stopped several times a period for commercial breaks.

Attempting to get Americans to stop observing physical activity and begin engaging in it is a tall order. In spite of constant warnings about the consequences of excess weight and physical inactivity, we Americans just keep sitting and getting fatter. We seem somehow to be able to mentally filter out consequences like cancer, strokes, heart failure, blindness, amputations, and the like from the simple act of reaching for more French fries.

Ask the typical American why he or she isn't losing weight and getting in shape, and the predictable answers could fill volumes. The most common first answer concerns time constraints. Like we'd all be out there walking or riding our bikes if we only had the time.

But time is a central problem for both sedentary and physically active people. Those of us who are sedentary say "finding the time" is the primary reason we're not working out, and those of us who exercise regularly say our biggest problem is "making the time."

Time availability is not always what actually separates those of us who are sedentary from those of us who are active. Most of us are busy and never seem to have enough time. What separates the two groups, at least in part, has to do with priorities.

Some of us, no matter how busy we may be, manage to work regular exercise into our lives. Exercise does not magically become high-priority for active people. It only does so only after we have managed to be physically active for a reasonable period of time and have begun to realize the benefits: when we realize that we don't function well in the many other aspects of our lives unless we are physically active. The trick is to somehow get ourselves started and to stick with it long enough until we reach a point when we choose not to do without it, until it becomes a high priority.

We'll now take a look at the people who make the time. Who are they, why did they begin, and why do they persist? Do the reasons change with experience? Do age and gender play a role? Learning about what motivates the men and women who have successfully incorporated regular exercise into their daily lives can be helpful to those of us who want to get started. It might help us to be patient with ourselves and help us avoid some of the common mistakes that might otherwise cause us to give up and quit.

HOW MANY OF US EXERCISE?

If there ever was a fitness boom, a lot of us got left behind, and that fabled boom is clearly now a bust. The technology revolution has made it unnecessary for us to even experience the world, much less to move around within it. We can now sit at our computer keyboards and, as the old telephone company Yellow Pages advertisement suggested, "let our fingers do the walking." We can talk with friends, take care of our shopping needs, order and send gifts, shop for mates, avoid trips to the library, play chess with people across the globe, and even put our marriages at risk by working at home full-time instead of giving ourselves and our spouses some personal space for at least a few hours a day.

Despite access to media warnings regarding the dire consequences of an inactive life, we seem to find it increasingly impossible to get off the couch. In a report released in early April 2002 (paradoxically to celebrate World Health Day), our National Center for Health Statistics painted a distressingly bleak picture of sedentary America. Preliminary data analyses of the center's most recent data revealed virtually no change from the findings of the 1997 and 1998 survey, the last year for which complete data were available. That study, based on sixty-eight thousand household interviews, revealed that seven in ten adults do not exercise regularly, and four in ten are not physically active at all. It was found that only three in ten of adults met the national center's modest criteria for being physically active: a half hour of light to moderate exercise five times a week, or twenty minutes of vigorous exercise three times a week.[1]

Over the years many surveys have suggested that far fewer than three out of every ten of us are active enough to be even minimally fit. Interviewing people about their activity habits is open to error, since many of us are likely to overestimate our physical activity levels. The widely respected Surgeon General's Report on *Physical Activity and Health* concluded that only about 15 percent of adult Americans exercise with sufficient intensity and regularity to meet the American College of Sports Medicine's minimum recommendations for the improvement or maintenance of fitness.[2]

WHO ARE THE EXERCISERS?

There have been many fitness surveys over the years, and while findings differ somewhat by virtue of sampling a variety of different sports and settings, overall findings are remarkably consistent.

People who work out regularly are most likely to be white, well-educated, reasonably affluent males between twenty-five and forty-five years of age who are employed in management, education, and the professions. Women, the very young, the very old, and blue-collar workers almost always constitute the minority.

So why do the demographics of regular exercisers predictably fit this mold? One contributing factor is that reasonably affluent people in management and the professions are more likely not only to have more free time, hiring others to do service jobs for them, but are also more likely to have greater flexibility in their work schedules, which allows them to factor in time for exercise. There are far fewer women than men in management and professional positions, which accounts for a percentage of the predictable gender difference. Like the majority of men, most women are more likely to be working forty-hour-weeks with annual two-week vacations.

Women also typically earn less money than men. This can make regular exercise difficult, especially if circumstances dictate that an exercise program is feasible only by joining a health club. Also, in these days of split families, children are still more commonly living with their mothers. Often these mothers are employed and may not only have less income but also have less time to work out than the children's fathers, since they are often stuck with most of the domestic chores.

Men also have more freedom to exercise than women simply by virtue of being male. They can more safely engage in solitary outdoor exercise before or after work, even in darkness when winter days are short, and they can exercise in unpopulated areas where women would be more at risk. Men running about in skimpy shorts carrying no wallets are seldom targets of rape or robbery.

Evana Hsiao and Robert Thayer recently conducted a study of eighty-four men and eighty-four women in two San Diego fitness centers, and as is usually the case, the majority of the members were between the ages of twenty-five and forty-four, and were white. I mention this study because the education demographics were so dramatic: 53 percent of the men and women were college graduates, and another 23 percent had earned advanced degrees.[3]

Education clearly plays an important role as a demographics determiner. It's difficult to graduate from high school or college without becoming reasonably well informed about what constitutes a healthy lifestyle and which of our habits might cause us future health problems. Highly educated men and women also typically have the luxury of more flexible time schedules so that they can more easily find a place for exercise in their lives.

As we examine the motives for exercise, it will also become clear that those of us who work out regularly may do so more for the *effects* or *consequences* of regular exercise than for its *immediate rewards*. This learned capacity to tolerate frustration and delay gratification is a central factor with regard to initiating and sustaining regular physical activity. Thus, many adults who have incorporated exercise as an important component of their daily routines are self-selected, entering the world of exercise with a capacity to assume responsibility for themselves (and their health) and to routinely expend effort for more than just immediate rewards.

But there are many others who first arrive at the fitness centers with a variety of personalities and motives. At the far end of the spectrum are those who arrive motivated out of sheer desperation who could honestly say, "I've tried everything else and found no relief. This is my last hope!"

WHY DO WE DO IT?

The most common motives for engaging in regular exercise, which have consistently emerged from many investigations over the years, make a short list. They are

- health and fitness
- weight control
- personal challenge
- mood control
- general appearance
- self-image
- social (to seek companionship or find privacy)

These are clearly not completely independent motives. Weight control, for example, is involved in health, appearance, mood, and self-image.

About twenty years ago, I developed a test to measure the relative strength of ten important reasons or motives for regular exercise, and I conducted five studies that were primarily focused on distance runners. If running is not your cup of tea, don't lose faith here. The majority of the early research on exercise and its many effects on the psyches of athletes was, for several reasons, done on runners, and it's been found that the motives that fuel runners are the same common motives that fuel other athletes over a wide range of sports—a little more of this and less of that, depending on the sport, gender, age, and experience of the athlete.

Bear in mind also that aerobic endurance activities such as brisk walking, running, swimming, bicycle riding, rowing, and cross-country skiing are often the exercise forms of choice if another of our goals is to enhance the probability of living a long and healthy life. So learning about endurance athletes such as runners is a fortuitous choice. Since I will be drawing heavily from my own research, I want to introduce you to the participants.

THE RESEARCH GROUPS

It was in the fall of 1980 that I had the good fortune to meet a group of Stanford scientists while standing on the starting line of a ten-kilometer footrace in the cool morning shadow of Stanford Stadium. It turned out they were mainly scientists from the Center for Research on Disease Prevention, all male, all over the age of fifty, and *all practicing what they preached.*

From that chance encounter, the Fifty-Plus Runner's Association was born, a nonprofit group dedicated to educating and encouraging fitness among men and women over the age of fifty and further dedicated to providing a data base of members to serve as subjects for research on the physiological and psychological effects of exercise on older adults. Now called Fifty-Plus Lifelong Fitness, the organization is still alive and well, with some of the members now having been a part of longitudinal studies of arthritis, disability, and the like, which have spanned twenty years. After ten years of primary involvement, I now serve on the Advisory Board.

Fifty-Plus membership comprised a rather impressive group of lean, active, nonsmoking men and women who had lived more than a half-century, long enough to know that their lives were time-limited, long enough to know that they would like to avoid disability in their later years, and long enough to know that the primary responsibility for their own health and longevity belonged not in the hands of repair-work doctors but with themselves.

I figured that these older, experienced men and women ought to know what they were talking about, and I recruited about four hundred of the early members to do two studies that inquired about their reasons for beginning and continuing to run. Our average male member in those early days was fifty-seven years old and had been running thirty-five miles a week for eight years. The average female was fifty-five years of age had been running twenty-four miles a week for four years. One member reported running 110 miles weekly, another had been running for forty years, and a third, who began competitive running at age seven in a boys' school in the United Kingdom, had logged 110,000 miles. No sneaker dilettantes these.[4]

I also invited readers of a then-popular running magazine, *Running Times*, to take my test and send a copy of their scores to me, their payoff being that I would publish the results of the study in a future issue of the magazine so they could compare their individual scores with group averages. This particular running publication appealed to a hard-core group of readers, since its primary focus was on competition as opposed to spandex fashions and diet supplements. Even so, I was surprised when 723 readers from all fifty states and some from as far off as Europe and Australia sent me their tests. As was usually the case, more than 70 percent of the runners were between the ages of twenty-eight and forty-eight, and only 21 percent were female. The men had been running an average of about forty miles a week for about eight years, and the women about thirty-four miles a week for about six years. This was a solid group of experienced and committed runners who might be able to tell us something of value about why they first began and why they continued to run.[5]

One of my graduate students, Barbara Edmiston, compared the profiles of the *Running Times* women with those of one hundred highly committed and experienced female aerobic dancers, and I later compared these same women runners with a group of English-speaking world-class woman marathoners.[6]

PERSONAL CHALLENGE AND SELF-IMAGE

I began my inquiries into the motivations of distance runners by conducting a pilot study of Fifty-Plus members in order to get the necessary information to construct a motivation test. The pilot study form invited participants to rank a list of the common motives that other investigators had uniformly found to be important. It also included a large space where men and women were invited to list additional motives that had played a role in their running history. Personal challenge, competition, self-image, and addictions control were commonly mentioned in the write-in space. These motives had seldom or never appeared in previous motivational surveys.[7]

The most common write-in motive was personal challenge, a motive ignored in earlier research. This motive appeared to be extremely important to these older men and women. Time and time again they related that it was central in both getting them started and keeping them running over the years.

Personal challenge is not the same thing as competition, which refers to measuring one's self against others. Personal challenge means attempting to accomplish something one has never done before or to better one's previous best effort: to become one's own personal hero.

A sedentary and aerobically unfit individual, who like most of us can't walk up a flight of stairs without running short of breath, might decide that it was time to begin a program of exercise and set an explicit goal, such as being able to jog for an entire mile without stopping. Weeks or months later, having attained that goal (with a nice boost of self-esteem to reinforce the behavior), a new goal might be set that involved running farther or faster, perhaps even finishing a ten-kilometer (6.2-mile) race in a year's time. Thus, a sense of challenge may not only help *initiate* a program of exercise but may later be central in *maintaining* it by virtue of the self-affirming qualities built into the process.

I started running quite unintentionally and without goals of any sort. My son Mark was a college diver who had began to do regular two-mile afternoon runs up the mountain from our home. He needed to strengthen his lower body to help deal with the force of impacting the water after a ten-meter free fall. I began to run with him occasionally, perhaps simply to see whether or not I could do it, or perhaps because my body was whispering messages to me about how much it missed being used as it was intended. I was slower than he, and being guys, it eventually came to pass that I was getting early handicap starts and the two of us were racing neck and neck up the final hill to the house.

Looking back, it was clear that that challenge played a central role in my so effortlessly incorporating running into my daily routine. I began to supplement my occasional afternoon runs with my son with solitary morning runs, gradually venturing farther and farther from home. I started to keep a calendar of times and distances. Very heady stuff: my own personal Wild West frontier adventure taking place on quiet village byways.

Then one day, instead of heading home at my most recent turnaround point, I impulsively kept going, risking a circle route that I knew would take me farther than I had ever dared run. It turned out to be my first five-mile run, and when I crested the last big climb, I stopped momentarily, raised my arms, and started yelling. I felt like Superman. Under my ordinary street clothing secretly dwelled this fifty-year-old man who could step into a phone booth, change into my big "S" T-shirt, and run five whole miles!

No one with whom I worked knew that I had become a runner, and they would not know that I had run my first marathon six months later. This was my personal secret. I wasn't running for anyone else. Just myself. And the knowledge that I was more aerobically fit than more than 95 percent of the entire male population, irrespective of age, was far too precious to be made public. My thing. As the months went by, I began to run ten-kilometer races, using other runners to pull me along to finish times I could never dream of accomplishing while running alone, gradually bringing down my personal best times.

That being said, I wasn't too surprised to find that personal challenge was the single most powerful motive for the 723 men and women who took part in the *Running Times* study. Number one for both sexes, challenge also turned out to be central in the motive profiles of the older men and women in my Fifty-Plus group. It was the second-most powerful motive for men (after fitness), and third-most powerful motive for women (after fitness and weight control) when both sexes ranked their reasons for beginning to run. When asked about why they currently ran, the strength of challenge held steady for both sexes.

Personal challenge and self-image (becoming Superman or Wonder Woman) turned out to be very powerful motivating forces for both initiating and sustaining exercise for the more than twelve hundred men and women (aged eighteen to ninety-three) in my studies. The opinions of these highly committed and experienced men and women deserve serious consideration. This interplay between challenge and self-image, and the resulting elevation of both, is very valuable information for those of us who are thinking about beginning to exercise. Personal challenge and self-image have a symbiotic relationship, each feeding the other. A successfully met challenge elevates self-image, which, in turn, promotes the setting of new goals and further affirmation of self.

However, a word of caution is in order here for the reader who is about to embark on an exploratory journey into the world of exercise. When getting started, it's important that we set very *modest, attainable goals*, allow plenty of time to attain them; experience the self-affirmation that follows; then use that affirmation to set reasonable and attainable new goals. We all have a Wonder Woman or a Superman caged within us, and they yearn to be set free. But they need to be treated with tender and loving care, perhaps considered as infants with great potential.

HEALTH AND FITNESS

Loss is one of the experiences all of us share in common. If we love, we will inevitably experience loss, be it the death of a puppy, the end of a love affair, or the death of family member. My Fifty-Plus members related many stories about how loss had been central in getting them started exercising.[8] Perhaps it was suddenly finding themselves middle-aged, overweight, and divorced. A common theme was that of the woman who had devoted her life to being a mother suddenly faced with an empty nest with no apparent role, identity, or purpose in life. Often it was the untimely death of a friend or family member or the shocking news that an apparently healthy and robust forty-five-year-old neighbor had died of a heart attack while mowing the lawn. Sometimes it was a physician's stern warning to either change his ways of living or anticipate a heart attack, stroke, or diabetes. Imminent death can be one hell of a motivator for change.

When we go to funerals, I assume that some of the tears we shed at those gatherings are for ourselves: that at those times we are forced to stop and look into our own waiting graves and grieve over our own inevitable mortality. We're truly fortunate if we become aware of what all those tears are about and even more fortunate if we have the courage to stay with that realization, not to distract ourselves and flee from the reality of our own mortality. Genuinely coming to grips with the fact that this lifetime is likely a one-time-around affair can open the door for us to take a serious look at who we truly are and how we are living.

Confronting our mortality can lead us into an existential crisis, sometimes precipitating a lingering depression, since that realization may demand that some impossibly hard choices and changes be made. But against the backdrop of our own mortality, the magnitude and consequences of those choices pale. If we can avoid fleeing from this crisis and the anxiety and depression that it can engender, it may allow us a freedom to know and be ourselves in a manner that we have never experienced.

Coming to grips with our own mortality can serve as a springboard for us to take personal responsibility for our mental and physical health. It can help us to make lifestyle changes that will enhance our chances of a enjoying a satisfying, vigorous, disability-free, and long life. Unsettling as it may be, it is a good thing to consider the possibility that life may be a one-time-around affair.

Most studies concerning the reasons for exercising have consistently found general health, cardiovascular health, and fitness to be primary motives, often the most important motives for men, and always ranked very high by women as well. The older men and women in my Fifty-Plus studies ranked cardiovascular health and fitness as their number-one motive for both beginning to exercise and for continuing to do so.[9]

The somewhat younger men (average age thirty-eight) in the *Running Times* study ranked fitness second only to personal challenge. The *Running Times* women (average age thirty-five) and the dedicated female aerobic dancers we studied also ranked fitness very highly. However, the world-class women marathoners ranked it low in contrast to other motives.[10] No surprise that the primary motives of these elite professional athletes turned out to be personal challenge, competition, identity, and fame and fortune. Being superbly fit and lean was yesterday's news, something to be taken for granted.

WEIGHT CONTROL

With most of us fighting a losing battle with the bathroom scale, it should be no surprise to learn that weight control has consistently emerged as a central motive for regular exercise. In some studies weight control has been packaged as a part of a larger physical health and fitness motive or as part of an appearance and attractiveness motive. However packaged, it invariably shows up as a primary motivating factor, is consistently more important to women than to men, and typically becomes less important to women as they age.[11] Our Fifty-Plus women turned out to be an exception to that age factor rule.

Our female aerobic dancers ranked weight control as their single most important reason for working out. It was ranked number three by the one hundred fifty *Running Times* women, who averaged thirty-five years of age. However, our Fifty-Plus women, who averaged fifty-three years of age, ranked it as their second-strongest reason for exercise (Fifty-Plus men ranked it third). These fifty-something women don't fit the mold of some other groups studied where it has been found that weight control loses importance with aging. While the importance of weight control diminished somewhat with experience for the Fifty-Plus men and women, this probably reflects that they (like the elite marathoners) lost unwanted pounds early on, assumed they would remain lean throughout their lives, and were later importantly fueled by other motives that would emerge with experience.

Weight control is such a primary issue for so many of us that a later chapter of this book will be devoted exclusively to it. Most of us know that exercise should be a cornerstone for successful weight loss, but we don't know much about the ideal parameters of exercise that will maximize shedding pounds.

MOOD IMPROVEMENT

While exercise can alter how we feel about ourselves, it can also alter how we feel. One in five of the Fifty-Plus men, and one in four of the women who took part in my pilot study, reported that they began running to reduce anxiety and depression.[12] That's a substantial percentage, especially since these men and women began to exercise on their own at a time when there was little or no information available suggesting that exercise might have a favorable impact on mood. Most, for one or another reason, had turned their backs on tranquilizers, antidepressants, and psychotherapy. They were searching for an alternative therapy to ease their troubled minds.

The stories of these men and women suggested that exercise affected their moods in two critical ways: how they felt while exercising and how they felt following exercise. When I constructed my test, I named the first of these motives "centering" and defined it as "space to be alone, to clear my head, and to simply experience the world around me *while* exercising." I labeled the second motive "afterglow," defined as "the elevated mood and reduced tension that *follow* regular exercise." These postexercise feelings of euphoria, decreased anxiety, and enhanced well-being (sometimes labeled as "runner's calm") have been reported in eight other investigations—solid testimony to the importance of afterglow as a central motive for exercise.[13]

CENTERING

Men and women in my research ranked "centering" as very important: both sexes, highly motivated to find distraction and relief from their troubles, found it in the more immediate centered state provided by vigorous exercise. Another aspect of the pilot study also revealed that this state of being centered or removed, which often meant thinking about nothing, was the mental process or state most commonly experienced while running. In other words, my older runners spent the majority of their time while out on the trails thinking about nothing in particular, simply experiencing themselves in a very primitive manner. I called this centered state *existential drift*: the here-now awareness of self and just the bare essentials of one's most immediate world. This most commonly experienced phenomenon while running turns out not to be a runner's high. It's more of a drifty, disconnected, languorous state.

When we ride bikes, walk, or run in places where we must pay constant attention to external risk factors such as traffic lights, automobiles, and pedestrians, that wonderful release into existential drift just can't happen. We'd wind up maimed or dead very shortly if our attention drifted off. Nor can it happen when we have an exercise companion with whom we often rehash our problems instead of finding relief from them. Riding a bike or being on foot on trails, where there is little or no traffic, opens the door to the existential drift experience and the relief that follows. Swimming laps (if we can find a time when the pool isn't overcrowded) does the same thing. Existential drift requires that we be alone in a safe environment that demands only the most minimal attention.

Runners often report settling into this kind of drifty state after warming up a mile or so into a trail run. They tell stories of being surprised later to discover suddenly that they'd run several miles without having realized it. A few have reported that this time warp is similar to what they've experienced when high on marijuana.

Swimmers often lose track of lap numbers when they start drifting and have to come up with strategies to keep count. I figure that there must be a switch from left to right brain activity. Sometimes when I'm running along a road where there is occasional traffic a driver will pull over and ask rudimentary questions like, "What's the fastest way to get to the freeway?" I always experience the question as staggering, leaving me momentarily speechless. I can't suddenly get my left brain back in gear. As often as not, when the driver has pulled away I realize I have given stupid or even wrong directions. The driver has jerked me back into the real world.

I don't believe I am unique in this regard. Other runners have often told me they share my difficulty in trying to do even the simplest arithmetic while on a run. Attempting to compute running speed (simply dividing minutes by miles run) is overwhelming. It's a wonderfully freeing and seductive state, this existential drift.

My runners also reported that sometimes, when they are *totally focused* on their breathing and running techniques while doing serious training, running assumed a marvelously freeing, mantralike meditative quality.

Whether the result of unfocused existential drift, or seemingly focused mantralike activity, runners report a surprising spontaneous upwelling of *creative solutions*. Thus, the music composer who is confronted by a compositional impasse and takes time out for a run in the nearby forest and the technology engineer who has struggled all morning with an impossible design solution and decides to take a noon run along the levee have reported similar experiences. Solutions often seem to dance into awareness from out of the blue at a time when these men and women are doing nothing more than trying to distract themselves from even thinking about their problems. The spontaneous upwelling of creative solutions was the third-most common mental activity reported by the runners I surveyed.

This phenomenon is no surprise to me, after decades of clinical psychology practice, where I often observed that patients discover that giving up sometimes leads to the solution of all sorts of problems. Examples might be giving up the notion that we can truly control other people in our lives, or giving up the struggle to become who we are not and settling for being our imperfect selves.

In an article titled "If We Are So Rich, Why Aren't We Happy?" the philosopher Mihaly Csikszentmihalyi discusses a concept he has labeled the "autotelic experience" or "flow," which may bear some relationship to what I call existential drift. He points out that flow "describes a particular kind of experience that is so engrossing and enjoyable that it becomes autotelic: worth doing for its own sake even though it may have no consequence outside itself. Creative activities, music, sports, games, and religious rituals are typical sources for this kind of experience. Autotelic persons are those who have such flow experiences relatively often, regardless of what they are doing."[14]

Csikszentmihalyi tells us that such experiences may have both intrinsic (flow) rewards and extrinsic rewards, such as a composer feeling flow while creating music but also knowing that she will be receiving monetary rewards for her work. He makes it clear that flow is not the same as "going with the flow," abandoning one's self to what feels good at the time. Flow, he relates, requires skills, concentration, and perseverance that lead to subjective well-being. His ten thousand interviews with people around the world suggest that *autotelic persons are happier* than those of us who experience flow relatively infrequently.

Distance running does involve skill and perseverance but rarely involves a great deal of concentration, other than during hard training days or on race days when total focus is vital. Both states appear to deliver subjective feelings of well-being. Whatever the case, distance runners, while engaged in the act of running, and autotelic persons, while engaged in a variety of activities, both experience enhanced moods.

AFTERGLOW

Afterglow is that marvelous tension-free, languorous, relaxed mood that *follows* vigorous exercise and may last a few hours. It's very similar to the "peaceful easy feeling" we experience when we come out of a hot tub or sauna. Afterglow is consistently ranked as more important than the centering experience by both men and women, suggesting that the psychological rewards that follow exercise might be more important than those experienced while performing it.

In years gone by, when beta-endorphin was first discovered, we heard a lot about it perhaps explaining the so-called runner's high. But most runners don't report experiencing such a high while running, and those who do report it say that it doesn't happen with any regularity. However, almost without exception, athletes report feeling the lovely "afterglow" or "runner's calm" that follows a workout.

The one hundred fifty women runners in the *Running Times* group ranked afterglow significantly higher than did the men, ranking it higher than fitness and second only to challenge. The men and women in the Fifty-Plus group, who averaged about twenty years older, also ranked afterglow very high. The female aerobic dancers ranked it as the highest of the psychological motives. The predictable afterglow that follows exercise is a very powerful motive indeed, and it appears to be more important for women than for men.

EXPERIENCE AND MOOD

The effects of experience on the importance of motives that relate to mood are remarkable. The only motives that increased significantly in strength as experience accrued for my Fifty-Plus women were all psychological motives: afterglow, centering, and self-image. Two of the only three motives that increased in strength with experience for the Fifty-Plus men were also psychological: afterglow and self-image. These findings of an upward shift in the importance of mood as a motive for exercise have been reinforced in other studies that have addressed the question.[15] The most recent was a cross-sectional study of men and women (beginners, intermediate, and experienced) at two San Diego urban fitness centers where the investigators found that exercising for mood improvement became much more important as experience accrued.

Certainly the *acute* mood-altering effects of vigorous exercise—centering and afterglow—become apparent early on, even after a single bout of exercise. But the studies that find a delayed awareness of the mood-enhancing effects of exercise suggest that regular exercise might also have a *chronic* effect on mood: altering our baseline mood levels—how we feel most of the time. (We'll explore the validity of that possibility in a later chapter.)

For the reader who's interested in using exercise to smooth out the extremes of her mood swings, it's critical to think in terms of sticking with exercise long enough to experience the powerful psychological impact that it has to offer. We're talking a few months here. The reader should not expect overnight change. She should plan to stick with it, practice moderation, and be certain to set modest goals. Doing too much, too hard, or too frequently can cause us to injure ourselves or give up and quit, preventing us from ever experiencing the impressive mood benefits that regular exercise can offer.

The really good news is that if you can stick with regular exercise for a few months and experience its many psychological and physical rewards, you may be unable to stop. You may be hooked, possibly for life. I'm encouraging healthy dependence and commitment here.

GENDER, EXERCISE, AND MOOD

Throughout my research I found evidence that exercising to control moods may be more important for women than men. The women in the *Running Times* group rated afterglow significantly higher than men, even more important than fitness. A greater percentage of women than men in the Fifty-Plus group began running in order to find relief from anxiety and depression, and while mood-relevant motives gained importance with experience for both men and women in the older group, the increases by the women were more impressive. So why does it appear that women exercise more for mood benefits than do men?

The more than twelve hundred men and women who took part in these studies came from an essentially normal and functional population. When we look at the personality structure of normal men and women, we consistently find gender differences, and these differential personality patterns appear to parallel the sorts of mental disorders that men and women are most likely to suffer in their lifetimes. Let's take a look at how normal personalities are structured and see if it offers some answers to our question about men, women, mood, and exercise.

Like other experts in the arena of human personality, the British psychologist Hans Eysenck, using the accepted factor analysis technique, reduced the myriad normal personality traits to a few central supertraits or families of related subtraits.[16] Some personality experts reduce the multitude of personality traits into families of five supertraits. Eysenck reduced them to three, and subsequent analyses by Marvin Zuckerman fine-tuned those three.[17] For simplicity and brevity, we'll consider Eysenck's three supertraits.

No gender differences were found on the introversion-extroversion supertrait. Men and women had similar average scores on this supertrait, which includes a family of subtraits such as sociable, lively, active, and carefree.

However, men had higher average scores than women on the psychoticism supertrait. It includes a group of tough-minded antisocial subtraits such as aggressive, cold, impersonal, impulsive, unempathic, and antisocial.

Women, on the other hand, had higher average scores than men on the neuroticism supertrait, which includes subtraits such as anxious, depressed, tense, emotional, irrational, and moody.

Men and women share the same personality traits, and while similarities far outweigh differences, there are clear gender differences.

When a combination of genetic predisposition and stress push normal men and women into a mental disorder, the disorders essentially exaggerate normal personality structures. Men have higher rates of antisocial personality disorder and higher rates of the substance abuse and dependency disorders. They act out more than women, who have higher rates of anxiety and depressive disorders. It follows that normal women would be somewhat more likely to utilize exercise to regulate moods to a greater extent than would men.

The percentage of men and women in America who suffer one or more mental disorders during their lifetimes is identical (about 48 percent), but they are predisposed to suffer different kinds of disorders. Men and women are simply not wired the same.

Evana Hsiao and Robert Thayer, in addition to using a *Reasons for Exercising Inventory* in their research, also employed the neuroticism and socialization scales of a widely used personality test, Costa and MacRae's *NEO PI:FFI*.[18] They found that both men and women who scored higher on the neuroticism scale rated mood improvement as a stronger reason for exercise than did those who scored lower. In other words, the more emotionally unstable the individual, the greater was the importance of mood improvement as a reason to exercise. Underlining this was the finding that the higher the neuroticism, the less important was the health and fitness motive. Men and women who suffered to a greater extent from emotional instability were at those fitness centers fueled importantly by a need to reduce anxiety and depression.

SOCIAL MOTIVES

Like most other researchers, I found social motives to be the weakest of the reasons that compelled people to exercise. This appeared to be the case whether they are those who participate in largely solitary sports such as swimming or running or those who take part in group activities. Hsiao and

Thayer tested men and women who exercised in the social setting of mixed-gender fitness centers and found socialization to be the weakest of the five major motives they tested. Social motives were also ranked rock bottom by our one hundred female aerobic dancers who, like others who at fitness centers, exercised in a social setting. In settings such as fitness centers, many people are interested in maintaining social distance and simply getting on with their workouts.

Making new friends at the gym is often a low priority for many participants. I have a neighbor who simply cannot find it within himself to exercise regularly on his own. While his wife and her dog do daily morning runs, he can only find the motivation to work out in an organized and led group program at a fitness center.

It is also the case that many men and women choose solitary activities to find privacy in a world where work and family routinely demand far too much social interaction during most waking hours. Some look forward to their hour's commute to find such relief, while others swim laps, go for solitary walks, or relate to their free weights in the basement.

There is, however, some experimental evidence that the social motive does become more important as we age.[19] I also recall interviewing a widowed eighty-something highly active male runner. A year or so after his wife died, he began to run occasionally at a community college track a few miles from his home. The track was quite busy in late afternoons. Much to his surprise and delight, he found that many of the collegiate runners truly enjoyed running along with him and doing some cross-generational chatting. Before long he sold his house and bought a condo across the street from the stadium.

And there are, of course, physical activity groups and venues where exercise is clearly secondary to socializing. Organized club sports, hikes, ski trips, dancing, and other physical activities for singles groups are examples.

COMPETITION

Competition does not appear to be an important motive for most of us who exercise regularly, and its strength varies with gender, age, experience, and kind of exercise. Men in my studies were fueled more powerfully by competition than were women, but this was true mainly for younger and less-experienced runners. This gender difference was large in the *Running Times* group. And competition was more important among my Fifty-Plus runners when they first began running, but both men and women became less competitive with age and experience. Thus, it appears that competition may play an important role in keeping us working out during the early stages of a program of regular exercise. There are, of course, men and women who for a variety of reasons are significantly fueled by competition periodically or throughout their lives: people who might not exercise without it.

There were clear differences with regard to the importance of competition among various groups of women I tested. Competition and personal challenge were the two premier motives for the world-class marathoners. On the other hand, competition was of no consequence among the aerobic dancers, who, as you might expect, also enjoyed their physical activity more than the women runners. Dancing to hard rock in an air-conditioned studio, decked out in spiffy spandex, and performing in front of huge mirrors or street windows is much more fun than running ten miles on a hot, humid day.

The individual who is thinking about beginning a program of exercise should be very cautious about competition. For some, the intensity, social interaction, and demanding focus of competitive team sports make such sports the only acceptable form of exercise. Team sports may, for some people, be the only kinds of physical activity that can fully engage and distract them from their troubles. Someone who finds typically solitary endurance activities such as lap swimming and running insufficiently distracting, unbearably boring, or far too lonely might thrive playing volleyball, basketball, or tennis. Depending on the venue, such games can be same or mixed gender, and the competition can range from social-friendly to cutthroat. However, some of us are uncomfortable in such competitive venues.

Whether we find peace of mind in social sports or in solitary endurance activities, it's important to be cautious about competition during the early stages of our athleticism. If used prudently, as a means to motivate or challenge ourselves, it can help keep us going. But if used imprudently, it can reduce our immune function and leave us constantly battling upper respiratory infections and feeling run down and weary most of the time. When our preferred exercise is no longer fun we may simply quit. Bad news. What's more, overtraining can result in serious overuse injuries that might force us to take a long sabbatical from an activity with which we were beginning a sizzling love affair. If wounded badly enough, we may decide to never risk loving again and retreat to the nurturing comfort of the couch.

ADDICTIONS

Taking up exercise to deal with addictions was a central motive for relatively few of the Fifty-Plus runners. Nonetheless, those who began and stuck with running to end an addiction succeeded. Tobacco and alcohol were the usual suspects. Our sample, of course, included only the success stories. There are a lot of folks who have attempted to use exercise to end an addiction and failed to do so. Our Fifty-Plus members were a select group of men and women who succeeded using exercise as a major recovery tool and incorporated it as a significant aspect of their daily lives. In the case of tobacco addiction, they typically reported that if they continued to run regularly, increasing distance and speed, at some point they had to make a choice: giving up cigarettes or running. What these findings do suggest is that at least some of us may successfully use exercise as a tool to stop drinking or smoking independently of any formal cessation program.

SUMMING UP

Distressingly few Americans exercise enough to maintain even minimal fitness levels, and there is no evidence that more of us are beginning to do so in spite of media warnings that physical inactivity has serious health consequences.

Those who work out regularly are predictably few, probably about only 15 percent of Americans. As indicated earlier, they are mostly white, reasonably affluent, well-educated managerial and professional men between the ages of twenty-five and forty-five. The very young, the very old, blue-collar workers, and women are underrepresented.

Surveys on the nature of motives that initially impel and later sustain exercise in those who have made regular physical activity an important part of their lives reveal remarkably consistent findings that are summarized below.

The Central Motives: Health and fitness, weight control, self-challenge, general appearance, mood control, self-image, and social (seeking companionship or time alone).

Gender Differences: Men are more motivated than women with regard to fitness and competition. Women are more motivated than men with regard to weight control and mood control.

The Effects of Aging: Weight control becomes less important, and socialization becomes more important as we move into middle age and beyond.

The Effects of Exercise Experience: Mood control and self-image both increase in importance the longer we exercise.

Personality Differences: Mood control is far more important to those of us who suffer from greater emotional instability.

That said, this chapter's overriding message is that in spite of being surrounded by masses of overweight and sedentary Americans, there exists a legion of men and women who have embraced regular vigorous exercise as an essential element in their daily lives, and their stated reasons for doing so constitute the very foundation for above average physical and mental health. A second message, which cannot be ignored, is that it is never too late to join them.

Perhaps one day as you stroll through the mall doing a little window-shopping, if you listen very carefully, you may hear a pair of homeless sneakers whispering your name.

3.
SOME BASIC CONCEPTS

As you read these pages, you'll keep running into a number of basic exercise physiology terms such as "aerobic," "VO_{2max}," and "heart rate reserve." It will make things easier if you become familiar with these terms before going on. Otherwise you may find yourself coming back to this chapter over and over again in order to make sense of what you're reading. This chapter also contains the important basics on how to monitor your own exercise intensities should you decide to begin a program of physical activity.

As you sit reading this book, your "resting" pulse rate is probably close to the national average of about seventy-four beats a minute. Is that good or bad? Maybe average is good. Maybe it isn't. Perhaps our more active ancestors enjoyed a lower average rate and were better equipped to deal safely with stress.

Lance Armstrong and other Tour de France elite bicycle racers have resting pulse rates down around thirty beats a minute. Why is that? Maybe their parents supplied them with a genetic combination of the right stuff, or maybe riding hundreds of miles a week has something to do with it. Maybe a combination of the two explains it. And why would you want a lower pulse rate if you're not planning to take part in the Tour de France or the Boston Marathon? It turns out that there are a number of excellent reasons. Exercise, especially aerobic exercise, which has the predictable effect of lowering our resting pulse rates, has a magnificent array of life-giving benefits.

Let's begin with examples of aerobic and anaerobic exercise. Assume that you are a sedentary person who, for some compelling reason, must suddenly begin to vigorously run for some considerable distance. Not long after beginning, you'll experience feeling "out of breath," even though your rate of breathing has speeded up and you're breathing more deeply. If you manage to keep going for a few minutes you may also begin to feel some burning pain in your leg muscles, signaling a build-up of lactic acid and lactate. If you manage to stick with it, you might experience "getting your second wind," which feels like some sort of physiological switch suddenly gets flipped to replenish your energy. What happened is that it took about two minutes for your heart and lungs to get up to speed and deliver sufficient oxygen to your working muscles, so it could be used to break down fuel to provide energy. Your "second wind" signaled a switch from anaerobic- (without oxygen) to largely aerobic- (with oxygen) fueled exercise.

ANAEROBIC AND AEROBIC ENERGY PRODUCTION

For those of you who are interested in the specifics of how energy is produced, and how aerobic and anaerobic forms of exercise are physiologically differentiated, this short section outlines the basics.

It turns out that all motion requires the breakdown and rebuilding (resynthesis) of a substance called adenosine triphosphate (ATP). It's a high-energy molecule consisting of a base, a sugar, and three phosphate groups. When one of those three phosphate groups is broken down, ATP is transformed into adenosine diphosphate (ADP). That process releases energy to power muscle contractions or other cellular work. So far so good. The problem is that we can store only a tiny bit of ATP in our muscle cells, and it becomes depleted after only a few seconds of maximum effort. Thus, our stored ATP gets us through those first few seconds of our run. Then what happens?

There are three interrelated metabolic processes that can resupply ADP molecules with needed phosphate to convert them back to usable ATP. The first, and most immediately available, resynthesis source is a high-energy phosphate-bearing molecule called phosphocreatine. It recharges the energy system by converting ADP back into ATP. However, phosphocreatine is not abundant, so it can recharge the system for only about five to ten seconds before it too is depleted.

Our second resupply process is called *anaerobic glycolysis*, where cells break down glucose (sugar) and glycogen (stored sugar) in our muscles to release the energy necessary to resynthesize ATP without the use of oxygen. But anaerobic glycolysis comes at a price, as it yields a buildup of lactic acid in our working muscles after about two minutes. Lactic acid and its metabolite, lactate (the by-product of lactic acid breakdown), cause burning pain in those muscles and can eventually cause those muscles to cramp up and become temporarily dysfunctional if we don't ease up. Anaerobic glycolysis can therefore be relied upon only for brief bursts of intense exercise.

The third process by which we resupply our ATP molecules is called *aerobic glycolysis*, and it largely involves the breakdown of glucose and glycogen (sugar) and fat (free fatty acids) in the presence of oxygen. This process supplies ATP for vigorous and continuous endurance activities such as a long run, swim, or bike ride. Since this process takes about two minutes to kick in, our body must depend on the first two anaerobic processes during that time period.

Lactic acid and lactate continue to be produced during sustained aerobic exercise, since the two anaerobic processes continue to function at lower levels, but fortunately these substances are carried away by our blood to be degraded (broken down) by muscles less actively involved in our exercise, as well as in our livers.

Let's work this whole business into an example with a soccer player, who is seldom still for two forty-five-minute periods. She is mostly walking briskly or jogging, but she frequently punctuates these less-demanding activities with high-intensity sprints. She functions largely on aerobic glycolysis. However, this energy source has an upper threshold. She can supply her working muscles with only as much oxygen as her level of conditioning allows. When this limit (VO_{2max}) is exceeded during high-intensity sprints, anaerobic glycolysis supplements energy production. When the sprint ends, her working muscles return largely to aerobic glycolysis, and the other energy systems recharge for the next sprint. Thus, anaerobic processes are important energy sources, not only during the first few minutes of vigorous exercise but also during brief periods when energy demands exceed the supply provided by aerobic glycolysis.

You may have experienced exceeding your aerobic capacity and going into "oxygen debt," finding yourself forced to stop, lean over, and gasp for air. You may also have experienced leg muscle cramps, caused by a buildup of lactic acid, when you overdid it.

AEROBIC TRAINING AND CARDIORESPIRATORY FITNESS

While the word "aerobic" literally means "with oxygen," the term "aerobic exercise" has come to have a broader specific meaning. The term was coined and popularized by cardiologist and fitness guru Kenneth Cooper of the Cooper Institute for Aerobic Research in Dallas. Aerobic exercise refers to exercise of a (1) *kind*, (2) *intensity*, (3) *duration*, and (4) *frequency* such that there is a *training effect*: an increase in *cardiorespiratory fitness*. Aerobic fitness is measured as an increase in VO_{2max} (maximal oxygen uptake). It is the maximum volume of oxygen (millileters per kilogram per minute) we can bring into our lungs and perfuse into red blood cells, deliver to our working muscles, and channel into continuous physical activity.

If you ask an aerobically fit runner if he can run as far as ten miles, the response might be, "How fast?" The ability to run that distance, and to do so in a given time, would reflect that runner's VO_{2max}, or level of cardiorespiratory fitness: how hard and how long he can run. While most of us are unfit and are unable run around the block, much less ten miles, a reasonably fit runner could cover ten miles in less than two hours, and an elite marathoner could do so in less than a single hour.

An average fit man has a VO_{2max} of about forty. Mine was fifty-five, six months after I began running and training for my first marathon. Tour de France champions such as Lance Armstrong and Miguel Indurain test out at around an astounding eighty, which reflects rare throws of the genetic dice together with grueling training. Lance and Miguel can cycle for hours at intensities very close to their VO_{2max}.

When you hear athletes talk about doing a "cardio" workout, they're talking about aerobic training, the sort of exercise that is specifically designed to increase *cardiorespiratory* fitness. Goals of other forms of exercise are strength, flexibility, and balance. *Cross training* typically refers to a workout that includes cardio and strength (resistance) components.

THE 1998 ACSM FITNESS REPORT

Perhaps the most highly regarded source for information regarding guidelines for exercise and fitness is the American College of Sports Medicine (ACSM) and its journal, *Medicine and Science in Sports and Exercise*. Its most recent position statement on "The Recommended Quantity and Quality of Exercise for Developing and Maintaining Cardiorespiratory

Fitness, Muscular Fitness, and Flexibility in Healthy Adults" was published in 1998.[1]

The 1998 position statement incorporates the findings of 262 investigations (and includes references to several other of its position statements: recommended exercise programs for individuals with coronary heart disease, hypertension, osteoporosis, and obesity and weight control). We will mainly concentrate on the ACSM recommendations that focus on the kind, frequency, intensity, and duration of training to achieve cardiorespiratory fitness.

Aerobic exercise involves *large muscle groups*, is *rhythmic* or *repetitive*, and can be *continuously maintained*. Brisk walking, running, swimming, rowing, bicycling, or mimicking those kinds of activities on exercise machines are examples—boring for some but an elixir for others.

The frequency and duration of exercise required to achieve aerobic fitness are interrelated. ACSM guidelines suggest that a training effect requires a workout of twenty to sixty minutes, three to five days a week, depending on workout intensity. An example of this interaction might be briskly walking four or five days a week as against running three days a week. Training fewer than two days a week yields negligible fitness increases. Because of the potential hazards and adherence problems associated with high-intensity training, moderate-intensity exercise is recommended for adults (who are not training for competitive events).

The older 1990 ACSM recommended workout *intensity range* required to bring about an increase in aerobic fitness was 60–85 percent VO_{2max}. A substantial period of continuous exercise was also recommended. The most recent 1998 recommendations have been broadened to include 40–85 percent of our individual VO_{2max}. These changes acknowledge research that has demonstrated that physical activity that is not of sufficient intensity to result in dramatically increased aerobic fitness still has substantial benefits, including reducing the risk of cardiovascular disease and diabetes.

Several studies have demonstrated that workout intensities as low as 40 percent of VO_{2max} and short periods of intermittent training could both result in moderate increases in aerobic fitness.

One such study involved a group of healthy women ranging from sixty-seven to eighty-nine years of age who walked at least three days a week for ten weeks at either 40 or 60 percent VO_{2max}. Both groups significantly, but not differently, increased average VO_{2max} after the ten weeks.[2] Other studies support these findings: that low-to-moderate training intensities are effective, especially with older, sedentary men and women. Bear in mind, however, that low-to-moderate training intensities do not increase aerobic fitness to the extent that higher intensities do.

The new guidelines also report that investigations have demonstrated that one's aerobic workout need not be a single continuous one. In one such study, forty middle-aged sedentary men were assigned to two groups whose workouts consisted of jogging for thirty minutes at 65–75 percent VO_{2max}. Members of one group did single thirty-minute sessions, while those in the second group did three ten-minute sessions, each separated by four hours. At the end of eight weeks, the intermittent group had an average VO_{2max} increase of 7.6 percent, and the continuous group had an average increase of 13.9 percent.[3] It's good news to learn that short bouts of regular exercise, which can be worked into busy schedules, can improve fitness. However, longer periods of exercise result in greater gains, if that is an eventual goal.

Why can't we exercise at 100 percent of our VO_{2max} instead of restricting ourselves to working out below the currently recommended 85 percent limit? The answer is that the 85 percent limit is similar to the RPM (revolutions per minute) redline limit for our automobile engines. Most cars have an automatic ignition cutoff when engine revolutions hit that redline limit. This prevents the engine from turning over too fast and self-destructing. We don't have such an automatic mechanism to protect our hearts, so we must monitor ourselves to avoid inviting an arhythmia or other untoward cardiac event that might occur if we push the limit.

Superbly trained elite world-class athletes can exercise dangerously close to their maximum aerobic capacities for amazingly long periods. Lance Armstrong's trainer was interviewed on television during the 2003 Tour de France. He indicated that Lance's prerace training involved riding up mountains at a steady 80–88 percent of his VO_{2max} for periods of four hours. World-class marathoners, who run a steady five-minute-mile pace to finish a 26.2-mile race in scarcely over two hours, also run right up next to the redline. Hardly anyone can do that, much less do it safely.

MONITORING TRAINING INTENSITY

If we decide to take up exercise and wish to monitor our exercise training intensity, just exactly how do we measure our personal VO_{2max}? The simple answer is that we cannot. A maximal treadmill test in a physiology laboratory is required to make that determination. This is not always convenient or affordable for some of us, and once our VO_{2max} has been established, there's no practical way that we can utilize this knowledge to assess our training intensity while we're out there sweating.

Fortunately, the ACSM provides us with a simple and cost-free alternative that allows us to monitor exercise intensity as we work out. It's based on our maximum allowable heart rate (HR_{max}): the highest pulse rate we can safely experience without putting ourselves at risk. Our individual HR_{max} can be computed by subtracting seven-tenths of our age from 208. This personal redline limit can then be used as a benchmark to compute various levels of aerobic training intensities.

It turns out that 55–90 percent of our HR_{max} corresponds quite closely with 40–85 percent of our VO_{2max}, so all that is necessary to monitor our personal training intensities is to check our pulse rate while working out and see whether it is within our desired intensity range. HR_{max} workout intensity ranges are shown in table 3.1. Intensities that result in increased aerobic fitness begin at 55 percent HR_{max}, and the 55–65 percent range is the recommended range for unfit, elderly, and overweight or obese individuals who are just beginning an exercise program.

Table 3.1. Relative intensities of maximal heart rate percentages

>35%: very light	**65–74%: medium**
35–54%: light	**75–89%: hard**
55-64%: moderate (aerobic effect begins at 55%)	

In case you have difficulty figuring out your personal training intensities, here are a couple of examples.

Fifty-year-old sedentary Luke is overweight and unfit, so he should initially exercise at a moderate intensity. Luke's HR_{max} would be 208 minus $(50 \times 0.7) = 173$, a pulse rate not to be exceeded. His range for low-intensity aerobic training intensity would be 55–64 percent of his HR_{max} of 173, pulse rates of 95 to 110 beats per minute.

Sandra is a twenty-year-old healthy and somewhat active woman. Her HR_{max} would be 208 minus $(20 \times 0.7) = 194$. A reasonable beginning training range for Sandra might be 65–74 percent of 194, or pulse rates of 126 to 143 per minute, a range she could easily adjust up or down depending on her assessment of effort. A not-to-be-exceeded limit for Sandra would be 90 percent of 194, a pulse rate of 175 beats per minute. As beginners, Sandra and Luke should avoid even approaching their HR_{max} limits.

Pulse rate monitors can be purchased at fitness stores. While wearing one, you can simply glance at your wrist monitor and see whether you're exercising within your desired range. Or you can buy an inexpensive digital wristwatch and learn to take your own pulse. Here's how.

Many of us begin walking as our first choice for an exercise program, so let's use walking as an illustrative example. As you walk along, place a thumb or finger on the big artery on the underside of your wrist, just behind your first thumb joint. When you can feel a strong pulse, check out your watch for a convenient start point, abruptly interrupt your walk and count your pulse for ten seconds. Multiply this pulse rate by six and see if this rate falls within your desired intensity range. The ten-second limit is set because your pulse rate will slow considerably over the course of a full minute if you monitor for such an extended period while at rest.

It's much easier to locate the carotid artery on your neck, but putting pressure on it can signal danger to your brain, resulting in an elevation of cardiac activity and an inaccurate reading, so you should learn to take your pulse on your wrist. As your fitness increases, your need to monitor will decrease. Experience will generally make it very easy for you to read your body and quite accurately estimate the intensity of your workout. When I was very actively racing and frequently running with others who were training for coming races, we were all able to very accurately estimate our pace (minutes per mile) without ever having to consult our stopwatches.

RESISTANCE TRAINING

The ACSM position statement recommends that resistance training for those younger than fifty should work the major muscle groups two to three days a week with weight loads that allow eight to twelve repetitions, while those who are older should choose loads that allow ten to fifteen repetitions.

The report includes some interesting new findings. One is that, over a year's time, multiple sets of eight to fifteen repetitions produce only slightly greater benefits than a single set. This is exceptionally good news for those of us with busy schedules, since it means we can reduce our workout time expenditure from an hour or so to only twenty minutes each day and still get almost identical benefits at the end of a year or more.

Other conclusions are that regular resistance training reduces heart rate and blood pressure elevations when lifting, but even regular circuit weight training (moving from one lift set to another with only fifteen to thirty seconds between) elevates VO_{2max} only about 6 percent. Thus, while resistance training is a critical component in fitness, its effect on aerobic conditioning is not great. (However, in a later chapter we will find that resistance training can substantially reduce the risk of heart attacks.)

HEARTBEATS IN THE BANK

Before closing this chapter, let's examine one of the many reasons that aerobic fitness is a good idea, even if we're not planning on swimming the English Channel or running the Boston Marathon.

Regular aerobic training can reduce our risk of suffering America's leading cause of death: a heart attack. High cardiorespiratory fitness is like having money tucked away in a hidden Swiss bank, the "heart rate reserve." This account can help us get through tough times, times of severe illness and acute, life-threatening stress. But instead of dollars in our savings account, aerobic fitness puts bonus heartbeats in our banks. An above average VO_{2max} and the resulting lower pulse rate is one of the genuine life insurance policies available to us.

You've probably by now figured out that life insurance companies don't offer life insurance at all. They sell death insurance, but it would be a tough sell if it were honestly labeled as such. While life insurance premiums don't insure a longer life, our heart rate reserve account pays off by substantially increasing our odds of enjoying greater longevity.

Our aerobic savings account consists of the number of heartbeats that separate our resting heart rate from our HR_{max}: the limit above which a disaster such as a sudden-death heart attack might occur. A predictable consequence of regular aerobic training is a lowered pulse rate, so our workouts constitute deposits in our account to keep a safe reserve balance. Here are two examples of how it works.

We'll compare the mortality risks of two women, both fifty years of age and sharing a HR_{max} of 173 beats a minute. Andrea is an unfit, overworked, and chronically stressed woman with an elevated resting heart rate of eighty-five. The difference between her resting pulse rate and her 173 HR_{max} is her heart rate reserve: eighty-eight beats in the bank, available for her to draw upon for emergencies.

Kimberly, in contrast, is a highly fit woman with a resting pulse rate of fifty, which subtracted from 173, leaves her with a heart rate reserve of 123, thirty-five more beats in the bank than sedentary Andrea. Kimberly can demand a great deal more of her heart before reaching her HR_{max}. She is more likely than Andrea to survive an encounter with an acute illness or other stressful circumstance because she has those extra thirty-five heartbeats in the bank to draw upon before her heart rate moves into the disaster zone. In an emergency it could save her life, or she could save the life of someone else.

You may be wondering what exactly happens to our cardiorespiratory systems as our aerobic fitness increases and our pulse rate is gradually reduced. Just how does our body adjust to such strong demands for continuous hard effort? We'll examine the specifics of cardiorespiratory adaptations and the many health benefits of aerobic fitness in chapter 8, but for now you have the necessary vocabulary and concepts both to read on and to monitor yourself should you begin to work out.

PART 2:
EXERCISE AND MENTAL HEALTH

4.
MOODS AND
SELF-ESTEEM

The Sampsons were new to the neighborhood. They'd finally stopped renting and were able to buy their first house. Bill and Jenny both worked full-time; he designed computer software, and she taught middle school. Their two kids attended an elementary school within walking distance. They soon became acquainted with their new neighbors, and friendships began to form.

Newcomer Jenny found herself immediately interested in Beth, whose home was just across the street. The two had a lot in common. Both were responsible and emotionally mature working mothers of about the same age with kids in the same school and on the same soccer teams. Jenny was a somewhat shy, reserved, and cautious woman. It was both her nature and her considered judgment to let her potential friendship with Beth develop slowly. Beth, on the other hand, was very sociable, trusting, and open, with few filters muting what she felt or thought at any given moment. Beth's nonneurotic and unreserved manner simply fascinated Jenny.

But soon a mysterious side to Beth began to emerge. In the very early mornings when Jenny was waking up and thinking about making breakfast, getting the kids ready for school, and getting herself ready for work, Beth would arrive home. Where had she been, what had she been doing, and for how long?

It was weeks before Jenny felt comfortable enough to inquire. Beth quickly explained that five days a week she arose before dawn, drove five miles to the reservoir, and worked out for an hour with her rowing team before coming home and getting on with the rest of her life. Her four-person team had placed second in the nationals the previous year. During the off-season she spent those morning hours at the gym on the rowing machine. Weekends were recovery time and family time, except for meets during the rowing season.

"How do you do it?" was Jenny's first reaction to this news. Both women had huge responsibilities: husbands, kids, house, and work. Beth said she simply made the time, that it was a matter of priorities. She explained that a few years earlier she'd been mildly depressed, feeling like she was going through the motions of living. She recalled that it seemed like everyone else's needs were controlling her. Perhaps out of desperation she had staked out a time claim. She'd had enough and decided that a part of her life simply had to belong to herself alone, and everyone else had to work around those few hours each week that she devoted strictly to herself. Without those hours, she realized that she had little to give to anyone else. This, she said, turned her life around.

As time went on Jenny observed Beth engage in this daily ritual in sickness and in health, in darkness and in light, and in both fair and foul weather. It made her wonder if this behavior had some sort of compulsive pathological roots. Maybe there was more to Beth than met the eye: a dark side. One early summer morning, during a break in heavy downpours, Jenny was out getting the paper when Beth drove up. Beth was soaked. Her hair was limp and bedraggled. She wore the gaunt face of someone who was seriously dehydrated and totally spent. But her eyes were very much alive. It was time for Jenny to ask the big question.

"Why do you do this?" she asked. Without missing a beat, Beth matter-of-factly replied, "*It makes me feel good.*"

At that point the downpour recommenced, driving them indoors, abruptly ending their conversation. A few days later, over coffee, Jenny pursued the puzzling response—"It makes me feel good." "It's as simple as that," said Beth. "Sometimes I feel powerful and great when I'm doing it, like, 'This is who I am,' or 'This is what I am for,' sometimes not. Sometimes I have to exert great will just to get out of bed and drive out to the boat house, but always, always afterward, I feel good. I'm not saying that I never felt good before I began rowing, but in my lifetime I have never felt so consistently good, so alive, and so in control as I do now. No matter how tired or miserable I feel before working out, I always feel energized after I finish. Hard to believe, but it's true. And I'm way less moody nowadays.

"Maybe it's the result of my deciding that I matter enough to make a couple of hours a day my own. Maybe it's my newfound self-discipline and how it has made me feel better about myself. Maybe it's not the exercise at all. Maybe I could stop working out and still feel good." She paused and thought for a moment, then added, "but I wouldn't even dream of taking that risk."

Beth speaks for the millions of us who work out regularly. If asked why we do what we do, our first answer is almost invariably, "It makes me feel good." That's a whole lot of testimonial. But before examining what science tells us about the relationship between exercise and mood, we must define some terms.

JUST WHAT ARE MOODS?

This sounds like an unnecessary question, since we all know what moods are. It's a term we all toss around casually and frequently. We all have them, have routinely observed them in other people, and have noticed that some of us are moodier than others. But some sorting out is in order here, since some things that appear to be moods aren't moods at all, and some things we consider to be moods may be a bit more serious and fall into another category.

Moods refer to *predominant emotional states*. They may be positive or negative, and there are all sorts of them. We sometimes feel euphoric, sad, apprehensive, silly, angry, guilty, energetic, distrustful, scornful, enthusiastic, frustrated, lustful, or foolish, to name just a few.

A psychiatric dictionary might refer to moods as *normal* fluctuating *affective* states. Note the emphasis on normal. Moods are not psychiatric disorders. *Affect* is psychiatric jargon for feeling. Thus, an affective mental disorder is a mood disorder such as depression, as opposed to a thought disorder such as schizophrenia. In building a diagnostic framework, the mental health professional might refer to a troubled patient as having "flat affect" or "inappropriate affect." Thus, a patient may be without feeling in circumstances that would normally evoke strong feelings in most of us or might be laughing in another situation where most of us would be sad or perhaps angry. All of us talk about how this or that *affects* us, which typically includes how something makes us feel.

We, and the professionals, would agree that moods are typically *situational*.

Falling in love or lust, getting a promotion, getting cut off on the freeway, waiting for a biopsy, coming home to find the cat took a dump on your pillow, or experiencing the death of our dog all affect our moods.

There's usually a clear reason for how we feel. A significant change in a friend's mood, without an obvious situational explanation, is always a cause for our concern. Women commonly deal with this circumstance at once by asking, "Are you okay?" A sensitive New Age guy, when talking to a woman friend, might inquire, "Do you want to talk about it?" With two close male friends the opener might be, "Harry, you're looking like crap today." Styles differ.

So does the intention of the inquirer, which can often have unconscious underpinnings. Inviting people to talk about their sudden mood change could be a ploy to establish or reinforce dominance in a relationship (defining who's got it together and who needs help). It could be the first brick put down in a foundation of future trust and a deeper relationship or the foundation of future blackmail. It could be seductive. It might be designed to make the inquirer feel better about himself or to suggest to others that he or she belongs to the grim, selfless legion of do-gooders who absorb the pain of others but have no fun themselves. It might also be the result of only moderately contaminated unconditional love. Whatever the case, mood changes are interesting.

We, and the professionals, would also agree that moods can be relatively *brief* or very *long-lasting*. Here's brief. I recall a day early last summer when I walked into Trader Joe's. As I entered the store, a group of three clerks approached: a forty-something woman, whose face suggested that she'd lived a lot but remained good humored, in charge of two young men who were making identity statements with facial hardware and shaved skulls. I'd never spoken to the woman, but I smiled a greeting: my usual semisquinty-eyed, closed-lip number. She returned the smile and surprised me by stopping directly in front of me and motioning for her two young companions to come over. She looked up at me, maintained eye contact, while over her shoulder said to her two companions, "Does this guy look like Steve McQueen or what?" As they passed by, the two young men gave each other a blank look, but my mood was changed big time for the next few hours. I'd always been a huge McQueen fan; we'd even ridden identical Husqvarna off-road motorcycles in the California deserts and mountains a quarter century earlier.

Here's briefer. A couple of months later I was in Trader Joe's again, reaching for some world-class Marin County sausage made with lean chicken, dehydrated apples, and chardonnay. I was reaching because I was leaning over a clerk who was crouched down as she finished stocking the lower level. It turned out be my second meeting with the woman who had "made my day" in June. She looked up, smiled, and without hesitation said, "Steve's back." With that, she straightened up and began walking away toward the stockroom.

I laughed and replied, "Hey, I can't help it." There was a noticeable pause before she responded. Then, without looking back, she said, "There are some things you just shouldn't mess with." I once again walked around with a silly smile on my face for all of ten minutes, before I ran into one of my graduate students. He asked about my smile and dutifully displayed his own expectant half-smile as I told him the story. When I finished, he paused for a bit as his smile faded, and then he asked, "So who's Steve McQueen?"

Moods can also be very long lasting. The First Noble Truth of Buddhism is that suffering is a fact of life. The second is that the cause of suffering is attachment. We Westerners do get attached, and we do suffer. Loss, whether it is the result of abandonment, being told we are no longer loved, or the death of a loved one can precipitate moods that can predominate for months. Sometimes the moods caused by loss are so severe that the symptoms are identical to those of a major depressive episode, and if those symptoms persist unabated, our normal bereavement may have evolved into a mental disorder.

Mental disorders differ from moods in terms of the number, severity, and duration of symptoms and the degree of dysfunctionality those symptoms incur. There are also some rule-outs. (The differences between moods and disorders will be specifically spelled out in the chapters on anxiety and depressive disorders.)

Finally, moods should not be confused with *personality traits*, which are our individual predictable ways of behaving, regardless of situation. For example, some of us are predictably social, trusting, open, warm, optimistic, or nurturing throughout our lives over a wide range of situations. Others of us may be predictably cool, reserved, assertive, unsentimental, or emotionally controlled. Thus we hear, "You can always depend on Bill to listen to your problems or lend a hand," or "It's no accident Sarah became a cop." We might also hear that "Poor Jane is going to come totally unglued when she gets the news," since degree of emotionality itself is a central personality trait. Some of us predictably overreact in circumstances in which the majority of us react in a more measured fashion and where others of us are remarkably unaffected.

Some of us are "high strung" while others typically "laid back," with most of us falling in between the two extremes. Men and women in the less emotional, laid-back group often fit into jobs in which a capacity to perform under circumstances of great stress is a central requirement. They may become emergency room nurses, Green Berets, fighter pilots, or members of a SWAT team. Jane, on the other hand, might find a home on stage.

Personality traits are mostly set in place before we reach the age of twenty, and they are almost set in concrete by age thirty. This does not suggest that people never undergo later significant personality changes as a result of "life-changing" or traumatic experiences, but an average of about 50 percent of each of our personality traits is the result of genetic predisposition. While heredity is not destiny, some gene combinations are difficult to counter. The basic extroversion-introversion personality trait, for example, is about 70 percent genetically predisposed. The sensation-seeking, risk-taking trait is almost as strongly tied to genes.[1] If you're skeptical about these examples, I suggest you try remake an introvert into a socially outgoing party animal, or convince someone who won't go to scary movies to make a solo parachute jump.

It's a good bet that the person you decide to marry at age twenty has a basic personality structure that isn't going to change a whole lot over his or her lifetime. So when you're blind in love, it's a bad bet to marry, thinking that your semiperfect partner, who has a few minor problematical personality traits, will change "if he or she really loves you." Don't even think about it. Remember, you're blind and may be coming up against some heavy-duty genetic storm troops, among other things. Lasting relationships typically involve partners who do not require major reshaping.

So moods are not enduring personality traits and are not mental disorders. Moods are normal, predominant feeling states. They fluctuate, are typically related to a situational circumstance, and can be short-lived or long-lasting. Now that we're clear on what they are and what they are not, let's see what science has to tell us about how they may be affected by exercise.

THE WAYS OF SCIENTISTS

Science progresses in reasonably predictable stages. In the case of exercise and mood, an interested scientist first might notice that out in the natural world, people who exercise regularly typically seem less depressed and anxious than those who are sedentary. This kind of anecdotal evidence might motivate interested scientists to conduct some quick, simple, and inexpensive studies to see whether any kind of consistent relationship emerges when the moods of large groups of normal active and inactive people are compared.

There are many ready-made circumstances where active and inactive populations, along with those of interested scientists, all coexist. University and college campuses are ideal laboratories. A simple study might be to compare the moods of college students who take physical education classes or are on athletic teams with the moods of students who attend only lecture classes and are largely inactive.

Such studies have the advantage of being both quick and inexpensive. Their weakness is that all they can determine is whether or not there is some sort of consistent association or relationship between mood and physical activity. These *correlational* or *cross-sectional* studies are *preexperimental* in that they don't delineate cause and effect. They leave us with the classic question of which came first, the chicken or the egg? Do people swim each day because they feel good, or do they feel good because they swim each day? However, if many such studies consistently show that active people tend to feel significantly better than inactive people, scientists are inclined to invest more time and effort into further exploration of the issue of cause and effect.

So, the first and least expensive question is, "Do the moods of active and inactive people appear to differ in a consistent manner?" Then, if it appears that active people are typically less depressed, the next logical question is, "What happens to the moods of inactive people if they become active?" Here again, this somewhat more complicated question doesn't necessarily demand a huge investment of time or money, since there are so many ready-made experiments out there in the natural world, circumstances where sedentary people for one or another reason begin to exercise.

A student working on a master's degree might, for example, measure the moods of a large group of college students at the onset and end of a semester, then compare the mood changes of those who were enrolled in physical education classes or played team sports all semester with the students who were normally sedentary. An even quicker study would be to measure the moods of students before and after an hour of strength training or fencing and compare them with moods of others before and after an hour of classroom lecture.

These kinds of studies are called *quasi-experiments*, "quasi" meaning "looks like, not quite, or almost a true" experiment. In contrast to correlational studies, which measure moods of naturally occurring active and inactive groups a single time, quasi-experiments always include *before* and *after* measurements. They allow for a much stronger implication of cause and effect. If many such quasi-experiments consistently suggest that exercise appears to result in improved mood, scientists become willing to invest more time, money, and effort into even more rigorous, controlled true experiments.

In *true experiments* our college students would not self-select themselves into active groups (I think I'll take a class in swimming this semester) or inactive groups (lecture classes only). When students self-select, it's impossible to know whether subsequent mood changes were caused by the exercise itself or the fact that certain students *chose* to exercise and others did not. Perhaps students who enroll in physical activity classes have learned in the past that regular physical activity helps them to deal with the stresses of college life. In true experiments, the students or *subjects* are *randomly assigned* to a sedentary *control* group and one or more active *experimental* groups. This kind of more rigorous design allows investigators to assign cause and effect with greater assurance.

THE EARLY STUDIES

Dozens of studies have now examined the relationship between mood and physical activity, and it's interesting to look back at some of these early correlational and cross-sectional investigations. They not only provide a great deal of information relating to the fundamental question but also reveal other interesting findings that relate to our ways of life and their consequences.

A word here about correlation. It's a term that gets tossed around a lot, but many of us who use it aren't really clear on what it actually means. "Correlation coefficients" are numbers that refer to the direction and degree to which two things co-vary or correlate. A perfect positive—"the more, the more" or "the less, the less"—correlation would be 1.0, and a perfect negative—"the more, the less"—correlation would be –1.0. Such perfect correlations almost never exist. Correlations around zero suggest no relationship.

Here are some examples. There would be a positive but imperfect correlation between adult heights and weights (tall people typically weigh more), a zero correlation between driver's license numbers and IQ scores (makes no sense), and a negative correlation between degree of obesity and longevity (the greater the obesity, the lesser the chance of a longer life). Examples of proven significant positive correlations would be the correlation between smoking and rates of lung cancer and between amount of media violence viewed and aggressive behavior on the part of viewers. An example of a significant negative correlation would be the correlation between children's exposure to lead and their IQ scores. Such relationships clearly suggest cause and effect.

This is also a good time to acquaint you with what is meant by the word "significant" in scientific literature. A "significant difference" is a statistical term that spells out the odds that the difference in average scores found between two groups may or may not be due to chance. For example, differences that reach the .01, or the more stringent .001, "levels of confidence" tell us that the odds are only one in a hundred, or one in a thousand, that the differences found between the groups being compared are due to chance. Throughout this book, when you read that groups "differed significantly," it will mean that the differences being discussed were subjected to statistical tests and were found highly unlikely to be due to chance.

Let's take a look now at some examples of correlational and cross-sectional studies that have examined how mood and exercise correlate.

My colleague Wesley Sime of the University of Nebraska did a study focused on occupational stress among seven hundred workers. All of these men and women were given tests to assess their moods and a questionnaire that inquired about their leisure-time activities. How did they feel, and what did they do in their spare time: a simple one-time, in-and-out, inexpensive study.[2]

Sime found that higher depression was most significantly correlated with amount of recreational drug use: a positive correlation, as you might expect. Do depressed people turn to drugs, does frequent drug use cause depression, or is it a little of both? The correlation doesn't answer that question, but the relationship cannot be argued. There's clearly something there.

Sime also found that depression was positively correlated with the number of hours spent watching television. Here again the study didn't reveal whether this means that depressed people watch more mindless television, that television has a depressing effect on people, or that both phenomena are involved. However, many subsequent studies now consistently tell us that watching a lot of television does, in fact, have a depressive consequence. A patient once related to me that during a major depressive episode years earlier, she had for several weeks spent her daylight hours on a couch looking at a blank TV screen. I jokingly suggested to her that she was lucky she lacked the energy to turn the thing on and make herself really ill!

So what about the negative correlations? What kinds of leisure-time activities characterized the lives of the workers whose depression scores tended to be on the low side? Two things: reading and engaging in sports. Sime also found that anxiety scores were positively related to TV-viewing time and negatively related to both reading and sports participation. Thus, those people who read and exercised during their leisure time tended to be both less depressed and less anxious.

Meanwhile, a Purdue University research team compared groups of sedentary and physically active men using a test called the Minnesota Multiphasic Personality Inventory. Originally designed only to sort out basic forms of psychopathology in severely ill people, the MMPI contains scales such as paranoia, depression, schizophrenia, and psychopathic deviate. The inventory is now one of psychology's most widely employed research tools, since it's become apparent that one's individual test profile, while not indicating serious pathology, does reveal useful personality patterns. It's a very helpful tool when used on normal individuals.

The Purdue investigators administered the MMPI to two groups of healthy, normal men aged forty to sixty. One group comprised typical sedentary Americans who had engaged in no aerobic exercise for the past ten years, while the second group was composed of highly fit runners who had been working out three to five times a week for three to ten years.[3]

As expected, the average scale scores of the two groups fell well within the normal range. No pathology here. However, the average scores of the two groups differed significantly on two of the ten basic scales. The runners, as a group, tended to be somewhat more extroverted than their sedentary brothers. But the largest, and the most significant, difference between the two groups was found on the depression scale, where the sedentary men scored higher than the runners.

Since the average scores of the two groups fell well within the normal range, the difference had to reflect a difference in mood (rather than pathology). Of course there was no way to know for sure whether the runners were happier because they ran or ran because they were happy. But this pioneering finding suggested that regular vigorous *physical activity might have its greatest impact on mood*, specifically on depression, rather than on other common dimensions of psychopathology as reflected by the MMPI.

These and other early correlational and cross-sectional studies typically found that physically active men and women had lower depression scores than did sedentary people. Meanwhile, other scientists were beginning to ask the question, "What happens to the moods of sedentary people who take up regular exercise?"

SOME QUASI-EXPERIMENTS

Another colleague, Bonnie Berger, now at Bowling Green State University, has systematically researched the relationship between exercise and mood for years.

Like so many other scientists who study mood, Berger most commonly used a psychological test called the Profile of Mood States (POMS) in her studies.[4] The POMS is a short paper-and-pencil test designed for use by psychotherapists, who could administer it to patients on a regular basis in order to get some kind of objective measure of changes in overall mood as therapy progressed. It has since become the most widely used inventory in research concerned with the effects of exercise on mood.

The POMS has six scales: From left to right they are tension, depression, anger, vigor, fatigue, and confusion. Since it was designed for clinical use, all but one of the moods (vigor) included were negative, thus higher total scores reflected a more negative overall mood state. The POMS attracted the attention of exercise/mood researchers back in 1980, when William Morgan published his now-classic "iceberg profile."

Morgan administered the POMS to a group of highly conditioned male runners. The average scores of these elite athletes formed an almost perfect iceberg-shaped profile, with the one positive mood, vigor, rising sharply above the surface (the average score for a large population of normal men and women) and the five remaining negative moods scores falling below. This dramatic pyramidal profile suggested that elite runners appeared to feel better than the typically sedentary average guys on the street.[5]

One of Berger's interests concerned the acute effects of exercise on mood. What happens to mood as the consequence of a single vigorous workout? Berger and D. R. Owen administered the POMS to groups of students enrolled in swimming classes both before and after a single workout. They did the same for an equal number of students who were enrolled in lecture classes.

They found no mood differences between the swimmers and lecture students in the pretest. However, the swimmers had significant reductions in depression, tension, anger, and confusion following their workouts. The swimmers also significantly boosted their vigor scores. These changes were greater than changes found in the lecture groups.[6]

These two investigators later examined the effects of a variety of college classes on moods of students whom they tested before and after classes on three occasions during the course of an entire semester. The students were enrolled in (aerobic) swimming, (anaerobic) weight training, fencing, yoga, and lecture classes.[7]

The greatest improvements in mood were in two yoga classes, with after-class profiles tending to move from a rather flat average configuration into a more classic positive iceberg shape. The weight lifters elevated only their fatigue scores, and the fencers elevated their scores on vigor. Students in health science and physical education lecture classes showed no significant changes.

In light of research findings reported in professional journals, the investigators had predicted that the students in the aerobic swimming class would show the greatest positive gains in mood. However, the before-after profiles of the swimmers turned out to be essentially identical, almost perfect iceberg patterns. There was nothing to improve on. This finding points to an inherent weakness of quasi-experiments, where participants self-select themselves into various groups. It seems likely that these happy swimmers had discovered in the past that spending a few hours a week in the pool made university life far better.

There have been many such experiments on various university campuses. At Pennsylvania State University, the POMS was used to assess the moods of students in jogging and English classes at the onset, middle, and end of a semester. By mid-semester, the tension and anger scores of the students in the English classes had elevated greatly, and by the semester's end those scores had returned to the same level as at the onset of the semester. However, the joggers substantially reduced both tension and anger by mid-semester and held on to those gains until the semester's end, suggesting that exercise might be useful for reducing the stresses of college life.[8]

By far the most impressive of the quasi-experiments was one done at the University of Virginia by Robert Brown and his colleagues.[9] They enlisted 561 volunteer students to take part in an experiment to examine the effect of exercise on mood. At the academic quarter's onset, students chose whether or not they wished to exercise, and how much (a minimum of thirty minutes either three or five times a week) for a period of ten weeks. The students were tested for depression and mood before and after the ten-week quarter.

When investigators take a close look at student populations, it is inevitable that they will find some members who are mildly or moderately depressed but getting along well enough to not require medication or psychotherapy. This was the case at the University of Virginia, where a Zung depression scale[10] pretest revealed that there were 101 mild-to-moderately depressed men and women among the 561 volunteers. Thus, the study involved six groups: sedentary normal students, sedentary depressed students, active normal students who worked out either three or five times a week, and active depressed students who worked out either three or five times a week.

Brown's sedentary students, whether normal or depressed, showed no changes in average depression scores over the ten weeks. However, all four of the active groups, whether normal or depressed, significantly reduced average depression scores over the same time period. The active depressed students showed the greatest average reductions. It was interesting that the students with the very highest pretest depression scores chose to exercise five as against three times a week, and their average depression scores dropped about twice as much as those depressed students who chose to exercise only three times a week.

Both of Brown's groups of active normal and depressed students also showed significant changes in other moods over the course of the semester: reduced anger, fatigue, and anxiety as well as elevated general activation. While Brown's focus was largely on depression, some comments about exercise and reduced anger are in order here.

Brown's findings are consistent with many other studies, which over the decades have time and time again shown that physical activity reduces anger. These findings lend validity to folk wisdom that has known this relationship to be true since time immemorial. Bickering children have been told to go out and play, and a father who comes home angry from work has been told to go out and mow the lawn or chop some wood. There are reasons for enduring folk wisdom.

This is a sedentary and aggressive culture in which we live. Frequently the violence we observe at sporting events takes place in the stands rather than on the playing field. And a large percentage of the calls responded to by police have to do with domestic violence. Perhaps America would be a less violent and safer place for all of us if more of us were physically active.

Returning now to Brown's ambitious quasi-experiment, I should point out that it had some obvious weaknesses. Students were allowed to choose whether or not they wished to exercise and how frequently they would like to do so. Furthermore, exercise was not monitored, so the degree of compliance was an unknown. However, the findings contributed by such a large sample lend some credence to the proposition that exercise may have a positive effect on mood and depression for both normal and mildly depressed university students.

What we've seen so far is that pioneering correlational and cross-sectional studies have consistently reported a positive association between exercise and improved mood. Quasi-experiments, which include before and after assessments of mood and carry a stronger implication of cause and effect, suggest more strongly that exercise positively affects mood.

Let's move on now to look at a few of the more rigorous "true experiments," which allow us to delineate cause and effect more clearly. Subjects for such experiments are typically drawn from normal, nonclinical university populations and are randomly assigned to control (sedentary) and exercise groups. Moods are assessed before and after a period during which some have exercised and others have not. Exercise is carefully monitored, as are its physiological consequences.

TRUE EXPERIMENTS

We will examine a series of four illustrative experiments that were carried out by William Morgan and colleagues at the University of Wisconsin. I chose this particular group of studies because they examined whether the (1) duration, (2) frequency, (3) intensity, or (4) kind of exercise affected mood.

The first examined the question of how the *duration* of exercise might affect mood.[11] A group of college men whose preexperiment POMS scores indicated that they were not depressed were randomly assigned to a sedentary control group or one of three exercise groups that ran three times a week for twenty weeks. The sessions were forty-five, thirty, or fifteen minutes in duration for the three groups.

As you might expect, at the end of twenty weeks, all three of the exercise groups showed increased aerobic power in direct proportion to workout duration. However, none of the groups showed a decrease in average POMS depression scores. This result was not totally unexpected, since this was a carefully selected *nonclinical* sample of men who were not depressed before taking part in the various exercise programs.

A second study examined the *frequency* of exercise, and once again a carefully selected group of nondepressed college men took part. They were randomly assigned to an attention-placebo control group or to groups that ran one, three, or five days a week.[12] Once again, aerobic power increased in direct proportion to workout frequency, and once again none of the groups of men showed reductions in average depression scores. These two rigorous experiments, which carefully documented increased aerobic fitness, suggest that perhaps we need to be at least moderately depressed for aerobic exercise to have a healing effect. The following two experiments support this suggestion.

The first examined whether the *kind* of exercise might differentially affect mood. A large group of *unselected* college men volunteered to exercise two to three days a week for six weeks. They were randomly assigned to swimming, running, cycling, circuit weight training, and sedentary control groups. After six weeks, the runners showed the greatest increases in aerobic conditioning, but all of the exercise groups had greater aerobic gains than the sedentary control men. Once again, none of the groups significantly reduced average depression scores.

However, an examination of the pretest depression scores revealed that scattered among the 140 men in the various groups were eleven who had clinically significant levels of depression before beginning the weeks of exercise. When the pre-exercise and postexercise scores of these eleven men were analyzed, a significant decrease in depression scores was found.[13] Apparently, if exercise is going to elevate mood, a variety of kinds will do the job, provided your mood needs elevating.

The final study, which examined the acute effects of exercise of varying exercise *intensities* on mood, also took into account the pre-exercise mood states of the participants. Six college women with normal POMS depression scale scores and six other women with elevated depression scores took part. They exercised on a stationary bicycle at 40, 60, or 80 percent of their maximum aerobic capacity in a random manner for three days. Preworkout and postworkout POMS testing revealed significant depression score reductions for the six mildly depressed women on each of three days of testing, regardless of the exercise intensity. The decreases were transitory. No such depression score reductions were found for the other six women who had normal POMS scores.[14]

These four selected studies suggest that there is a mood ceiling that limits exercise-mediated reductions in depression in groups of reasonably happy and highly functioning university students. They have further suggested that individuals who are the most depressed to begin with typically experience the greatest reductions in depression following exercise. The people who most need it experience the greatest relief.

You may recall that in an earlier chapter that Hsiao and Thayer found that those men and women who scored high on a test of neuroticism (describing themselves as depressed, anxious, moody, apprehensive, fearful, etc.) rated mood improvement as a much more important reason for exercising than did other, less troubled, fitness club members. You may also recall that in research discussed earlier in this chapter, Brown found that students who were the most depressed were more likely to choose to exercise five rather than three times a week. Thus, exercise might be more eagerly embraced as a potential healing agent by those who need it the most. In a later chapter, we will see that the same appears to be true even with individuals hospitalized with major clinical depressions.

THE EXPERIMENTAL EVIDENCE: CONCLUSIONS

There has been no shortage of experimental research on the relationship between physical activity and mood. Over the past several decades, there have been dozens of such studies. The results are mixed, but about 75 percent of them support the proposition that exercise has a positive effect on mood, according to a review by University of Toronto professor Larry Leith.[15] There is considerable imperfection in this accumulated data, and as you might suspect, as the rigor of research increases, the percentage of positive findings tend to decrease.

Many of the studies on mood have not included measures of fitness, nor have they quantified exercise intensities. Some of the research involved assessing mood before and after single bouts of exercise, and there has been no real consistency as to just exactly how long before or after exercise those measures are taken, a factor that can be critical when dealing with transitory mood changes following different kinds of exercise. For example, one of the studies discussed above found that the only significant mood change following weight lifting was increased fatigue. Perhaps positive mood changes would have become apparent an hour or two after that sort of strenuous workout ended.

Other studies have assessed mood changes after weeks or months of chronic exercise, and if the population studied was sufficiently large, significant positive mood changes were often found. Brown's research, which involved 561 men and women, illustrated this. Groups of normal men and women who exercised either three or five times a week had significant positive mood gains after ten weeks. But many studies have compared small groups, and for mood changes to be of significance, those changes must be both large and consistent within such groups. This is not likely when dealing with groups of essentially healthy, nondepressed college students.

Reviews of mood research suggest that length of workout does not seem to be critical in determining mood but that fifteen to twenty minutes appears to be a minimum, and while mood may improve after a single bout of exercise, working out a minimum of three days a week appears necessary to impact mood in a more durable way.[16]

There have been at least twenty reviews of the accumulated experimental evidence on mood and physical activity, and the reviewers are consistent in concluding that there is cautious support for the hypothesis that physical activity is associated with positive changes in mood. The caution is a result of the kind of research-design weaknesses discussed above. However, when we leave the world of college campuses behind and venture out into a broader world, epidemiological evidence that physical activity enhances mood is very strong.

EPIDEMIOLOGICAL EVIDENCE

Epidemiological research is very different from experimental studies, and each kind offers unique strengths and weaknesses. While well-executed and controlled true experiments offer conclusions in which we may place considerable confidence, they lack the huge sample sizes and fail to tap the diverse members of the general population examined in epidemiological studies. Small groups of very bright, reasonably high functioning, and mentally healthy college students are a whole different ball game than tens of thousands of adults living out there in the real world. Such real world households are not even close to being Ivy League campuses. Households are filled with men and women of varying ages and functionality and include some members who have very serious mental health problems.

Three epidemiological studies involving nearly sixteen thousand adults carried out during the 1990s in Great Britain were reviewed by Stuart Biddle of Loughborough University.[17] All three surveys found emotional well-being to be positively related to increased physical activity for both sexes. Two of the surveys found this relationship to be unrelated to health status: that is, even among the men and women who were least healthy, those who exercised reported significantly greater feelings of emotional well-being than those who did not. While this relationship was apparent across all age groups, there was some evidence that the effect of exercise might be greater among older adults.

Thomas Stephens did a similar review of four studies conducted in Canada and the United States that involved a total of fifty-five thousand people.[18] In his 1988 *Preventative Medicine* article, he wrote:

The inescapable conclusion of this study is that the level of physical activity is positively associated with good mental health in the household populations of the United States and Canada, when mental health is defined as positive mood, general well being, and relatively infrequent symptoms of anxiety and depression. This relationship is independent of the effects of education and physical health status, and is stronger for women and those 40 years and over than for men and those under 40. The robustness of this conclusion derives from the varied sources of evidence: four population samples in two countries over a 10-year period, four different methods of operationalizing physical activity, and six different mental health scales.

"Inescapable conclusion" constitutes very strong language on the part of a scientist. Nevertheless, well-conducted studies that involve more than seventy thousand people deservedly carry considerable weight. The persuasive and consistent epidemiological findings he reviews offer great hope for those of us ordinary folks out in the real world who are looking for an effective and economical solution to moods that seem to be controlling our lives. And the best news from the more rigorous experimental studies is that the greater our depression or anxiety, the more likely physical activity will provide relief.

TOO MUCH OF A GOOD THING

Mood improvements have been demonstrated over a wide range of both aerobic and nonaerobic activities, from aerobic dancing to yoga. Improvements have also been demonstrated over a broad range of exercise intensities. However, evidence is beginning to accumulate that suggests that exercise of moderate intensity is as effective in producing positive mood change as is high-intensity exercise. What's more, it's becoming clear that when people get carried away and begin to work out too hard, too long, and too often, moods predictably worsen.

Expert Patrick O'Connor of the University of Georgia reported that by 1994 more than forty very high-quality studies had focused on the phenomena of *overtraining* and *staleness*, and these two conditions, as well as the mood disturbances associated with them, are now well documented.[19] First, some definitions.

Overtraining refers to a short period of intense exercise where highly motivated and fit athletes engage in training loads that are maximal or near maximal in order to boost performance that has plateaued after a long period of training. These overtraining periods can last for only a few days or weeks, since exercising for as long as a month at such intensity would be impossible. Thus, overtraining involves short-term exercise regimens that are more intense, of greater duration, or more frequent (often twice a day).

Motivation for such focused exercise is varied, ranging from careful controlled preparation for the Olympic trials to outright pathological. For competitive athletes to reach their performance potential, at least one period of overtraining is necessary during each training season. But many athletes—competitive and recreational—are often unwilling to stop progressive increases in training after their performances plateau. If these increased demands continue without interruption, typically one of two negative consequences will occur: injury or staleness.

Fortunately, most of us nonelite types who are in the simple pursuit of personal bests are most likely to incur an injury. After one or two injuries and the dreadful consequence of being unable to engage in our beloved activity for extended periods of time, most of us learn to avoid overdoing it. Better to be able to continue doing our favorite thing than to periodically be unable to do so because of injury, or even worse, be unable to ever do it again.

The alternative to injury is *staleness*, a psychobiological malady. The main physical symptoms are fatigue and a reduction in athletic performance. Not so very long ago, the standard prescription for staleness was rest, perhaps six months to a year being required before an athlete even felt like working out again.

Eventually it was noticed that the symptoms of staleness and depression looked very much alike, and in 1987, William Morgan reported that 80 percent of stale athletes were clinically depressed.[20] The elite American marathoner Alberto Salazar overtrained and went stale for more than a year, then Prozac arrived on the scene to get him up and moving again.

It seems highly likely that the stresses of unremitting increased physical demands, *like any other chronic stress*, can dysregulate mood-relevant neurochemical systems and result in depression. The fact that antidepressant medication enhances recovery from staleness strengthens that possibility.

While we're discussing the consequences of overtraining and staleness here, it may not be a far reach to move from the locker room to the office or factory and think in terms of overwork and burnout. As you read on about the mood changes that delineate physical overtraining and staleness, consider whether or not they seem to parallel those you have observed in yourself or others whom you know well who are experiencing overwork and burnout.

Staleness has circulatory, immune system, metabolic, dietary, neuro-muscular, endocrine, and psychological markers. Without resorting to invasive and costly laboratory testing, the POMS has offered scientists, as well as coaches and trainers, a simple and economical way to assess both over-training and staleness. It turns out that each of these two states has its own predictable mood markers.

O'Connor relates that a number of studies have examined the mood disturbances associated with overtraining and staleness in a wide variety of athletes and performers and that the findings are quite consistent.[21]

Negative moods are closely related to training volume. In one investigation, the POMS was used to chart the moods of two hundred male and female swimmers over the course of a seven-month period.[22] The daily distance swum during the first month was about one mile, and as the months went by it increased in rather linear fashion to about seven miles during month five, then dropped to about six miles during month six, and back down to about one mile during month seven. Plotted graphically (with distance swum on the vertical and months on the base), it looked like a pyramid with a steep right side.

These swimmers also took the POMS each month during that period of differential physical demands. You'll recall that the POMS was designed for clinical use and had five negative moods and only a single positive mood (vigor). When you add the negative mood scores and subtract that of vigor, you have an overall mood score. The higher the score, the more negative one's overall mood. A plot of the swimmers' average overall mood scores was *virtually identical* to the plot of the miles swum per day over the seven months. The more miles swum, the more negative the general mood: going up with increased mileage and down again when mileage decreased.

The most consistent and replicated finding in this area of research is that increased training demands are associated with increasingly negative mood states, and reductions in load are associated with improved mood.

The two POMS moods that are most sensitive to overtraining are *fatigue* and *vigor*. Anger, confusion, and depression show the least reaction to overtraining. However, if overtraining continues and staleness sets in, *depression* and *anger* are the predominant markers.[23]

You may have observed the same progression of symptomatic mood changes in people you know well as they move from a period of overwork into one of burnout and reduced productivity. Reduced vigor and increased fatigue mark the demands of overwork, and if burnout occurs, anger and depression become the major mood markers. The burned-out worker whose productivity has taken a dive and who no longer wants to go to work looks a lot like the stale athlete whose performance has fallen off and no longer wants to train.

These predictable mood markers are important for those of us who choose to challenge ourselves or others in physical activities. Many of us, for various reasons, become quite obsessed with improving our performances. It's useful to know that when *fatigue* and reduced *vigor* become our predominant moods, it may be time back off or face the consequences: injury or staleness, both of which can leave us feeling *angry* and *depressed*.

With regard to exercise, we can clearly get too much of a good thing. Many of us who become regular exercisers, especially during our midlife years, go through a "born-again" period. We may rediscover youth or for the first time discover a youthfulness we never had previously experienced, discovering what our bodies are actually capable of doing and what we're capable of becoming. These are huge discoveries: very reinforcing and very seductive. This type of birth or rebirth frequently results in hard-learned lessons.

CHANGING HOW WE FEEL ABOUT OURSELVES

Exercise can certainly affect how we feel (our moods), but can it affect how we feel about ourselves? Can it affect our self-esteem and self-concept? And what are those things anyway?

Self-concept basically refers to the picture that we have of ourselves: This is who I am. We sometimes may have some difficulty differentiating our real self from our ideal self, but we do the best that we can. *Self-esteem* refers to our evaluation of this self-portrait and all of the components that contribute to it. Because it's virtually impossible to look at these many aspects of our self-concept without making a judgment about them, the terms self-esteem and self-concept are sometimes used interchangeably.

Self-concept is a multidimensional structure, probably Gestalt in nature, since the whole package is more than the simple sum of its parts. It has many subcomponents, which in turn also have their own subcomponents. For example, one component that contributes to overall self-concept is personality, which in turn has subcomponents such as emotionality, introversion-extroversion, sociability, intelligence, and so on. Another self-concept structure would include attitudes and beliefs, such as "I am a 'Right to Life' Christian," or "I believe drugs should be legalized." Character is another factor.

Expert Robert Sonstroem of the University of Rhode Island has discovered a *physical self-worth* component that contributes to the self-esteem and ultimately the self-concept of men and women. Physical self-worth includes four major factors: (1) one's skills, (2) degree of conditioning, (3) strength, and (4) attractiveness. Sonstroem and other investigators have found that of these, the physical attractiveness factor is the characteristic most closely related to positive self-esteem in people across our life spans.[24]

There are many contributors to our global self-concept, and it's very difficult to differentiate self-concept from self-esteem. How does one not evaluate one's attractiveness, intelligence, sociability, physical skills, and character? All of these, plus other components, contribute to our overall or global self-esteem, which turns out to be a rather important factor in our lives.

Low self-esteem has been linked to neuroticism, depression, anxiety, feelings of worthlessness, child abuse, adolescent relationship problems, and obesity. Hemiplegics and coronary risk patients, as well as alcoholics, often suffer from low self-esteem. Those of us with low self-esteem often feel that our lives are controlled by external circumstances, while those of us with high self-esteem are more adaptable and feel as though we have greater control over our lives. High self-esteem is also associated with above average social skills, achievement, and leadership. It's no surprise that a common goal in psychotherapy is improved self-esteem.[25]

During the 1960s and 1970s, there was an enormous output of investigations conducted in the area of "sport personality." How did the personalities of athletes differ from those of nonathletes, good athletes from poor ones, athletes in team sports from individual-sport participants, quarterbacks from tackles, male athletes from female athletes, and so on.[26] A veritable landslide of master's theses took place. However, there was little consistency in the findings, partially reflecting the poor quality of many studies but also reflecting the fact that personality traits are rather consistent and resistant to change. That landslide of research did, however, suggest that exercise seemed most consistently to elevate feelings of self-sufficiency.

By the early eighties, it was virtually written in stone that one could elevate his or her self-esteem with a pair of dumbbells or sneakers. However, that message turned out to be etched on crumbly sandstone. Many of the studies were flawed by virtue of failing to measure whether the increases in self-esteem were paralleled by increases in fitness, were lasting, or were the result of all kinds of other uncontrolled factors such as expectations, social experiences while exercising, attempts to please the experimenters, and so forth. However, since the mid-eighties, many quality studies have been carried out. Reviews of this entire substantial body of research allow us to draw several conclusions.[27]

Self-esteem may be elevated in normal populations through exercise. Weight lifting and jogging in particular have been shown to do so.

Interestingly, a number of studies have now demonstrated that self-esteem can be significantly elevated in groups of people who simply think that their exercise program has increased their fitness. For example, Abby King and colleagues assigned male and female aircraft workers either to a six-month, home-based, unsupervised aerobic training program or to a sedentary control group. Those in the training group showed significant increases on several self-esteem dimensions, but in fact, only 15 percent of the men and 9 percent of the women who worked out actually showed increases in fitness.[28] Other studies have also revealed that increased fitness does not always reveal parallel gains in self-esteem. To elevate self-esteem through exercise, *sometimes all that is necessary is the perception of increased fitness.*

Studies that have included follow-up measures suggest that *self-esteem elevated by exercise may have lasting effects.* In one such study, thirty-two depressed women who completed an exercise program maintained self-esteem gains for twelve months,[29] and a second study found that a group of women who completed a twenty-six-day Outward Bound (how to survive on your own in the wilderness) course maintained such gains for a similar period.[30]

It turns out that elevating self-esteem in so-called normal populations, such as college students, through exercise, is not as easy as was earlier believed.[31] A few recent quality studies have demonstrated that it is possible, but many others have not revealed such gains. Certainly we would expect that individuals with average or above average levels of self-esteem would run into a "you can't feel any better about yourself" ceiling sooner than those with initial low levels of self-esteem. This turns out to be true and leads us to another important conclusion.

People with low self-esteem may be considered as belonging to a special population, and several studies suggest that *certain special populations are more likely to respond to exercise with greater gains in self-esteem* than are normal college students. A review of studies reveals that such gains have been demonstrated for hemiplegic, paraplegic, coronary risk, and physical rehabilitation patients as well as obese teenagers, elderly adults, clinically depressed male and female adults, and individuals with initial low levels of fitness.[32]

Self-efficacy is certainly a factor in these findings. Our perceived self-efficacy reflects the strength of our belief that we can successfully perform a specific task (self-confidence is a broader concept). Albert Bandura wrote that self-efficacy expectations influence whether or not we will undertake a given behavior, how hard and long we will work at it, and, in turn, whether it will itself be influenced by the success of that behavior.[33] The clinically depressed patient who successfully becomes symptom-free through regular exercise may experience a significant increase in his feelings of self-efficacy: "I did it on my own, and I have the skills to do it again if I ever need to." These increased feelings of self-efficacy elevate self-esteem and feed into a more positive self-concept.

It seems safe to conclude that *exercise is most effective in elevating self-esteem in special populations, especially those where its consequences positively impact the reasons for the low self-esteem.*

Thus, exercise is most likely to deliver the gift of elevated self-esteem to those of us who most need it. Those of us who are depressed, over-weight, or belong to other special populations that characteristically suffer from low self-esteem are the people most likely to get the biggest boost in self-esteem as a result of a successful program of exercise.

5.
ANXIETY AND
ANXIETY DISORDERS

Exercise appears to have a positive effect on a number of the moods we commonly experience, but its effect is most noticeable in providing us relief from anxiety and depression. This constitutes very good news for many reasons.

Anxiety disorders are very widespread in the United States. The highly regarded 1994 National Comorbidity Survey (NCS) carried out by the National Institute for Social Research assessed the (1) twelve-month and (2) lifetime prevalence of the *most common psychiatric disorders* in a large representative sample of adults in the United States.[1] Like previous surveys, it found that these disorders fell into three major categories.

Individuals with substance-use disorders (abuse and dependency) had the highest rates, with 26.6 percent of those sampled having experienced one or another kind of abuse/dependency disorder during their lifetimes. While "substance" includes a broad array of prescription, over-the-counter, and illegal drugs, the great majority of abuse and dependency disorders reflect alcohol use.

The lifetime rate for those who had experienced anxiety disorders was nearly as high at 24.9 percent, and the lifetime rate for those who had experienced affective (depressive) disorders was 19.3 percent.

The survey also inquired about the incidence of the common disorders during the most recent twelve-month period in the lives of the people surveyed. Anxiety disorders had the highest twelve-month rate, 17.2 percent, while both the substance-use and affective disorders had rates of 11.3 percent.

Gender incidence differences, consistent with previous surveys, were also found. Women had a higher lifetime rate of anxiety disorders (30.5 percent) than men (19.2 percent) and higher lifetime rate of affective disorders (23.9 percent) than men (14.7 percent). Men had a higher lifetime rate of substance-use disorders (35.4 percent) than women (17.9 percent).

The NCS came up with a number of sobering findings. During the previous decade, substance-use disorders bypassed anxiety disorders to become America's most common mental affliction. What's more, the survey suggested that the prevalence of mental disorders may be considerably higher than we previously thought. Nearly half of the representative sample of eight thousand men and women who took the structured diagnostic interview reported having suffered one or more of the most common disorders in their lifetimes. However, less than 40 percent of those with lifetime disorders and fewer than twenty percent of those with a recent disorder had sought professional treatment.

Professional help comes at a price and is often considered a luxury. Psychotherapists report that caseloads predictably diminish when the economy takes a hard fall. Psychotherapy is expensive, can be long-term, and simply isn't acceptable to all people for a variety of reasons. Treating anxiety and depression with drugs can also be expensive and long-term. In addition, some such drugs are themselves dependency-producing, and virtually all drugs have side effects that many people find unacceptable.

When the early tricyclic antidepressants, such as Tofranil and Elavil, arrived, some patients stopped taking them, saying that they'd rather be depressed than fat. Others rejected the early MAOI (monoamine oxidase inhibitor) antidepressants because of potentially lethal side effects (if dietary restrictions were ignored). Some patients had to undergo detox from a dependency on antianxiety medications such as Librium and Valium during the time period when refills were easy to come by and the two were among the most widely prescribed drugs in America.

Fortunately, antidepressants have now been fine-tuned so that the most objectionable side effects ease off for most people after ten days or so; a new class of safe MAOIs has been synthesized; and antianxiety drugs are more restricted and more carefully prescribed. However, all drugs that treat mental disorders have side effects. Some, such as weight gain or loss of libido, can be problematical for those who suffer them.

There are some compelling reasons for exploring the alternatives or adjuncts to conventional treatments to manage anxiety and depression. Exercise may offer one such option, one that is inexpensive and with side effects that are largely beneficial.

Here we will explore research that sheds light on the question of whether exercise has proven to be an effective tool for us to control our own normal everyday anxieties. We will also consider the efficacy of exercise treatment with clinical populations who suffer more serious anxiety disorders such as phobias and panic disorder.

NORMAL ANXIETY AND ANXIETY DISORDERS

Normal anxiety differs from clinical anxiety disorders in terms of the kind, number, duration, and severity of symptoms as well as the degree of dysfunctionality it engenders. However, the boundary that separates normal moods from clinical disorders can be a hazy one, as in the case of the boundary that separates normal anxiety from the clinical syndrome labeled generalized anxiety disorder (GAD).

Generalized anxiety disorder frequently manifests itself as an incomplete recovery from a number of anxiety and depressive disorders or as a harbinger to another depressive episode. Some patients diagnosed with GAD experience a chronic state of anxiety that consistently interferes with their social or occupational functioning (dysfunctionality), while others experience a waxing and waning of symptoms just below the diagnostic threshold for long periods of time. GAD is often a "comorbid disorder," appearing in a given individual in conjunction with another disorder, such as substance abuse. It is a very serious disorder, and while treatable with anxiolytic drugs, full recoveries after two years of treatment occur in only about 20 percent of the cases.[2] GAD is definitely not just a series of bad hair days.

The diagnostic criteria for GAD, taken from the American Psychiatric Association's *Diagnostic and Statistical Manual of Mental Disorders: Fourth Edition* (DSM-IV) are as follows:

A. Excessive anxiety and worry (apprehensive expectation), occurring more days than not for at least six months, about a number of events or activities (such as work or school performance).

B. Difficulty in controlling that worry.

C. Anxiety and worry associated with three or more of the following six symptoms present for more days than not for the past six months (*Note:* only one is required for children).

    1. Restless or feeling keyed up or on edge

    2. Easily fatigued

    3. Difficulty in concentrating or mind going blank

    4. Irritability

    5. Muscle tension

    6. Sleep disturbance (difficulty falling asleep or staying asleep, or restless and unsatisfying sleep).

D. The focus of the anxiety and worry is not confined to the features of another Axis I disorder, such as panic disorder, social phobia, anorexia nervosa, separation anxiety, and so on.

E. The anxiety, worry, or physical symptoms cause clinically significant distress or impairment in social, occupational, or other important areas of functioning.

F. The disturbance is not due to a substance or general medical condition and does not occur exclusively during a mood, psychotic, or developmental disorder.[3]

ANXIETY IN NORMAL POPULATIONS

Anxiety is no stranger to us. While we may be unable to come up with a textbook definition, we all know what it feels like, and each of us can predict circumstances when it is likely to occur in our own lives. Anxiety is not the same as being anxious. Both involve physiological arousal, but the cognitive aspects of the affect (emotion) are dissimilar. Waiting at the airport arrival gate, anxious to meet our lover, who has been gone for far too long, involves a mixture of mainly positive affect and arousal. The element of *anticipation* is central.

It's a different story when we're sitting in our dentist's waiting room, listening to the muted sound of his whining drill, knowing that our root canal is next on his list of things to do. We are experiencing anticipatory anxiety here as well, but the affect is unpleasant, and *apprehension* is the central feature.

Then there are circumstances where the arousal can be intense, but a confusing blend of positive and negative affect. Suppose, for the first time in years, we unexpectedly meet a stranger to whom we find ourselves immediately attracted on many levels. It's a rare occurrence when someone such as this steps forth from the crowd. On the one hand, we're simply unwilling to let such an opportunity pass without seizing the moment, such as inviting this person for a drink or lunch, but on the other hand, there's the fear that the feelings might not be mutual and that we could well get summarily rejected. Such intense arousal can involve mixed and conflicting feelings as well as cognitive factors (weighing the risks and anticipating the future). Anxiety has many dimensions. It can be objective or subjective (imagining or magnifying threats) and involves feelings, cognitions, and physiological changes.

Anxiety is closely related to fear with regard to a predictable sequence of bodily changes. Our blood pressure elevates and our heart rate quickens, our muscles tense, and our digestive functions slow or stop (butterflies in our stomach). In the case of extreme fear, we often lose control of our excretory systems. Anxiety can, depending on the circumstances, intensify into full-blown fear or even panic, but when we speak of anxiety, we're talking about a kind of physiological arousal that is less intense than fear. Anxiety is unpleasant and typically has an anticipatory, apprehensive character.

HOW DO WE MEASURE ANXIETY?

Because anxiety involves cognitive and affective psychological states as well as predictable physiological changes, some scientists who wish to assess anxiety have developed self-report psychological tests, and others have used a variety of instruments to measure physiological changes in skin conductance (sweating), blood pressure, heart rate, and muscle tension. For a while, many scientists believed that the more objective physiological measures would produce more valid reflections of anxiety than the more subjective verbal reports of affect found in psychological tests. However, it turns out that measures of various physiological components that make up what was thought of as "nonspecific global arousal" don't correlate well with one another, either within a given individual when reacting to different stressors or between individuals when reacting to the same stressor. A number of inconsistent and problematic findings have led investigators to turn increasingly to psychological tests to assess anxiety.

The tension/anxiety subscale of the Profile of Mood States (POMS), described in the previous chapter, and the State-Trait Anxiety Inventory (STAI)[4] are two of the most widely used psychological self-report tests to assess anxiety in research concerning the anxiolytic effects of physical activity. Both have been shown to be valid instruments. Postexercise decreases in anxiety as reflected by these two psychological tests predictably parallel decreases in blood pressure and EEG activity, both common measures of tension.

The STAI assesses two dimensions of anxiety. The first is *state anxiety*, which reflects how an individual is feeling at a given moment. It is transient, can fluctuate, and can last for seconds, minutes, or hours. *Trait anxiety*, on the other hand, is a more enduring baseline condition reflecting the level of anxiety an individual typically feels over long periods of time. Those of us with high trait anxiety are more likely to experience anxiety and to experience a higher anxiety reaction to stress than those of us with normal or low trait anxiety. Thus, trait anxiety is more of a day-to-day predictable enduring condition.[5]

Some of us are more high-strung and reactive, while others of us are more laid back and less reactive. Those are traits that characterize us. Research on the effects of exercise on anxiety has examined the acute effects of a single workout on state anxiety, as well as the chronic effects of a long program of regular exercise on trait anxiety.

So our two basic questions are (1) can a single bout of exercise provide short-term relief (perhaps minutes or hours) from anxiety we may be experiencing during a stressful period, and (2) might weeks or months of regular exercise lower our day-to-day baseline anxiety level (make us somewhat less high-strung and jumpy)?

REVIEWS OF RESEARCH ON EXERCISE AND ANXIETY

There have been more than eleven hundred investigations inquiring about the effect of exercise on various aspects of mental functions and in excess of twenty reviews of those investigations that have examined the association between exercise and anxiety. The reviews of *epidemiological* surveys of more than seventy thousand household adults in three countries, discussed in an earlier chapter, offered convincing evidence that physical activity is associated with a more positive mood profile, particularly in lower levels of anxiety and depression. There have also been dozens of *experimental* studies targeting the effects of exercise on anxiety.

Larry Leith, author of *Foundations of Exercise and Mental Health*, reviewed fifty-six empirical studies that examined the specific effect of exercise on anxiety.[6] He reported that 73 percent of those studies found significant reductions in anxiety following exercise. His findings are in line with most other reviews, which largely conclude that single bouts of vigorous exercise are associated with decreased state anxiety, which persists for several hours in persons with either normal or above normal anxiety levels, and extended programs of regular exercise are associated with reductions in trait anxiety.

The problem with research on exercise and anxiety is not with a lack of studies, or with inconsistent findings, but instead with the quality of the research that is reviewed. A considerable number of studies suffer from one or another methodological shortcoming. These weaknesses can be partially dealt with (through coding and subsequent analysis of potential effect) by a statistical technique called meta-analysis, in which a large number of selected studies are packaged together and treated as a single large one.

Three of four meta-analyses, which all inquired as to the anxiolytic (anxiety-reducing) effect of exercise, found that it had a (1) moderate, (2) significant, and (3) highly significant effect. A fourth analysis failed to find a significant effect for either trait or state anxiety.[7] The most significant anxiolytic effect was found with a group of coronary heart disease patients who undertook a rehabilitative exercise program. Thus, three of four meta-analyses tend to support the conclusions of most reviewers, that exercise is associated with reductions in both state and trait anxiety in individuals with normal or above average anxiety levels.

These findings give rise to a number of questions for those of us who are seeking to find relief from our own personal demons. Are some forms of exercise more effective than others? How hard and how long must I exercise to reduce my tension, and how long will that tranquil feeling last? How many weeks or months must I exercise with regularity before I hope to feel a decrease in my everyday tension or reactivity to stress? Let's begin with a discussion of the temporary relief offered by a single bout of exercise: the reduction of state anxiety.

EXERCISE TO REDUCE STATE ANXIETY: WHAT KIND?

Investigators have studied the anxiolytic effects of a large variety of physical activities, including running, walking, cycling, swimming, aerobic dance, jumping rope, weight training, and fencing. The greatest number of studies have involved running and walking. In such experiments, state anxiety is assessed just prior to a single exercise session, which typically lasts twenty to thirty minutes, then is measured again following the termination of exercise.

While a few studies have found exercise to have no effect, the vast majority have found exercise to have a significant anxiolytic effect. The kinds of exercise that are most often associated with reductions in state anxiety are aerobic activities such as running, walking, cycling, and swimming, all of which are characterized by repetitive and rhythmic use of large muscle groups. There is also limited evidence that exercise that takes place in competitive sports may be effective in reducing state anxiety.

Research that has focused on the anxiolytic effects of resistance training is limited, and the results are equivocal at this juncture. Weight training is typically intermittent, performed at high intensity levels, and mainly involves anaerobic metabolism. Descriptions of two investigations that target the effects of weight training follow.

Indiana University professor John Raglin was the lead investigator in an experiment that compared the effects of cycling (aerobic) and weight training (anaerobic) on state anxiety and blood pressure.[8] His subjects were twenty-six well-conditioned college athletes with experience in both forms of exercise. They did thirty-minute workouts of stationary cycling or resistance training on two separate days. Intensity levels were controlled to fall between 70 percent and 80 percent of each person's predetermined maximal capacity. Blood pressure and state anxiety levels were assessed prior to each exercise bout and during the sixty-minute postexercise period.

Blood pressure and state anxiety levels fell gradually following cycling, and levels of both had fallen significantly *below* pre-exercise levels after sixty minutes. However, immediately following weight training, blood pressure and anxiety levels were significantly elevated (above pre-exercise baseline levels) and had returned to pre-exercise *baseline* levels at twenty and sixty minutes after exercise ceased.

A second study compared college students in a beginning weight training class with those in a lecture class.[9] State anxiety failed to decrease significantly after either fifty minutes of weight training or a similar period of sitting through a lecture. Blood pressure was elevated immediately following weight training and decreased following the lecture condition.

The number of studies that have examined the effect of resistance training on state anxiety is very limited, and at this early stage, results suggest that such training may not have a significant anxiolytic effect. Still, many questions need answering. For example, future experiments should carefully (1) examine the role of exercise intensity (for each individual), (2) control for what these individuals do during the postexercise period, and (3) make multiple assessments of state anxiety over several hours postexercise. It may be that state anxiety benefits occur only after a recovery period of considerable duration. But for now, it appears that aerobic exercise typically delivers a significant anxiolytic effect and that resistance training may or may not.

HOW HARD?

A large number of studies on aerobic exercise have addressed the exercise intensity question. Early findings suggested that exercise had to be of at least a moderate intensity for an anxiolytic effect to occur and that very intense exercise had a negative effect, actually elevating state anxiety. However, these early investigations didn't always control or directly measure exercise intensity, nor did they assess state anxiety over a reasonable time span following very intense exercise to see whether its anxiolytic effects might be delayed.

More recent studies have more carefully controlled and monitored exercise intensity by utilizing treadmills and stationary cycles and have often made multiple postexercise assessments of state anxiety. One such study found state anxiety to increase significantly immediately following twenty minutes of cycling at 70 percent of VO_{2max} but to decrease immediately following bouts of less intense cycling at 40 percent and 60 percent of VO_{2max}. However, the elevated state anxiety that immediately followed the most intense bout of exercise was transitory. State anxiety levels were similarly reduced for all three conditions sixty minutes after the exercise ended.[10]

It now seems clear that aerobic exercise over a very wide range of intensities will result in reduced state anxiety, although those effects are likely to be delayed after very intense exercise. Brisk walking delivers relief as effectively as does running. This is very good news for the those of us who are tentatively experimenting with bringing exercise into our lives. Those of us who are fit and sometimes exercise intensely may have already discovered that its anxiolytic effects are delayed.

DURATION?

A third important question is "How long do I have to exercise to feel better?" The great majority of studies that have focused on the anxiolytic effects of exercise have required subjects to work out for twenty minutes or more. Thus, it has been largely accepted that exercise bouts must last at least twenty minutes for individuals to experience relief from tension. However, two studies have reported that state anxiety has been lowered after only ten- and fifteen-minute workouts.[11] It may well be that future investigations will confirm that such short workouts are all that is necessary to lessen state anxiety, but for now it seems reasonable to stay with the twenty-minute minimum, since there is such a wealth of data supporting its significant anxiolytic effects.

DURABILITY OF EFFECTS

The reduced state anxiety that follows aerobic exercise doesn't last forever. A dozen studies have revealed that such effects typically last for about four to six hours. Nonetheless, while somewhat transient, the payoff of hours of relief from anxiety with an investment of only twenty minutes of moderate exercise is a bargain. Those of us who are going through stressful periods in our lives can readily put this knowledge to practical use. Here's how.

A highly anxious individual who commutes to work may be able to substitute walking or cycling instead of driving or using public transportation. If that's impossible, he can park (or get off the bus) a mile or so from work and briskly walk to the job, arriving with reduced tension, which should last until lunch break. No problem to work in a twenty-minute walk at lunch time to keep tension under control until he finishes work. At the day's end, he can take another tension-reducing walk to his ride home. If necessary, another walk before or after dinner will relax him for the evening and enhance sleep. What's more, while on the job, the individual can use every possible opportunity to move about, using stairs instead of the elevator and his feet instead of in-house e-mail or phones.

Burnout was a serious problem among my colleagues who worked at the university counseling center. After a few years of full-time clinical work, staff members often chose to return to less stressful classroom instructional duties. Two of my colleagues and I dealt with the emotional highs and lows produced by the stresses of clinical work by taking long lunch breaks on three days of the week. We'd head for the gym and the campus outdoor courts, where we played very serious doubles volleyball with hot-shot students whose skills had been honed on the sands of southern California. After a shower and a walk across campus, we returned to work feeling both relaxed and energized, ready to cope with whatever the afternoon dealt us.

This knowledge, garnered from treating my own personal chronic occupational stress, was a springboard for my beginning to prescribe exercise for my clients who suffered from depression and anxiety and eventually to sometimes go outdoors and walk and talk with them during therapy sessions.

TRAIT ANXIETY

Trait anxiety is everyone's predictable or baseline anxiety or tension level. It has been typically assessed with the STAI and the Taylor Manifest Anxiety Scale, both designed to measure trait anxiety.[12] Larry Leith reviewed twenty-eight studies that assessed the effect of regular exercise programs on trait anxiety, and he found that seventeen reported significant reductions.[13] Other expert reviews of the anxiety literature also report that the majority of studies have found such reductions. Three meta-analyses reported the same positive effect of chronic exercise on trait anxiety, while a fourth found no such effect.[14]

So while the findings are not entirely consistent, the majority of studies found that extended programs of aerobic exercise do result in significant reductions in trait anxiety.

The fact that some studies have not found such reductions in trait anxiety is not terribly unsettling in that most studies have been done on university populations of normal individuals who typically enjoy reasonably good mental health. How does one significantly lower anxiety in a population of people whose anxiety is not particularly elevated to begin with? It's no surprise that there is evidence to suggest that significant reductions in trait anxiety are most likely to occur in individuals whose baseline anxiety is elevated prior to beginning regular physical training. In other words, the more we need a reduction in our day-to-day baseline anxiety, the more likely a program of regular exercise will help.

There is also a suggestion that studies that have found no significant reductions of trait anxiety may have involved exercise programs that were too intense. One such study found significant reductions in trait anxiety after a ten-week training period for individuals who had exercised at 60 percent of their maximal heart rates three times a week for thirty to forty minutes, but there were no such reductions for those who exercised at 70 to 75 percent of their maximal heart rates.[15]

Reductions in trait anxiety are typically unrelated to the degree of fitness attained by individuals during the training period. And since high-intensity workouts increase the likelihood of participants dropping out, moderation should be the rule.

Most research on trait anxiety is based on programs that last eight weeks or longer, with workouts lasting twenty minutes or more, three times a week. So if we're looking to do something about our own baseline anxiety level, it's going to take a while. If we suffer from an above average level of baseline anxiety, it's more likely that the extended program will be of help to us. Other good news is that our workouts don't have to be intense or of great duration. A half hour of brisk walking three or four times a week (which would predictably provide us with relief for a few hours after each walk) could well make a noticeable difference in our baseline trait anxiety after several months.

THE MECHANISMS: PSYCHOLOGICAL THEORIES

The tranquilizing drug Xanax, psychotherapy, meditation, or a hot shower can all reduce *state anxiety*, so the anxiolytic effects of physical activity aren't unique. But just how does physical activity function to reduce anxiety? Exercise results in a number of neurochemical, physiological, and psychological consequences, each of which suggests theoretical mechanisms. Let's begin by considering some possible psychological mechanisms.

While exercise has a number of psychological and physiological properties, there is the possibility that all it offers us is a transient *distraction* or *time-out* from our current worries. More than a dozen studies have found a wide variety of time-out interventions to be effective in reducing state anxiety. Three studies are of particular interest.

In a now-classic study, adult male exercisers either walked on a treadmill at a medium intensity, engaged in autogenic meditation/relaxation, or quietly rested in recliners for twenty minutes. All three conditions resulted in significant, but not different, reductions in state anxiety. The results suggested that all three interventions offered distraction from worries.[16]

A second investigation compared exercise with quiet rest and found the anxiety-reducing effects to be the same under both conditions. However, the reduced anxiety that followed exercise was found to be more *long-lasting*, suggesting that exercise may offer distraction *plus* other physiological or neurochemical changes that also contribute to tension reduction.[17]

A third study compared state anxiety levels of college women who shared high trait anxiety before and after (1) moderately intense exercise, (2) exercise while studying, (3) studying only, and (4) quiet rest. The only condition that resulted in a significant reduction in anxiety was exercise-only, suggesting that the anxiolytic effects of exercise as a time-out from their worries might have been interfered with by studying.[18]

The anxiolytic effect of physical activity on *trait anxiety* may also have psychological components in addition to the possible cumulative effects of weeks and weeks of distraction or time-out during regular sessions of exercise.

One such possibility concerns *self-efficacy* and *skills mastery*. The individual who begins to exercise regularly quickly becomes aware that each session is predictably followed by few hours of relief from anxiety. This can lead to an increasing awareness that she is beginning to take charge of her own moods. In a world where stressful events inevitably *happen to her*, she may come to realize that she has the knowledge and power to *make things happen*, a partial shift from an external to an internal locus of control. There is the possibly that this sort of self-efficacy and skills mastery may in part account for the reduction in day-to-day baseline anxiety that is observed after many weeks of regular exercise: "I'm not so tense anymore because I know that whatever comes along, I can handle it."

PHYSIOLOGICAL MECHANISMS

A substantial body of research confirms that exercise produces a very widespread and objectively measurable physiological relaxation response.

Walking, jogging, and cycling at mild to moderate intensities have all been shown to reduce physical tension. And symptom relief is especially pronounced among those of us who suffer from chronic high anxiety. Such relaxation effects are reflected by reduced blood pressure and pulse rates. They are also measurable in the brain (increased hemispheric synchronization and alpha brain wave activity), in the dorsal spine (as reflected in certain reflex tests), and in skeletal muscles (decreased spindle activity as measured by an electromyograph, which reflects resting muscle tension).

The muscle relaxation that follows exercise is quite impressive, and it has been the focus of many investigations. Herbert de Vries has done a number of studies that have consistently demonstrated that exercise can significantly reduce electrical activity or tension in our muscles.[19] What is so encouraging about his findings is that this kind of significant physiological tranquilizing effect holds for both normal and clinically anxious men and women, and it has been demonstrated in young adults as well as in middle-aged and elderly men and women. Even better news is that the tranquilizing effect results from even brief periods of very moderate exercise and that it is measurable for at least an hour and a half after exercise ends.

In one experiment, de Vries selected ten elderly people from a group of sixty volunteers who believed they suffered from anxiety or tension problems. The ten selected all showed electromyographic evidence of above average neuromuscular tension. They were tested three times before and after five different conditions: (1) walking at a heart rate of a hundred beats a minute, (2) walking at a heart rate of one hundred twenty beats a minute, (3) ingesting four hundred milligrams of meprobamate (a tranquillizing muscle relaxant), (4) ingesting four hundred milligrams of placebo, and (5) a no-treatment (control) period.

Only a single condition reduced tension to a greater extent than the no-treatment control condition. After walking at a hundred-beats-per-minute pace, muscular electrical activity was reduced significantly from pretest levels at thirty, sixty, and ninety minutes. The one hundred twenty-beats-per-minute condition approached, but did not quite achieve, statistical significance (a trend). These findings led de Vries to conclude that "at least in single doses, exercise of an appropriate type and intensity had a significantly greater effect on the resting musculature than did meprobamate, which was one of the most frequently prescribed tranquilizer drugs at that time." He suggests that moderate exercise might be used as an alternative to tranquilizing drugs in the treatment of the normal anxiety that we periodically experience and that "rhythmic exercise such as walking, jogging, cycling, and bench stepping from 5 to 30 minutes at 30 percent to 60 percent of maximum intensities was effective."[20]

Because reductions in muscle tension can be produced by simply warming our bodies, some observers suggest that the acute relaxation response produced by exercise is probably nothing more than the result of the higher body temperatures that it generates. The jogger we see moving along the roadside may have a core temperature as high as 103 degrees Fahrenheit: his own portable sauna.

The knowledge that warming our bodies produces relaxation is not a new idea. Some American Indian tribes began erecting sweat lodges thousands of years ago; upper-crust Europeans began visiting the hot baths at Baden during the Middle Ages; and Scandinavians have been taking saunas for centuries. These ancestors knew all about the effects of heat on their bodies, but they didn't bother to verify it scientifically or assign it a dignified label. Contemporary scientists have now demonstrated significant reductions in both state anxiety and muscle tension following saunas or even a five-minute very warm shower. They refer to it as the *thermogenic effect*.

This raises an intriguing question: Is elevating our body temperature an *essential* condition to bring about the general relaxation response, or is it merely *sufficient* (perhaps only one of several factors that might have the same effect)? Perhaps vigorous exercise, in the absence of an elevated core temperature, would do the job just as well. Over the years, scientists have come up with marvelously creative investigative schemes to manipulate and measure core temperatures while subjects exercised.

Core temperatures of subjects who wore skimpy running apparel have been compared to others who wore layers of insulating clothing while doing calisthenics. Some subjects were exposed to whole body cooling by being immersed in very cold water before exercise. Others have exercised in shoulder-deep water of varying temperatures. Scuba divers have exercised while wearing minimal swim wear or while wearing wet suits in waters of varying temperatures.

University of Wisconsin expert Kelli Koltyn, in an extensive review of research, points out that there is considerable inconsistency in the findings of such research. Some studies demonstrate that the reduced anxiety following vigorous exercise is associated with elevated core temperature, while others demonstrated that reduced anxiety follows exercise when there is no increase in core temperature. Even when an association has been found between reduced anxiety and elevated core temperature, there is a lack of evidence to support a causal link. Nonetheless, after reviewing a large body of research, Koltyn concludes that the thermogenic hypothesis remains a tenable one.[21] Generations of Swedes would comment, "Of course!"

NEUROTRANSMITTER MECHANISMS

Our brain manufactures chemicals that are similar to many drugs that can alter our mental functions. Our brain synthesizes its own antidepressants, hallucinogens, and anxiolytics. It also makes its own marijuana (anandamide), its own morphine (beta-endorphin), and a host other chemicals that affect our mental processes (psychotropic chemicals).

The word "endorphin" is an abbreviated form of two words: "endogenous" (produced within or native to our own bodies) and "morphine," a member of the opioid family, which has the capability to reduce pain and alter mood. Morphine was named after Morpheus, the Greek god of dreams, because it produced dreamlike mood changes, drowsiness, and euphoria. Beta-endorphin was discovered in the mid-1970s, at about the same time as American Frank Shorter's surprising Olympic marathon win. His victory motivated thousands of American men and women to take up distance running.

Before long, researchers found that blood plasma elevations of beta-endorphin and its metabolites (the chemical by-products of beta-endorphin breakdown) appeared to be associated with exercise. Some suggested that exercise-generated increases in beta-endorphin activity could be a causal factor for the so-called runner's high.

Beta-endorphin is a *neurotransmitter*, one of many kinds of chemical molecules that transmit messages from one neuron to another across tiny liquid-filled gaps called *synapses*.

A number of scientists have attempted to determine whether the reduced anxiety reported by individuals following exercise was associated with higher peripheral (to the central nervous system) blood plasma beta-endorphin metabolite levels. They also wondered whether the postexercise afterglow would be interfered with if the individuals were pretreated with opioid antagonists (drugs such as naloxone and naltrexone, which block beta-endorphin effects). Their thinking was: If exercisers who received naloxone (as against a placebo) failed to experience postexercise afterglow, then it could be assumed that beta-endorphin plays an important role in the mood improvement.

Such research on human subjects has seldom found an association between postexercise reduced anxiety and higher beta-endorphin levels, and the bulk of research suggests that opioid antagonists, such as naloxone, do not block exercise-induced mood improvement.[22]

But the problem with these human studies is that they all have involved assessing beta-endorphin and its metabolites in peripheral blood plasma rather than plasma in the central nervous system (brain and spinal cord). The blood-brain barrier is virtually impenetrable by beta-endorphin, so in order to study the effects of exercise on beta-endorphin concentrations within the central nervous system, it has been necessary to turn to animal subjects such as rats.

An excellent study (that eliminated many of the contaminating stress factors that had been problematic in earlier investigations) was conducted by expert Pavel Hoffman at the University of Göteborg in Sweden.[23] Some of his rats were offered the opportunity to run voluntarily by virtue of a free-access exercise wheel attached to the side of their living cages. Others were not. Rats in the optional running group were all running regularly within three to five weeks, with some running as much as three miles in a twenty-four-hour period. They liked it.

After five to six weeks of voluntary running, samples of cerebral spinal fluid revealed elevated (above baseline) beta-endorphin concentrations not seen in the sedentary rats. Perhaps Hoffman's most interesting finding concerned how long these elevated beta-endorphin spinal fluid concentrations persisted in animals that had been exercising vigorously for weeks. Most research on humans has suggested that the exercise-mediated elevated beta-endorphin metabolite concentrations found in peripheral blood plasma return to normal within an hour or two.

However, when access to activity wheels was blocked, Hoffman's active rats retained above-average spinal fluid concentrations of beta-endorphin twenty-four and forty-eight hours later, returning to the levels of the sedentary control rats only after ninety-six hours. Whether similar exercise-mediated beta-endorphin concentration longevity occurs in the central nervous systems of humans has yet to be determined.

Further supporting evidence for the role of beta-endorphin in tension reduction comes from animal research that has focused on the large muscles that are used in aerobic exercise. Recall here that research on thermogenesis revealed that elevating core temperature through passive heating or exercise was sufficient, but not essential, to result in postexercise reduced blood pressure, reduced heart rate, and reduced state anxiety. Such consequences have been demonstrated when individuals engage in vigorous exercise *without increasing core temperature*.

Several investigations have now examined the effects of prolonged rhythmic low-frequency electrical stimulation of nerves in various large leg muscles of conscious rats. The muscles responded to the electrical stimulation by rhythmically contracting, which simulated prolonged aerobic exercise such as running or swimming. The post-stimulation consequences observed in these studies included decreases in blood pressure, an increase in pain threshold, and behavioral calm. These consequences were reversed by high doses of naloxone, an antagonist that blocks beta-endorphin receptors. These findings suggest that aerobic exercise, per se, stimulates afferent nerve receptors, which, in turn, facilitate the release of beta-endorphin.[24]

While beta-endorphin appears to play a role in the reduced state anxiety that follows exercise, none of the currently approved anxiolytic drugs target beta-endorphin. Drugs such as Xanax and Valium target a neurotransmitter called GABA, and other effective anxiolytic drugs target serotoninergic (serotonin) and noradrenergic (norepinephrine) neurotransmitter systems.

Anxiety symptoms can be induced in patients with panic disorder by blocking serotonin receptors. Anxiety disorders, such as panic disorder, are most commonly treated with selective serotonin reuptake inhibiting drugs (SSRIs), which serve to increase serotonin activity. Thus, serotonin often acts as a brake mechanism in brain neural activity. (In the next chapter, we will discover that exercise increases brain levels of serotonin, suggesting another possible mechanism to explain the anxiolytic effect of exercise.)

While activating serotoninergic systems relieves anxiety, suppressing the effects of norepinephrine has similar anxiolytic effects. Drugs that activate norepinephrine release increase anxiety, and those that decrease norepinephrine activity relieve anxiety. So with regard to the transmission of anxiety messages along norepinephrine pathways in our brains, serotonin functions as a brake, in opposition to norepinephrine, which can be thought of as an accelerator. We will shortly discuss a second anxiety brake mechanism: the neurotransmitter GABA.

Dopamine and beta-endorphin are sometimes referred to as "feel good" brain chemicals. Both can alleviate pain and produce euphoria. Dopamine is the dominant neurotransmitter in the brain pathways and structures that deliver pleasure and as such is central in nearly all the substance dependencies with which we contend. Dopamine release in the pleasure pathways of our brains is reinforcing, encouraging us to repeat whatever behavior we engaged in to produce it. Methamphetamine (speed) and cocaine positively flood our brain's synapses with dopamine and are perhaps the two most powerful reinforcing substances.

There is the possibility that vigorous exercise might also deliver a smaller, but nonetheless pleasurable, reinforcing dopamine hit. Peripheral blood plasma levels of dopamine metabolites quickly elevate to about 300 percent above baseline and remain at that level in experienced marathoners who are competing in a 26.2-mile race.[25] After an initial bounce up to about 600 percent above baseline when the race ends, levels return to normal within an hour or two. Studies estimate that from 20 to 60 percent of the peripheral blood plasma concentrations of dopamine metabolites have central nervous system origins, so there is a possibility that exercise-induced elevations of dopamine may play a role in postexercise calm.[26]

We shall see shortly that the neurotransmitter GABA, which also plays a central role in anxiety, can also be affected by exercise.

SUBSYNDROMAL ANXIETY: MECHANISMS AND TREATMENTS

The anxiety that many of us suffer, either periodically or rather constantly, is usually subsyndromal in that it is not sufficiently severe to satisfy the criteria for generalized anxiety disorder (GAD).

Those of us who visit our family physician complaining of anxiety typically are given a prescription for one of the many benzodiazepines (BZs), such as Xanax, Valium, Serax, or Ativan. Benzodiazepines act as modulators of a neurotransmitter called GABA (gamma-aminobutyric acid). GABA serves as a fast-acting inhibitory agent throughout the brain and is especially common in the orbital frontal cortex, where the neural mechanisms of anticipatory anxiety are thought to reside; in the amygdala, where our emotional reactions to sensory stimuli primarily occur; and in the locus coeruleus, a brain stem structure that is the primary norepinephrine arousal center. Mild electrical stimulation of the locus coeruleus produces anxiety and panic in monkeys. On the other hand, destroying the locus coeruleus norepinephrine neurons produces genuine "no fear" monkeys.

GABA has a significant role in inhibiting anxiety, and the benzodiazepines function by lending GABA a helping hand. GABA A receptors are found on the dendrites of postsynaptic neurons and act as "gatekeepers" for a chloride channel. When those receptors are occupied by GABA molecules, the channel opens, resulting in increased chloride conductance through the channel and an immediate inhibitory effect on the postsynaptic neuron. GABA has a large role in inhibiting the transmission of anxiety messages.

However, the GABA receptor complex also contains receptor sites for benzodiazepines, alcohol, barbiturate, and both convulsive and anticonvulsive drug messengers. GABA, when working alone, can only influence conductance to a certain extent, and during prolonged stress its capacity to reduce anxiety may be insufficient. If we then take a benzodiazepine, such as Xanax, both GABA and benzodiazepine receptor sites become simultaneously occupied. The Xanax causes a large amplification of GABA's ability to conduct chloride through its channel and have an inhibitory effect on the postsynaptic neuron. In the absence of GABA, benzodiazepines have no effect; thus, they are modulators, which amplify GABA inhibitory activity.

It should be no surprise that alcohol also appears to have a modulating effect similar to that of the benzodiazepines. It certainly serves as an over-the-counter effective anxiolytic to help us relax in uncomfortable social situations. Thus, an overtaxed GABA system that is attempting to keep anxiety in check during stress can get "a little help from its friends": alcohol or benzodiazepines such as Valium or Xanax.

While these two kinds of helpers offer the advantage of fast, effective relief from anxiety, both are sedating and both can result in dependency. Fortunately, there are alternatives.

The serotonin partial agonist (enhances serotonin activity) Buspirone is an effective anxiolytic that avoids the negative effects of the benzodiazepines. But, like antidepressants, it requires a few weeks to become effective. Clonidine (a norepinephrine alpha 2 autoreceptor agonist, which also requires a few weeks to become effective) serves as an anxiolytic by reducing the release of norepinephrine. Sometimes beta-blockers serve as effective anxiolytics (by blocking norepinephrine beta–receptor sites).[27] These newer anxiolytic agents, which act on serotonin and norepinephrine activity, do not offer the immediate anxiolytic effects of the benzodiazepines, but on the plus side, they do not produce dependency.

Finally, it's important here to recognize that exercise may also play a role in GABA activity and anxiety reduction. University of Georgia exercise psychologist Rod Dishman and his colleagues have found changes in GABA levels and receptor frequency in the brains of rats as a *result of chronic exercise*: changes that are consistent with behavioral anxiolytic effects.[28]

EXERCISE TREATMENT OF ANXIETY DISORDERS

While there has been a great deal attention paid to the anxiolytic effects of exercise on normal populations, only a limited number of studies have targeted populations with diagnosed anxiety disorders. Three such studies came out of Norway in 1989, each of which examined the effects of exercise with hospitalized patients diagnosed with a variety of anxiety disorders. We'll begin with a description of these three investigations and then move on to pay special attention to panic and phobic disorders and how exercise can play an important role in their treatments.

In a purely exploratory study, the eminent Norwegian psychiatrist Egil Martinsen examined the effects of exercise as the *primary treatment* for a group of ninety-two patients who had voluntarily committed themselves to a hospital for eight weeks. They were a select group who had previously not responded well to or had rejected psychoanalytic treatment. They had a variety of diagnoses.[29] (We will deal with the entire group in a later chapter, but now we will focus only on the thirty-six who suffered from various anxiety disorders.)

These patients received the regular clinic treatments, including group therapy once a week, but medications (especially anxiolytic drugs) were stopped if at all possible. The core treatment was an hour of aerobic exercise (50–70 percent maximum aerobic capacity) five days a week for eight weeks.

Our thirty-six patients all increased their aerobic capacity, and anxiety scores decreased significantly in all of the anxiety disorder diagnostic groups, with the exception of those with social phobia. So, as a group, patients with anxiety disorders had good short-term gains.

However, a one-year follow-up revealed that those patients who suffered from agoraphobia with panic attacks did not fare as well over the long term, perhaps because some of them continued to be medicated while hospitalized. Agoraphobia involves a fear of leaving home alone, and panic disorder involves unpredictable episodes of terror. Both will be fully defined shortly.

However, the follow-up revealed that the patients diagnosed with generalized anxiety disorder and those diagnosed with agoraphobia without panic attacks did maintain their treatment gains. These findings are encouraging, suggesting that further research concerning exercise treatment for these two disorders is warranted. These findings further suggest that individuals who suffer from GAD might (after consulting their physicians) personally experiment to see whether a program of exercise is helpful in reducing or controlling their symptoms. Exercise might possibly negate the need for, or allow a reduction in, their required dosage of anxiolytic drugs.

In a second experiment, Martinsen explored the effects of aerobic versus nonaerobic exercise in a group of seventy-nine adults, all hospitalized with various anxiety disorders. Nearly two out of three were diagnosed with agoraphobia with panic disorder. In addition to the regular hospital treatments, these men and women exercised for an hour three times a week for eight weeks. Half of them engaged in a controlled walk/jog program at 70 percent of their maximal aerobic capacity, and half engaged in stretching, muscle relaxation/breathing exercises, and moderate strength conditioning.

As you might suspect, only the patients in the walk/jog group significantly increased their aerobic conditioning, but Martinsen found that patients in both groups significantly decreased both phobic avoidance symptoms and resting anxiety levels. This has some significance in that the majority of the patients suffered from agoraphobia with panic attacks. However, these patients were not followed up, so we don't know whether their gains were long lasting. Finding that both aerobic and nonaerobic exercise reduced anxiety and phobic avoidance symptoms equally well, Martinsen suggested that the psychological mechanisms of distraction and skills mastery might be the best explanation for the effectiveness of the two treatments.[30]

In a third Norwegian study, hospitalized patients who were diagnosed with anxiety and depressive disorders were assigned to either walk or jog groups in order to examine the effects of exercise intensity on clinical symptoms. Patients in one group jogged at 70 percent of their maximal heart rates, and those in the second group were instructed to walk at a comfortable pace three or four times a week for thirty minutes over the course of eight weeks.

At the end of the treatment period, there were no differences between the two groups with regard to aerobic gains. However, both groups had reduced anxiety and neurotic symptoms to an equal extent. The overall dropout rate was 25 percent, but the joggers had significantly more dropouts than the walkers. A six-month follow-up revealed that most of the participants remained active and that both symptomatic and physical gains were maintained. Since the only difference between the two groups was dropout rate, the investigators suggested that low-intensity exercise should be the preferred treatment.[31]

Taken together, these three studies suggest that exercise helps reduce the symptoms of several anxiety disorders during the time of hospital treatment, and those treatment gains appeared to be maintained with patients suffering from generalized anxiety disorder. However, treatment gains may not persist after discharge for patients suffering from agoraphobia with panic disorder. Panic disorder offers some treatment challenges.

PANIC DISORDER

A panic attack is a *single episode of terror*, with all of the physical symptoms that characterize extreme fear, along with feelings of unreality or detachment and a fear of losing control, going insane, or dying. It typically lasts for less than thirty minutes, with symptoms most severe about ten minutes after onset.

Panic attacks occur in some individuals who are diagnosed with a social phobia, agoraphobia, or a specific phobia. Phobias of all kinds always involve *situational avoidance*, whereas individuals diagnosed with *panic disorder*, uncomplicated by phobic disorders, suffer *unexpected, spontaneous attacks* that seem to come out of nowhere. Panic attacks are typically not a one-time episode. They can occur even during the night, and they predictably generate a postattack period (as long as a month) of persistent concerns of having another attack or concern that the attack might actually signal a more serious condition such as an impending heart attack or going insane.

Panic disorder affects about 5 percent of American women and 2 percent of men during their lifetimes,[32] and it has a strong genetic predisposition. There is a concordance rate of 40 percent in identical twins, and 15 to 20 percent of relatives of those diagnosed with panic disorder are similarly diagnosed.[33]

Panic disorder is typically treated with drugs. The patient is started off with a high-potency and fast-acting benzodiazepine, such as Xanax or Klonopin (to provide immediate relief), plus one of the panic disorder-approved SSRIs (to be used over the long term). Usually after a few weeks, the increased serotoninergic activity produced by the SSRI will inhibit anxiety sufficiently, allowing the potentially dependency-producing benzodiazepine to be discontinued.[34]

Traditional talk psychotherapy does not have a history of effectiveness with panic disorder. However, Panic Control Treatment, a variant of cognitive-behavior therapy, shows promise. It involves progressive relaxation training, cognitive procedures directed at eliminating catastrophic thoughts, and exposure to the physical sensations experienced in panic attacks.[35]

The unfolding story of the relationship between exercise and panic disorder is unusually interesting, one that generates considerable optimism about future use of exercise as a primary or adjunctive treatment for this disorder.

The story began with a 1967 *New England Journal of Medicine* article that reported that panic attacks could be induced by an intravenous infusion of lactate.[36] Since physical activity generates lactic acid and its metabolite lactate, the authors of the article cautioned readers that exercise might set off panic attacks in people who were diagnosed with the disorder.

The article provoked immediate concern on the part of other scientists. Two studies followed very quickly, and their findings revealed that the original study was flawed and essentially invalid. However, the notion that exercise was unsafe for people diagnosed with panic disorder has persisted among many health professionals. Now, fifteen studies involving a total of four hundred twenty people diagnosed with panic disorder revealed that only five of those individuals suffered panic attacks while taking part in vigorous exercise. The studies also found that patients who completed maximal exercise tests had postexercise plasma lactate levels far higher than normal subjects, which indicated that they tended to be less fit than controls.[37]

These studies have clearly demonstrated that very vigorous exercise is safe for people who suffer panic attacks, but the lack of fitness among this population suggests that vigorous exercise may be more than simply safe. It's possible that regular vigorous exercise could have a therapeutic effect. It's certainly no accident that people who dread panic attacks are less fit, since the impressive physical arousal that accompanies vigorous exercise must be frightening. In the past, that high state of arousal had often signaled an impending panic attack, leading to an avoidance of vigorous exercise.

Years ago I would, on occasion, take patients who suffered from panic attacks (*but were in good physical health*) to a nearby mountain park for a therapy session. I would walk them briskly up a long, uphill trail until they were in a high state of arousal and out of breath. I would then encourage them to have a panic attack. Sometimes I pleaded with them. None ever did, but my idea back then was that patients might learn that it was possible to experience a high state of arousal without it signaling a coming panic attack. Looking back, I think I should have done this on a weekly basis and emphasized between-session aerobic training for the patients.

It wasn't until 1998 that psychiatrist Andreas Broocks and his colleagues at the University of Gottingen in Germany put that idea to the test.[38] They randomly assigned forty-six outpatients diagnosed with moderate to severe panic disorder to one of three groups for ten weeks of treatment: (1) running three times a week, (2) the serotonin reuptake inhibitor clomipramine (112.5 milligrams per day), or (3) daily placebo pills.

It was found that clomipramine improved anxiety symptoms earlier and more effectively than did exercise. However, both exercise and clomipramine treatment resulted in a significantly greater symptom reduction than did the placebo. In addition, it was found that both treatments also significantly reduced patient *depressive* symptoms, while the placebo did not.

Broock's findings suggest that exercise could play a role in the treatment of panic disorder, particularly as a form of self-prescription. It seems possible that individuals (with their physician's approval) with moderate panic disorder might discover that they can use systematic exercise to reduce or eliminate the need for medication.

PHOBIC DISORDERS

The word "phobia" is frequently misused in contemporary society. Normal individuals with strong attitudes or opinions are sometimes routinely labeled as being this or that kind of phobic, suggesting that they suffer from a mental disorder. However, phobias are more than just strong attitudes. They are serious disorders that are characterized by marked and persistent fears that interfere significantly with a person's daily routine, occupational functioning, or social life and cause significant distress to the individual. There are three kinds of phobias.

The NCS reveals that, following major depression and alcohol dependency, *social phobias* are the third most common lifetime mental disorder in America, with 11.1 percent of men and 15.5 percent of women having had to deal with it during their lifetimes.[39]

A social phobia involves an extreme irrational fear of social or performance situations in which individuals are exposed to strangers and scrutiny, and embarrassment or humiliation is anticipated. A social phobia is not just extreme shyness, contrary to what current television advertisements peddling SSRIs might suggest. It often has an onset around puberty and may last a lifetime. Expert Stephen Stahl points out that two-thirds of those suffering from social phobia are single, divorced, or widowed, that more than half did not complete high school, and that one-fifth are sufficiently dysfunctional that they are unable to work.[40]

Specific phobias are our fourth-most common lifetime disorder. The NCS found that men and women had lifetime rates of 6.7 and 15.7 percent. Such phobias involved intense, irrational fears about specific situations or objects. Fear of heights, flying, enclosed places, and dogs are examples. After having been involved in a serious automobile accident, a substantial number of people either curtail or stop driving completely. Some become phobic and others develop posttraumatic stress disorder. Automobile accidents are responsible for producing a large number of phobias in America.

Agoraphobia literally translates into "fear of the marketplace." Agoraphobia is most commonly the result of having experienced a panic attack while alone and away from home, and the subsequent fear of having another such attack somewhere where help might not be available. After such a panic attack, the individual's anxiety-free space often becomes more and more restricted, eventually making it impossible to drive or even leave home alone.

Some individuals who experience panic attacks live reasonably normal lives between attacks, but about a third of them develop a "fear of fear" and become agoraphobic. About 65 percent of agoraphobics have panic disorder, while the remaining 35 percent typically develop agoraphobia as the result of a single terrifying experience such as an auto accident, rape, assault, or animal attack.

SSRIs are typically the first-line treatments for all forms of phobias. However, fast-acting and powerful benzodiazepines are sometimes prescribed for social phobias. While SSRI treatment is often successful, its effects are not always permanent. The phobic response reappears for many people after drug treatment is terminated. Relating the freedom from phobic symptoms to taking pills, and feeling apprehension about the consequences of stopping taking them, is a no-brainer.

Traditional talk psychotherapy has not proven to be an efficacious intervention in the treatment of phobias, but behavior therapy has shown remarkable success. Current behavior therapy treatment almost always involves *exposure* to the feared object or circumstance, so that the intense fear can be experienced and gradually extinguished with repeated exposures—in essence, getting back on the horse that threw you.

"Flooding" is the treatment of choice. It involves the therapist's repeatedly accompanying the patient to the feared object or circumstance at which time the patient is flooded with anxiety. Exposure is the central essential factor, and considerable research suggests that the *fear must be experienced* during *exposure* for the fear response to be permanently extinguished.

It was the British psychologist Arnold Orwin who reasoned that exercise might be a powerful tool to use in the treatment of agoraphobia and situational (specific) phobias.[41] He pointed out that the "physiology of conversion," which characterizes religious practices in some cultures, often involves drumming, dancing, and chanting to the point of exhaustion, and this state appears to facilitate relief from sin, evil, and the anxieties associated with them. Orwin reasoned that since the physiological state exhaustion is incompatible with anxiety, perhaps it might be useful in the treatment of certain anxiety disorders.

Physical exhaustion produced by running became central in the highly effective technique that Orwin developed for the treatment of both specific phobias and agoraphobia. It combines exercise with exposure, and it has several advantages over conventional treatments. I've used Orwin's technique a number of times to deal quickly and effectively with agoraphobia that is the result of a panic attack. Here's how it works.

Agoraphobics are homebound, typically shackled by a fear of the predictable intense anxiety they experience when alone out in the world where a panic attack might occur and when familiar help is not available. This means that the agoraphobic requires a driver just to get to my office for a first appointment. Most often that person, typically a family member, can be recruited and trained to be a part of the treatment team. The first office visit involves sitting with the two of them, educating them about panic and agoraphobia, outlining the treatment, and extending hope.

I explain that panic attacks have a strong genetic component, which often is a relief to the afflicted patient, who sometimes blames herself for the disorder. I also talk about how common panic attacks and resultant phobias are and how amenable such phobias are to treatment. I specifically outline the learning process that occurred when the patient's agoraphobia took shape and then help them to understand how anxiety played a central role in gradually restricting the patient to the home. I explain that exercise is one of the most potent antianxiety forces available and that it will play a central role in therapy. I further point out that treatment will take place both at the patient's home and in the mostly deserted parking lot of a shopping center in the early morning hours.

Prior to session two, the patient is instructed to contact her physician and get medical clearance that her health is such that it is safe for her to engage in brief sprints.

Session two takes place at the shopping center's parking lot, where we seek out a peripheral area devoid of traffic. Our goal that morning is to determine just exactly how far the patient must run (as hard as she can) in order to bring on a state of exhaustion and breathlessness, which, in turn, requires her to stop to recover. For most unfit individuals, that distance is not great. After several runs, we will have determined the average distance and the length of the breathlessness period that follows each run.

During the remainder of session two, I talk to the two about home treatment. Since agoraphobia involves both an avoidance of approaching a strange, crowded, and unsafe place (a mall) and leaving a safe place (home), I recruit the patient's significant other to spend some time working with her each day at home. My new assistant therapist is instructed to stand in clear view on the sidewalk in front of the patient's home while she runs swiftly away to the point of breathless exhaustion. At that point, she is instructed to continue to walk away during the moments required for her to recover. When the first twinges of anxiety are experienced, she is then to turn around and walk slowly back to my assistant. This sequence, which requires very little time, is to be repeated three times each day.

Session three takes place back in the mall parking lot, where the patient does a single trial run to establish an accurate distance to the point of exhaustion. I then measure off that distance from the mall entry door to the starting point where I will stand. The patient's task is to run from me to the entrance, where she will arrive in a state of breathless exhaustion. I assure her that her state of physical exhaustion will prevent a panic attack. After arriving at the mall entrance, she is then instructed to walk around there recovering her breath until the first hints of anxiety are experienced, then walk back to me. This task is repeated several times during the session, with the patient typically spending a greater amount of time near the mall entrance doors after each run.

Successive sessions at the parking lot largely follow the above format. However, the patient is instructed, on arrival at the mall entrance, to walk inside and stay until the first twinges of anxiety would be the signal to return to the therapist (who is standing farther and farther away with each successive session). When it becomes clear that the patient can stay inside the mall as long as she chooses, I sometimes encourage her to try to faint or have a panic attack upon entering. Patients usually treat this as a joke.

At the close of each parking lot session, I check with the patient with regard to the home exercise therapy. Typically, runs there become longer as the patient becomes more fit and as anxiety-free space expands. Then, as the anxiolytic effects of exercise are realized and extinction of the fear response gradually takes place, patients often begin to run from home without the reassuring presence of their assistant therapist. By this time, the patient is likely to begin to drive alone to mall sessions.

I've found that often only a half-dozen sessions are required to effectively treat agoraphobia. The number of sessions needed depends upon the degree of cooperation extended by the assistant therapist, the severity of the patient's symptoms, and the degree to which the symptoms have come to have secondary psychosocial rewards (which may outweigh the inconvenience of the agoraphobia).

So what exactly happens in Orwin's running therapy? Basically, a very simple kind of conditioning procedure takes place (the fear response is extinguished through repeated exposure to the feared circumstance). However, exercise contributes some unique benefits that extinction procedure, by itself, does not offer.

For starters, the state of breathlessness and acute exhaustion is antithetical to panic and makes it possible for the patient to experience the feared stimulus *without drugs.* Also, the instinctive response to a feared object (to run away) is used to control it: the patient runs *toward* the feared mall and *away* from her safe home. Finally, at some level patients must cognitively redefine the high state of arousal experienced in the presence of the feared circumstance. Such arousal has a sensible explanation, and through repeated exposures, patients, perhaps unconsciously, learn that such arousal doesn't always presage a panic attack.

This form of treatment for specific phobias and agoraphobia has a number of strengths. Orwin reports that he has treated more than a hundred hospitalized patients with consistent success. He has found that the treatment is normally short-term, but the number of treatments varies with the intensity of the patient's symptoms and the secondary psychosocial gains associated with the symptom. Another obvious advantage is that another family member or a technician can be quickly instructed to administer the treatment. It follows that such treatment would be very cost-effective. Both of these are important considerations in a society where phobic disorders are so common.

Exercise treatment can also be an adjunct to psychotherapy when that therapy doesn't offer sufficient symptomatic relief or when the treatment for one or another reason is long-term. I've found that when treating phobic patients who show indications of repressed trauma, exercise can be a powerful adjunctive intervention. It can help control anxiety and keep a patient functional during a long psychotherapeutic process.

SUMMING UP

We have explored whether or not exercise might offer an inexpensive and effective way for us to deal with our daily anxieties, as well as offer us an alternative or an adjunct to conventional psychotherapy and anxiolytic drug treatments for more serious anxiety disorders.

A substantial body of research suggests that normal state anxiety can be successfully reduced from four to six hours following twenty minutes of moderate aerobic exercise, a large payoff for a small investment in time and effort. Baseline trait anxiety is also typically reduced after a few months of regular aerobic exercise. Both the short- and long-term anxiolytic effects of exercise are most pronounced for those of us who suffer from above average anxiety.

The major psychological theories that have been proposed to explain the anxiolytic effects of exercise are distraction (time-out), self-efficacy, and skills mastery. The thermogenic (elevated core temperature) mechanism turns out to be a sufficient but not essential element in anxiety reduction. Several neurotransmitters (norepinephrine, serotonin, GABA, dopamine, and beta-endorphin) play roles in anxiety, and exercise can have an effect on all of these systems.

Increasingly sophisticated and effective anxiolytic drugs (benzodiazepines and SSRIs) have been brought to bear on anxiety and anxiety disorders. Exposure to the feared object or situation (flooding) is central in effective psychotherapeutic approaches to treating phobias.

Exercise in itself shows promise as safe and effective in the treatment of panic disorder, and in combination with behavior therapy, exercise has been shown to be an efficacious treatment for specific phobias and agoraphobia.

ANOTHER VIEW OF ANXIETY

Anxiety has a bad reputation. Like mosquitoes, gophers, and other pests or inconveniences, it's something professionals and laypeople alike typically try get rid of. But anxiety is a normal and important part of our lives and, like nearly everything else, it has both positive and negative dimensions.

Carl Jung pointed out that fire has the capacity to both destroy (it can destroy a house) and create (forge steel). He suggested that the fires within human beings are our emotions, and that they, like a blazing fire, have a similar capacity to destroy and create. Anxiety does fuel psychopathology (agoraphobia is a good example). But Jung reminded us that embracing anxiety is sometimes necessary in order to break maladaptive defensive behaviors that isolate us from others and to create new ways of feeling, thinking, and being.

Nearly a century ago, when sedatives were the only drugs available in mental hospitals, Jung cautioned us against unthinkingly or indiscriminately medicating away anxiety, the very state that might be necessary for personal change.

Present-day psychotherapists concur that personality change is unlikely without experiencing anxiety, and it is a necessary and powerful force in psychotherapy. But there is such a thing as optimal anxiety, and if anxiety is excessive, it can cause such dysfunctionality that even psychotherapy is rendered ineffective. Exercise and anxiolytic drugs can serve as effective adjunctive interventions in such cases.

Anxiety plays a central role in the practice of those who practice existential psychotherapy. They typically embrace anxiety as a necessary and positive force in human change, be it within or outside the psychotherapist's office. They suggest that anxiety may sometimes be viewed as a clarion summons, an important signal that alerts us to avoided opportunities for living, chances passed by, potential unrealized, and risks not taken. For existential therapists, anxiety might not be seen as the cause but rather the consequence of a restricted existence or way of living. They contend that there are times when, however painful, it is best to embrace our anxiety, with the payoff being a fuller and richer life down the road.[42]

6.
DEPRESSION AND MOOD DISORDERS

Major depression is the most common single mental disorder in America, with 21.3 percent of women and 12.7 percent of men reporting that they had experienced at least one major depressive episode during their lifetimes. The next most common form of depression is dysthymia, and here again, women suffer higher lifetime rates (8 percent) than men (4.8 percent).[1] These two forms of *unipolar* depression will be fully described shortly. (Unipolar refers to forms of depression that only include depressed moods, disorders that have never included a manic episode, which delineates bipolar disorder.)

Even more than in the case of anxiety, our periods of depression can become so pronounced that they move into a gray boundary area that separates a severe normal depression from a clinical affective disorder. Let's address that gray boundary and begin by spelling out the DSM-IV criteria for a major depressive episode and dysthymia.[2]

CRITERIA FOR A MAJOR DEPRESSIVE EPISODE

To meet the criteria for such an episode, five or more of the following symptoms must have been present during the same two-week period, their presence must represent a change from previous functioning, and at least one of the two core symptoms (1) a depressed mood or (2) a loss of interest or pleasure must be present.

1. depressed mood most of the day, nearly every day, as indicated by subjective report (e.g., feels sad and empty) or observation (e.g., appears tearful). Note: In children and adolescents, it can be an irritable mood.

2. markedly diminished interest or pleasure in all, or almost all, activities most of the day, nearly every day (as indicated by subjective report of observations of others).

3. significant weight loss when not dieting or weight gain (e.g., a change of more than 5 percent in a month) or decrease or increase in appetite every day. Note: In children, consider failure to make expected weight gains.

4. insomnia or hypersomnia (excessive sleep) nearly every day.

5. psychomotor agitation or retardation nearly every day (observable by others, not merely subjective feelings of restlessness or being slowed down).

6. fatigue or loss of energy nearly every day.

7. feelings of worthlessness or excessive or inappropriate guilt (which may be delusional) nearly every day (not merely self-reproach or guilt about being sick).

8. diminished ability to think or concentrate, or indecisiveness, nearly every day (either by subjective account or as observed by others).

9. recurrent thoughts of death (not just fear of dying), recurrent suicidal ideation (thoughts) without a specific plan, or a suicide attempt or specific plan for committing suicide.

In addition, these symptoms must cause clinically significant distress or impairment in social, occupational, or other important areas of functioning. They cannot be due to the direct physiological effects of a substance (e.g., a drug of abuse or a medication) or a general medical condition (e.g., hypothyroidism).

And finally they cannot be better accounted for by bereavement, that is, after the loss of a loved one, the symptoms persist for longer than two months, or are characterized by marked functional impairment, morbid preoccupation with worthlessness, suicidal ideation, psychotic symptoms, or psychomotor retardation.

CRITERIA FOR DYSTHYMIC DISORDER

In order to meet the criteria for dysthymic disorder, an individual must have a depressed mood for most of the day, for more days than not, as indicated either by the afflicted individual's subjective account or by the observations of others, for at least two years. Note: In children and adolescents, mood can be irritable and the duration must be at least one year.

Two or more of the following symptoms must be present during the depression.

1. poor appetite or overeating
2. insomnia or hypersomnia
3. low energy or fatigue
4. low self-esteem
5. poor concentration or difficulty making decisions
6. feelings of hopelessness

There are also a number of rule-outs. The depressed symptoms cannot be due to a substance or general medical condition, and they must cause significant dysfunctionality. No major depressive episode can have occurred during the first two years of the disturbance (one year for children and adolescents), and the depression cannot be better accounted for by the diagnosis of chronic major depressive disorder in partial remission. Finally, the afflicted individual cannot have ever experienced a manic episode of any kind and has not met the criteria for cyclothymic personality disorder, and his disturbance cannot occur exclusively during the course of a chronic psychotic disorder.

* * *

An examination of the criteria for the two forms of depression reveals that they share common symptoms. However, there is a major difference between the two. Major depressive disorder is *episodic*, punctuated with substantial periods of normalcy, while dysthymia is *chronic*, punctuated periodically with brief periods of normalcy (perhaps two weeks). About 50 percent of us who are diagnosed with major depression suffer only a single episode during our lifetimes, but the rest of us are not so fortunate, since with each successive episode, the likelihood of additional episodes increases, suggesting a strong genetic predisposition. This genetic influence is further reflected by the 40 percent concordance rate for major depression between identical twins. (Concordance rates were explained in an earlier chapter.)

So how can we evaluate the severity of our own depression when we are going through stressful times? A recent survey conducted in three major American cities has revealed that there is no sharp boundary that separates the periods of severe depression (that many of us are likely to experience at least once in our lifetimes) from the clinical disorder, major depression. Depression is not a single unique disease entity, but it incorporates a range of symptoms of varying number and intensity.

In one of the three cities surveyed, Los Angeles, one out of nine of the 2,393 adults surveyed currently suffered from a depression of sufficient magnitude to create substantial dysfunctionality in their jobs and families. However, their symptoms fell in that gray boundary zone that separates an unusually depressed mood from a major depression. This group of people had, for a two-week period, and for no apparent reason, manifested two to four of the required five symptoms that define major depression. Yet their degree of disability or dysfunctionality was nearly as severe as those with five or more of the required symptoms. The investigators labeled this condition subsyndromal (not quite a full syndrome) depression (SSD).[3] An amazing 11 percent of the group surveyed in Los Angeles suffered from SSD, and only slightly over 4 percent met the more stringent criteria for major depression. You might be thinking that it's no surprise that living in Los Angeles is depressing, but the other two cities surveyed showed virtually identical rates. These findings underline just how common serious and disabling depression is in urban America.

It seems likely that the next revision of the American Psychiatric Association's *Diagnostic and Statistical Manual of Mental Disorders* will incorporate a new affective disorder something along the lines of subsyndromal depression.

The rather demanding diagnostic DSM criteria for major depression have for some time largely isolated it from the broad range of depressions that trouble most of us. As a consequence, decades ago scientists developed a number of psychological tests that could assess this broad range of subsyndromal depressions that failed to meet the rather stringent DSM-IV criteria for one or another depressive disorder. Such self-administered paper-

and-pencil tests typically yield depression scores that fall within specific ranges: none, mild, moderate, and severe. Much of the research concerning depression and physical activity that we will review here has been done with outpatients on campuses or adjacent communities, people who typically do not meet the DSM-IV criteria for major depression.

Outpatients and hospitalized patients in the investigations we will discuss have typically been evaluated with accepted tests such as the Revised Symptom Checklist-90 (SCL-90),[4] Research Diagnostic Criteria for the SCL-90,[5] the Zung Self-Rating Depression Scale (SDS),[6] and, most commonly, the Beck Depression Inventory (BDI).[7]

Our fundamental question in this chapter is whether or not exercise is a viable and efficacious treatment for depression. Let's begin by having a look at three meta-analyses that addressed this question.

META-ANALYSES: EXERCISE TREATMENT AND DEPRESSION

In the previous chapter, I pointed out that meta-analysis is a statistical technique in which a large number of investigations are packaged together and treated as a large investigation. The first large meta-analysis regarding exercise and depression included eighty studies completed prior to 1989. These studies all related at least one outcome measure of depression to exercise treatment or fitness.[8]

The initial meta-analysis found that exercise had an overall moderately significant effect in reducing depression, with its effects found to be particularly strong for groups of people who were undergoing various forms of medical rehabilitation. It also revealed that greater gains were made by individuals who exercised at home than for those who did so in various other facilities. Significant gains occurred in all age groups but were greater in middle-aged groups than in younger people. Gains were similar for both sexes, for all forms of exercise. Exercise proved to have a larger effect in reducing depression than all conditions with which it was compared, with the exception of psychotherapy, which was shown to be equally effective.

Perhaps the most striking finding of this meta-analysis concerned the effect of exercise program length. Exercise programs as brief as four weeks yielded significant antidepressant effects. Programs of five to sixteen weeks in duration had a greater effect on symptom reduction, but programs of five to six months in duration showed enormous gains.

Since the vast majority of experiments concerning exercise and depression have involved treatment periods of eight to twelve weeks, these findings suggest that the maximal physiological and psychological antidepressant effects may require more time. This is important information for the reader who is contemplating embarking on an exercise program for the purpose of mood elevation.

Each session of exercise offers a few hours of postexercise calm and serves to keep us going. However, four to six weeks of regular exercise are typically required to reduce depression, and the greatest mood benefits might not be realized until after five or six months of regular exercise. An exercise program should be carefully built on a foundation of moderation and patience, knowing that as time goes by our benefits will increase.

A second meta-analysis, conducted a year later, had parallel overall results, reinforcing the findings of the first.[9]

While meta-analyses are respected statistical devices, the results of such analyses are only as valid as the quality of the studies that are packaged together and analyzed. The two analyses just discussed were criticized by one reviewer who questioned the quality of some the studies that were included, pointing out that the analyses incorporated studies with different designs and methods, subjects with different initial levels of depression, and subjects who rarely suffered from very severe depression.[10]

A more recent 1998 meta-analysis confronted one of those criticisms by carefully selecting thirty studies that assessed only groups of subjects who met the criteria for clinical depression. It is no surprise that this analysis found exercise to be far more effective than did the first two. It also revealed that the effects of aerobic and nonaerobic were equal, and that exercise, psychotherapeutic treatments, and behavioral treatments were equally effective. Finally, it found that magnitude of exercise effect was greater for those groups who were initially classified as moderately to severely depressed (in contrast to those initially classified as mild to moderately depressed).[11]

While this third meta-analysis carries more weight than the previous two, it does not fully cancel out several of the criticisms that have been leveled at such analyses. An alternative approach is to examine a number of well-designed experiments that have included only subjects who met the criteria for depression. Such subjects have typically been classified as mildly, moderately, or severely depressed on one of the commonly used diagnostic tests, such as the Beck Depression Inventory, or have been diagnosed on the basis of DSM criteria.

Within those parameters, we will examine research that compares exercise treatment to no treatment, placebo treatment, meditation/relaxation therapy, individual psychotherapy, group psychotherapy, and antidepressant drug treatment. We will also compare the effectiveness of aerobic versus anaerobic exercise for both outpatient and hospitalized populations. I have selected studies that should answer most of the questions readers might have concerning how they might utilize exercise to find symptomatic relief from depression. Let's begin with a look at some illustrative epidemiological and experimental studies of outpatient groups, adults who mainly suffer subsyndromal depressions (not severe enough to meet the criteria for major depression or dysthymia).

EPIDEMIOLOGICAL INVESTIGATIONS

Some epidemiological surveys go beyond simply comparing levels of depression in large population groups of active and inactive people at a given time. Of special interest are four prospective studies. Prospective studies assess both physical activity levels and levels of depression in an initial survey (baseline), then again after several years.

One study of 1,497 men and women revealed that women who had, at the time of the initial survey, reported that they engaged in little or no physical activity were twice as likely to develop depression eight years later than those who had initially reported that they engaged in moderate or much physical activity. There was no such significant relationship found for men over the same time period. However, initial depression at baseline was a strong predictor of depression eight years later for the men.[12] Variables such as age, income, employment, education, and chronic illness, which could affect the results, were all statistically taken into account in this study.

In a second study, a large group of California adults provided baseline depression scores and physical activity levels in 1965, 1974, and 1983. Their activity levels were categorized as low, medium, and high in 1965 and again in 1983.

At the first follow-up in 1974, the relative risk (RR) of developing depression was higher for both men (1.8) and women (1.7) who had been inactive in 1965 compared to the reference group of men and women who had been high active in 1965 (and were assigned a RR of 1.0). Those men and women who had been medium active in 1965 had 1974 relative risks that fell between those of the initially low- and high-active groups (1.3).

At the 1983 follow-up, four categories were created that reflected reported activity levels at baseline and eighteen years later: (1) low/low, (2) low/high, (3) high/low, and (4) high/high. The low/high group (1.11) had no greater risk of being depressed in 1983 than the high/high reference group (1.0), suggesting that those initially inactive men and women who took up physical activity during the eighteen-year period seemed to have developed a protective shield that reduced the risk of becoming depressed. The greatest difference was found between the high/high reference group (1.0) and those who abandoned exercise in the interim. The high/low group had a RR of 1.6, which the authors concluded was a robust finding, since the odds ratio was unaffected by a host of potentially contaminating variables such as age, sex, health, social support, socio-economic status, and so on.[13] Thus, it appears that taking up regular exercise provides a protective shield, and abandoning regular exercise may well put us at risk for developing depression.

The well-known ongoing Harvard Alumni Study, which followed seventeen thousand male graduates who entered the university between 1916 and 1950, has periodically assessed the association between physical activity and several measures of physical and mental health.[14]

The researchers found that men who engaged in three or more hours of sports activity a week had a 27 percent reduction in risk of being depressed (at follow-up) than those who spent less than an hour a week in sports activity. The findings also revealed a close relationship between the risk of developing a clinical depression and the total number of calories expended per week in aerobic activities such as walking, jogging, stair climbing, and sports activity. The men who expended a thousand calories a week in such aerobic activities had a 17 percent reduced risk (compared to the least active men), and those who expended twenty-five hundred or more calories a week had a 28 percent reduced risk. These findings suggest again that engaging in sports and aerobic exercise may have a protective effect, reducing the odds of developing a clinical depression.

A fourth study found that within a sample of 1,536 members of a community in Bavaria, 8.3 percent were clinically depressed. Community members who were physically inactive were 3.15 times more likely to be depressed, and those who were only occasionally active were 1.55 times as likely to be depressed than those who were regularly active. However, in contrast to the three previous studies, a follow-up five years later found that low physical activity did not predict depression.[15]

These four studies all found an association between physical activity and depression, with low-active people having the greatest rates of depression, and in three of the four studies initially inactive people were found to be at greater risk to have developed depression by the time of the follow-up many years later.

Two Norwegian studies lend further support to suggestion that physical activity may have a protective effect. The first study found that soldiers who regularly engaged in sports were significantly less depressed after twelve weeks in a stressful life situation than those who were classified as sedentary.[16] The second study found that patients with a history of physical activity and sports participation were more responsive to treatment in a mental hospital and were less likely to undergo a relapse after discharge.[17]

Taken together, these six studies suggest that regular physical activity may have a preventive or protective effect with regard to depression. Regular exercise may help us avoid getting depressed, help us get well sooner if we are depressed, and reduce the odds of a relapse.

EXERCISE AND SUBSYNDROMAL DEPRESSION: EXPERIMENTAL STUDIES

University of Wisconsin psychiatrist John Greist had been a student athlete. Later in life, he came to appreciate how exercise had elevated mood and reduced anxiety in both himself and fellow athletes. As an increasing number of reports in the professional literature suggested that exercise produced such mood changes in normal populations, Greist wondered if similar changes would occur with depressed patients.

In 1973, he and a group of similar-minded colleagues conducted a pilot study that explored the possibility that exercise might be an efficacious treatment for depression. Because his project was the very first such investigation anywhere in the entire world, Greist had a problem selling the proposed pilot study to fellow psychotherapists at the university student clinic. He wrote that some of his colleagues felt that he was placing depressed students who had come for help at considerable risk by offering such "heretical" treatment, but his proposed study was eventually approved.[18]

A group of twenty-eight men and women who came to the clinic complaining of depression, how it substantially interfered with their lives, and whose SCL-90 RDC test scores confirmed that they were moderately depressed were selected for the study. They were randomly assigned for ten-weeks of treatment to one of three groups: (1) behavior-focused time-limited therapy: a brief semistructured therapy in which the focus was to identify and change the patient's self-defeating behaviors that perpetuated his depression, (2) traditional time-unlimited psychodynamic therapy, in which the focus was insight-oriented, and (3) walk/run therapy.

Those assigned to the two traditional psychotherapy groups met once a week for individual psychotherapy with highly experienced therapists. The walk/run patients met individually with a running therapist three times a week for thirty to forty-five minutes for the first few weeks, and less often later on, when patients exercised alone. The sessions contained pre-stretching and poststretching and track workouts that involved alternate periods of walking and running. The percentage of time spent walking gradually decreased and time spent running increased as fitness improved. At the end of ten weeks, all patients were able to run for the entire session.

Patient depression levels were assessed on intake, at several points during treatment, at termination, and at several points post-treatment.

All three treatment groups showed improvement, but running therapy and behavior-focused time-limited therapy appeared to have more powerful effects than did dynamic therapy. Six of the eight runners were symptom-free in three weeks, one in ten weeks, and one showed no change. One year after treatment terminated, 80 percent of the runners remained asymptomatic, while 50 percent of the patients in the two traditional psychotherapy groups were back in treatment at the counseling center. The durability of the running therapy treatment was in part explained by the fact that nearly all of the patients in that group were still running regularly a year after treatment ceased.

Encouraged by the results of that pilot study of student patients, Greist invited referrals of clinically depressed patients from psychiatrists engaged in private practice in Madison. One might surmise that the patients referred were likely to be those who were not responding well to traditional sit-and-talk therapy. These thirty depressed patients were treated according to the same walk/run protocol as was used with the university students. Twenty-four recovered promptly, and of the remaining six who didn't quickly recover, four never became runners.

This pioneering effort was groundbreaking in a number of respects. It revealed that a walk/run protocol was viable, that most depressed patients accepted and stayed with the treatment, that the treatment reduced depression as well as two conventional psychotherapeutic treatments, and that the effects of running treatment were unusually persistent.

The several deficiencies of this first pilot effort were corrected in a later outstanding investigation, once again carried out at the University of Wisconsin. This time, a member of the original research team, psychologist Marjorie Klein, was the lead investigator.[19]

More than two hundred Madison residents responded to an advertisement offering free treatment for depressed men and women who would volunteer for a university research project. After careful screening, sixty people who met the criteria for major or minor depression on the SCL-90 RDC depression cluster, who had no other psychological disorders, and who were not in any form of treatment were selected and randomly placed in one of three groups for twelve weeks of treatment.

Group psychotherapy sessions met weekly for two hours. These sessions encompassed a combination of cognitive and interpersonal approaches designed to help patients recognize and change problematic behaviors and thought patterns that played a role in maintaining their depressions. (A patient might, for example, come to recognize his guilt-provoking, passive-aggressive manner of dealing with his anger and attempt to be more direct and assertive in interactions with important people in his life, resulting in improved social relationships.)

Running therapy sessions lasted forty-five minutes twice a week. Warm-up and cool-down bracketed thirty minutes of walk/run. Individual patients met with individual running therapists who kept them focused on breathing and technique, disallowing any discussion of symptoms or problems. Patients were encouraged to run on their own between sessions and keep a log. All who completed the twelve weeks of treatment did so.

Meditation-relaxation therapy groups met weekly for two hours. It was similar to running therapy in that the focus was on body-awareness, breathing, and technique. However, there was no aerobic component. Like those in the psychotherapy groups, they were assigned homework sessions.

Attrition rates for the three groups were reasonably similar, but the patterns differed. Almost all of those assigned to the running group began treatment, but a substantial number dropped out before the treatment period ended. Attrition in the other two groups involved dropouts as well but mainly reflected no-shows when treatment began.

Significant reduction in depressive symptoms was apparent in all groups after four weeks of treatment, and at the end of twelve weeks, all three groups showed very significant, but not different, symptom reduction. The treatments were equally effective.

Follow-up assessments were made at one, three, and nine months, and it was here that differential treatment effects emerged. At three months and nine months, the psychotherapy groups average scores had regressed toward greater depression, while the gains of the other two groups remained constant.

These findings of durable treatment effects replicate those of the earlier Wisconsin pilot study. However, a smaller percentage of patients in Klein's running group continued to run after treatment ended: 76 percent after three months and 37 percent after six months. Nonetheless, the therapeutic gains persisted. Klein attributed the longer lasting effects of the meditation-relaxation and running groups to *skills mastery*.

Patients in both groups spent twelve weeks learning specific skills and monitoring their bodies. During that time they also experienced a reduction in their depressive symptoms (which they attributed to treatment). Many of the patients arrived in therapy with a reactive depression (the result of one or another stressful event) and were symptom-free when treatment ended. For them there was no significant reason to keep on running (or meditating), but they carried with them a set of learned skills that they knew they could put to work should they become depressed down the line. Klein attributed the backsliding of the psychotherapy group to a loss of group support.

An outpatient investigation carried out at Pennsylvania State University is also worthy of our attention.[20] Adult volunteers, solicited through public service announcements, displayed a range of depression scores. Those whose scores fell below the "mildly depressed" range were excluded, and the forty-nine men and women with mild, moderate, and severe depression scores were randomly assigned to three groups for ten weeks of treatment. The psychotherapy component of this study differed from that of Klein in that it was individual therapy.

1. *Walk/run therapy*: groups of six to eight patients met three times a week for a twenty-minute workout, preceded by stretching.

2. *Individual brief cognitive psychotherapy*: one session each week where patients identified irrational thoughts about self, the world around them, the past, and the future, and tested new ways of behaving between sessions.

3. *Combined treatment.*

The Beck Depression Inventory, the Profile of Mood States, and the State Trait Anxiety Inventory were administered at the time the patients came in seeking treatment; at weeks one, five, and ten of treatment; and two and four months post-treatment.

All three treatments were equally effective, with BDI depression scores significantly reduced by week five, further reduced by week ten, and remained reduced at the two-month follow-up. Exercise, by itself, proved to be as effective as a proven form of individual therapy and as effective as the two forms of therapy combined.

The STAI revealed that average state and trait anxiety scores were also reduced in all groups. The POMS revealed tension, anger, frustration, and confusion scale scores decreasing and vigor scale scores increasing over the course of treatment for all three groups.

A second study, also carried out at Penn State, involved a group of eighteen mildly and moderately depressed students who sought help at the campus counseling center. All received weekly counseling sessions, but half were randomly selected to walk/run for at least twenty minutes three times a week for the ten-week treatment period. Average pretreatment depression scores (in the moderate range) for the two groups were identical, but after ten weeks of treatment, the counseling-only group showed no significant gains, while members of the combined treatment group were largely symptom-free.[21]

Some readers may be wondering, "Where were the placebo groups or no-treatment groups in these studies?" By the time these studies took place, a large body of research had confirmed that psychotherapy was an efficacious treatment, shown to be more effective than no treatment in control group studies. Investigators therefore felt free to simply compare exercise treatment with a form of treatment already shown to be efficacious.

Exercise treatment has, however, been evaluated in several control-group and placebo-group investigations. One such study involved a large group of mildly depressed women. Women who engaged in aerobic dance, jogging, or running for an hour two times a week had significantly greater BDI score reductions after five and ten weeks (when treatment ended) than a waiting-list control group and a placebo group that engaged in relaxation exercises and brief walks four days a week.[22]

Baseline studies, where depressed individuals serve as their own controls, have also been utilized in some studies. In such research, depression levels are assessed during a pretreatment period of a few weeks, during which time the individuals receive attention/placebo treatment. Once baseline depression levels are established, exercise treatment is introduced.

In one such study, four women diagnosed with major depression exercised on a bike ergometer for thirty minutes, four times a week, at 85 percent of aerobic capacity, for six weeks. All four had significantly reduced depression levels at the end of treatment and at a three-month follow-up.[23]

In a second baseline experiment, fifteen mildly depressed men and women exercised at a gradually increasing intensity either walking, running, or on a stationary bicycle four times a week for fifteen weeks. Their average scores were significantly reduced from pretreatment baseline levels at the end of treatment, and those gains remained at both six and twenty-one month follow-ups.[24]

All these studies involved aerobic exercise, with walk/run protocols the most common. They demonstrated that the walk/run method works, doesn't demand any great expense, is convenient, and is easily monitored.

But what about anaerobic exercise? It has yet to be demonstrated that weight lifting has an anxiolytic effect. Will it reduce depression?

ANAEROBIC VERSUS AEROBIC EXERCISE

The first investigation, that addressed this question studied a large group of women who met the SCL-90 RDC criteria for minor or major depression. Some ran, others lifted weights, and some were placed on a waiting list to serve as controls. Treatment sessions lasted thirty minutes and took place four times a week for eight weeks. Both the runners and the weight lifters showed significant (but not different) reductions in average depression scores at the end of treatment, gains that were maintained at a one-month follow-up.[25]

This study was later replicated, comparing women who worked out four times a week for eight weeks. Some ran at 80 percent of their maximal heart rates; some engaged in circuit weight training at 50–60 percent of their maximal heart rates; and others served as waiting list controls. Once again both treatment groups made significant, but not different, gains in reduced depression, gains that persisted for one year.[26]

In the United Kingdom, a group of mildly and moderately depressed women engaged either in aerobic exercise (walk/jog for twenty to thirty minutes, three times a week) or nonaerobic exercise (stretching and strengthening) for eight weeks. After four weeks of treatment, only the aerobic group had significantly reduced depression, but by week eight both groups had similar significant reductions. Gains for both groups persisted at the twenty-week follow-up.[27]

These findings suggest that five to ten weeks of regular aerobic, anaerobic, and nonaerobic exercise all have similar and significant antidepressant effects on groups of men and women whose depressions are largely subsyndromal, ranging from mild to severe, but don't meet the criteria for dysthymia or major depression.

But does exercise treatment hold any promise for the most severely depressed men and women, those who suffer such dysfunctionality that they require hospitalization? Research from Europe provides some very encouraging answers.

EXERCISE TREATMENT WITH HOSPITALIZED PATIENTS

In a hospital on the west coast of Norway, psychiatrist Egil Martinsen selected forty-nine depressed adult patients for a pioneering investigation. These men and women all met the DSM-III criteria for major depression when admitted. They were seriously ill. They had experienced an average of eight previous major depressive episodes (about one a year), and their current episode had lasted at least six months. These were highly dysfunctional men and women with strong genetic predispositions for depression.[28]

All forty-nine patients received the standard weekly hospital treatments: one to two hours of dynamic psychotherapy, an hour of occupational therapy, and tricyclic antidepressants (if necessary). Half of them were randomly assigned to an aerobic exercise group. They walked, jogged, skied, or swam at 50 to 75 percent of their maximum aerobic capacity (light to moderate intensity range) for one hour, three times a week, for nine weeks. The remaining patients were assigned to an additional hour of occupational therapy three times a week for a similar time period. (Occupational therapists help physically, mentally, and emotionally disabled patients gain skills needed for daily activities at home, in the community, or at work.)

At the end of nine weeks, men and women in the aerobic group had significantly increased their fitness, and they had significantly reduced BDI depression scores to a greater extent than the control subjects in the occupational therapy group.

Martinsen found there was a significant negative correlation between degree of fitness and degree of depression at the end of the treatment period (the more fit, the less depressed) for the male patients. The female patients showed a similar trend. However, the correlation between fitness and depression for the women was too low to attain significance. This gender difference suggested to Martinsen that the antidepressant effects of exercise did not reflect increased fitness alone but may have multiple determiners.

A follow-up of these patients, which took place between one and two years after release, revealed that following release, the patients who took part in the study now constituted three groups instead of two. It turned out that following the nine-week experimental period in the hospital a number of the occupational therapy (control) patients had joined the aerobic program for several weeks. They tended to be the younger and more depressed patients, whose depressive symptoms had reduced less than others when the nine-week treatment experimental period had ended. So, after discharge, there were three groups: the occupational therapy control group, the aerobic treatment group, and the control-aerobic group (made up of occupational therapy group members who had spontaneously joined the aerobic program after the nine-week experimental period had ended).

At follow-up, members of the control group rated the psychoanalytic dynamic psychotherapy as the most therapeutic element in their hospital treatment, while members of both other groups rated exercise as far more important than any other element of their treatment.

A larger percentage of the two aerobic groups than controls were exercising at follow-up, although the number of patients still exercising was very impressive overall. Norwegians live in the northern latitudes where seasonal affective disorder (a unipolar depressive disorder caused by too little sunlight) is common. It is no accident that they are very active people. The percentages of the groups that were (1) engaging in *regular* exercise and (2) engaging in at least two hours of *aerobic* exercise a week were 54 and 23 percent of the controls, 91 and 53 percent of the aerobic group, and 100 and 100 percent of the control plus aerobic group. Members of the aerobic group, and especially members of the control plus aerobic group, had learned during hospitalization that exercise was a legitimate and effective intervention to reduce depression.

There were also promising trends that suggested that the members of the exercise treatment group had suffered fewer post-treatment depressive episodes, were using fewer antidepressant drugs, and had sought medical help less frequently.

Martinsen was puzzled by the gender differences revealed in this experiment. While both men and women in the aerobic group had significantly increased fitness and reduced depression, the correlation between increased fitness and reduced depression was statistically significant only for the men.

Martinsen determined to find out whether exercise had to be aerobic in order to have an antidepressant effect on hospitalized patients. He selected ninety-nine male and female patients who met the DSM-III criteria for major depression, dysthymia, or depressive disorder not otherwise specified and treated them for eight weeks. All received the standard hospital weekly treatments, but half engaged in aerobic training (walk/jog at 70 percent of VO_{2max}), while other half engaged in nonaerobic training (flexibility, strength, and relaxation exercises) for an hour, three times a week.

At the end of treatment, only the aerobic group members had significantly increased their aerobic fitness, but both groups had made significant, although not different, reductions in depression. There were no gender differences. Martinsen speculated that distraction might play a significant role in the antidepressant effects of the two forms of exercise.[29]

Martinsen's work was truly groundbreaking. He demonstrated that hospitalized patients suffering the most severe episodic depression were willing to exercise and would benefit from it, that it was safe for medicated patients to engage in vigorous exercise, and that a variety of aerobic and nonaerobic exercises were effective. Patients who exercised several times a week got well sooner, and there was a strong suggestion that they stayed well longer following release.

EXERCISE VERSUS ZOLOFT

Another groundbreaking experiment took place a few years ago at Duke University, where for the first time the effects of exercise treatment were compared to those of a widely prescribed and proven antidepressant drug. The investigation involved 156 adults, all of whom were diagnosed with major depression. No previous research on exercise treatment had included such a large sample and demanded that the outpatients meet the stringent DSM-IV diagnostic standards.[30]

The subjects were randomly assigned to three treatment groups: (1) exercise treatment, (2) Zoloft treatment, and (3) combined treatment. The exercisers engaged in brisk walking, jogging, or stationary bicycle riding three times a week. Their sessions included a ten-minute warm-up, a thirty-minute exercise period, and a five-minute cool-down.

At the end of the four-month treatment period, between 60 and 70 percent of the individuals in all three groups had "vastly improved" or were "symptom-free." All three groups were equally effective in reducing the symptoms of depression.

However, a follow-up study, completed ten months after the initiation of treatment, revealed a remarkable difference with regard to the durability of treatment effects. The follow-up analysis examined what percentage of subject, whose symptoms had fully remitted at the end of all forms of treatment had suffered a return of depressive symptoms. Thirty-eight percent of the Zoloft group, 31 percent of the combined treatment group, but *only 8 percent* of the exercise group experienced a return of symptoms. This difference in relapse rates found between the medication and exercise group was highly significant. Members of the exercise group who continued to exercise on their own during the follow-up period were less likely to be diagnosed as depressed at the end of that period. Investigator James Blumenthal said the findings suggest that exercise "is an effective, robust treatment for patients with major depression."

WALKING AND TALKING WITH PATIENTS

Toronto psychologist Kate Hays is the past president of the American Psychological Association's Division 47, Exercise and Sport Psychology. She recently wrote *Working It Out: Using Exercise in Psychotherapy*, a book written for mental health professionals who might want to incorporate exercise as a treatment component.[31]

However, the odds that therapists will recommend exercise, much less walk and talk with patients during psychotherapy sessions, appear to be meager. Hays reports that many surveys have found that 50–75 percent of psychotherapists engage in regular physical exercise themselves but that few recommend it for patients.

Hays personally conducted a survey of thirty-four male and thirty-two female therapists, all of whom exercised with regularity, and found that 92 percent of the female and 96 percent of the male therapists recommended exercise to at least some of their patients (10–90 percent). Recommendations were mainly made for patients who were depressed, anxious, overweight, and stressed.

Of the sixty-six therapists who placed great value on their own personal exercise, only three women and three men exercised with their patients during therapy sessions. The primary reasons given for this reticence were escalating litigiousness and an increased awareness of the potential for boundary violations (clear role definition and professional boundaries between client and therapist).

I personally walked and talked with patients less frequently as my professional liability insurance premiums dramatically increased over my years of practice. America is increasingly populated by legions of liability lawyers, and many citizens are encouraged by both the media and liability lawyers to think of themselves as victims. The consequences are that therapists are discouraged from using interventions that have great promise but may seem unconventional. This would especially be the case when treating patients whose diagnoses might predispose them to project blame and to litigate. Such patients may be less likely to get the high-quality help they need in these days of victims and litigation.

Nonetheless, there are professionals who do walk, and sometimes even run, with selected patients because they believe that the pay-off in patient progress is so impressive.

San Diego therapist Ozzie Gontang estimates that 75 percent of the people he has treated since 1973 have chosen to walk and talk during sessions (thousands of depressed people). He reports that walking side by side on the beach, through the woods, in a park, or even in the city during a soft rain helps the patient to look at life through a different filter. Like other walk/talk therapists, Gontang has found patients to be more open and in touch with their feelings in such circumstances. He tells of walking with a patient who had attempted suicide.[32]

During the first five miles of an eight-mile circle route, they chanted in unison, "I can't go on, I can't go on," mantra-style. They were forced to stop periodically while the patient uncontrollably sobbed and talked of his hopelessness. When the two returned the starting point of their journey after eight long miles, Gontang suggested that the patient could, in fact, go on.

Wes Sime is an exercise physiology professor at the University of Nebraska. Years ago, psychiatrists in the community frequently referred severely depressed patients to him for "stress reduction" runs. Sime details one such case.[33] The patient had recently spent thirty days in a drug detox center for benzodiazepine dependency and had received electroconvulsive therapy treatments for his suicidal depression. The patient was making little or no progress in analysis.

The patient's level of depression was measured several times during a two-month pretreatment period to establish a baseline, then Sime ran with him on nineteen of the next thirty-six days. Depression was measured each of those thirty-six days. It was discovered that on the days they ran, depression scores were dramatically reduced and remained low for about twenty-four hours. Sime reported that at that time, running appeared to be the only effective treatment and that it probably kept the patient alive.

Sime also related that the patient was unusually emotional during their runs, and he expressed the wish that the patient's therapist (instead of Sime) had been running with the patient at those times to more effectively deal with such catharsis. However, therapists mainly sit in their offices. Sime was so impressed with the effects of running with severely depressed patients that he went on to get a second doctorate, this one in clinical psychology.

My experiences in walking and running with patients have been similar to those commonly reported by others who walk with patients. My patients have seemed far less guarded when outdoors. I found that when exercise was vigorous (brisk walking for healthy unfit individuals), patients typically experienced and released more emotions of all kinds than when more passively sitting in comfortable office chairs.

I also found that very vigorous exercise seemed to be particularly helpful for depressed and guilt-ridden patients whose anger was typically repressed and that the high state of physical arousal often served to transform pervasive guilt into the anger or rage that guilt so often effectively conceals.

We often feel guilty about how we just can't seem to refrain from systematically rejecting or neglecting close family members or other important people in our lives. While guilt is unpleasant, it's usually less painful to deal with such guilt than to admit the true reasons behind our rejection or neglect of these people. Sometimes simply getting angry at a therapist who is pushing you faster than you want to walk opens doors to anger at other more significant people. Even if it does not immediately do so, expressing that anger at a therapist (and discovering that you both survive very nicely) is a move in the right direction for patients whose anger is typically contained.

I once treated a man whose unremitting obsession with guilt over his wife's suicide had rendered him highly dysfunctional. He was a hazard to other drivers on the highway, was in danger of losing his job, and was unable to be a father to his children effectively. His friends, his pastor, his family doctor, a psychologist, and a psychiatrist had all told him that he *shouldn't feel guilty*, that her suicide wasn't his fault. But nothing helped. He came to me as a last resort.

I utilized exercise and symptom prescription with him, actually prescribing guilt. We quickly agreed that trying to not feel guilty hadn't worked, and he said he was willing to try something different. The fact of the matter was that he *did* feel guilty. In order to sell my symptom-prescription intervention, I suggested that his guilt had to be purged and that by concentrating on feeling nothing but guilt for an a hour a day, he would be less preoccupied with it during the other twenty-three hours and could function better in all aspects of his life.

My prescription was that he walk/jog for an hour each evening and think about nothing except how guilty he felt during that hour. When I told him that feeling nothing but guilt for an entire hour was an almost impossibly difficult task, he laughed at me. I told him that if he could somehow stick with my prescription, he would likely be feeling much better in a few weeks.

He was desperate, and he embraced exercise/guilt prescription with intensity. However, each week he became increasingly angry at me, eventually telling me that I didn't know what I was doing. I recall his yelling at me that I should have known that it was impossible to feel nothing but guilt for an hour a day. I told him that if he wanted to get well he had to try harder, suggesting that he wear a rubber band around his wrist and deliver a punishing snap whenever his mind wandered from his guilt during his daily runs.

Paradox is a wonderful therapeutic tool. He came to me wanting to stop feeling guilty and was now complaining that he wasn't able to feel guilty for even a single hour a day. After a few sessions, the guilt he felt about his wife transformed into anger at her, and I got off the hook.

He still wasn't convinced that I knew what I was doing, but after six weeks of treatment, he had stopped taking antidepressants and tranquillizers, was sleeping better, driving safely, concentrating on the job, and was focusing more on helping his kids deal with their loss. His guilt was a thing of the past.

I have found that even leisurely walking with patients was more productive than sitting and staring at one another in the office. Patients are likely to be more defensive when they feel that they are being scrutinized for fifty minutes: that every change of expression or posture may be analyzed. It's a different story when both of you are outdoors, walking side by side and looking at the path ahead, instead of sitting and mentally slogging through the quagmires of the past.

WHEN IS EXERCISE TREATMENT APPROPRIATE?

All the studies on exercise treatment for depressed individuals have found it to be highly effective. These studies have examined exercise as the primary treatment of clinically depressed outpatients and as either an adjunctive or primary treatment for severely depressed hospitalized patients. While the body of research is relatively limited, it includes a number of very well-designed and well-executed studies. The consistency of findings is remarkable.

In light of such findings, the more reasonable question might be,

"When is exercise an *inappropriate* intervention for the treatment of depression?" There are at least three such circumstances.

The first, of course, is when physical activity might present a threat to one's health or life. A physical examination, perhaps including a stress test, is a must for those of us entering an exercise program.

A second circumstance is when regular exercise is doing such an effective job of keeping depressive symptoms at bay that it makes it unnecessary for us to attend to the problems that are actually at the root of our depression. Regular exercise can help keep us out of the psychotherapist's office when such professional assistance should clearly be the primary treatment of choice.

Perhaps, for example, we are locked into predictable behavior patterns that sabotage our important interpersonal relationships with friends and family members or on the job. Better to do something about those behaviors and put an end to the depressions that invariably result when we repeatedly act them out.

However, even if we are working on our problems in a professional setting, exercise can provide symptom relief as we struggle to find solutions. If safe, it is always appropriate as an adjunctive intervention for outpatient or inpatient treatment.

Finally, exercise by itself isn't always enough to deal with our depression. Sometimes hardly anything is.

I recall working with a woman who had suffered major depressive episodes twice in years past when she had experienced heart-breaking losses. She was doing well in psychotherapy and was running most days of the week. Then, in the course of a few weeks, her fiancé unexpectedly left her for another woman, and her father died. She swiftly became deeply depressed, stopped running, and spent most of her time in bed, where she compulsively binged. She only barely managed to function on her job, where she began having a series of uncharacteristic severe interpersonal confrontations.

After a few weeks, I was finally able to convince her that she needed medication (only after sitting with her and systematically going through the list of criteria for a major depressive episode with an open DSM-IV). Fortunately, an antidepressant put an end to her downward slide, and together with psychotherapy and running she began to put her life back in order.

Sometimes exercise, psychotherapy, and antidepressants in combination are insufficient to cope with the magnitude of our depression. When that occurs, electroconvulsive therapy (ECT) is the treatment of choice. It almost always swiftly drives a deep wedge into such a devastating depression, allowing medication and psychotherapy to again play major roles in treatment.

While ECT was portrayed as a barbaric and punitive procedure in Ken Kesey's *One Flew over the Cuckoo's Nest*, a panel of experts at the National Institute of Mental Health concluded that the treatment is both safe and effective for a narrow range of very serious disorders and that future psychiatrists should be trained in its administration.[34]

Exercise can also play a role in protecting us from the onset of a depression. It is a marvelous vessel to keep us afloat during the inevitable periods of stress we all must deal with in our lifetimes. Such periods don't always require professional assistance. They sometimes have no solutions: They must simply be gotten through.

HYPOTHESIZED MECHANISMS: PSYCHOLOGICAL THEORIES

Since exercise appears to be an efficacious and safe treatment for clinical depression, perhaps theorizing about just exactly how it works is irrelevant. If it works, it works! However, scientists are exceedingly curious people who pursue all kinds of ideas that may have little or no immediate applied value. This kind of "pure science" has proven time and time again to have enormous value down the line.

There is already a monumental stack of accumulated studies that inquire about whether the biochemical consequences of exercise might mimic those of antidepressant drugs, and the quest for answers has only just begun. Theories concerning psychological mechanisms have been formalized as a result of experimental studies but remain largely speculative.[35]

The major psychological explanations for the antidepressive effects of exercise are the same as for its anxiolytic effects: *distraction or "time-out,"* *self-efficacy*, and *skills mastery.*

The fact that such a wide variety of aerobic, anaerobic, and nonaerobic interventions have all proven to be equally effective in reducing the symptoms of subsyndromal depressions, as well as those of more serious clinical disorders, suggests that distraction or "time-out" may play a role.

Of course distraction undoubtedly has some additional help from the attention/placebo effects that are always a factor in research examining various kinds of treatment. Patients in all groups have an expectation to be helped and are regularly attended to by professionals who supervise their activities. And those professionals are typically kind people who reinforce patient expectations that whatever it is that they're doing will make them feel better.

It's difficult to separate out the effects of exercise from all the confounding factors that are a part of any exercise setting. For example, a group of mildly depressed elderly men and women were split into three groups that (1) individually walked outdoors with a student for twenty minutes twice a week, (2) had twenty minutes of individual social contact with a student twice a week, (3) or were waiting-list controls. After six weeks, the reductions in depression were the same for the two groups who had social contact with students, suggesting that the exercise was superfluous.[36]

All kinds of activities can help us take our minds off our problems and allow us to experience at least temporary relief. Each of us is aware of particular activities (physical, social, job-related) that will distract us and predictably elevate our mood or calm us down.

But these activities are typically short-term (acute) effects and don't explain the pervasive and longer-lasting (chronic) antidepressive effects that result from several weeks of regular exercise treatment. It seems unlikely that distraction, by itself, has a cumulative enduring effect. Some other cognitive processes must play a role. The most obvious candidate is self-efficacy.

The depressed research subject who jogs, lifts weights, or meditates several times a week shortly becomes aware that these activities are followed by predictable periods of elevated mood. This awareness can set into place the cognitive processes that lead to increased self-efficacy and a shift toward a more internal locus of control: "This makes me feel better, and I can do it on my own."

When John Greist published the results of his pioneering study in 1978, he speculated about the various mechanisms that might explain the antidepressive effects of exercise. He suggested that the acute mood-elevating effects that followed each workout could give the depressed individual a feeling of *hope* (that the depression might not necessarily go on forever) and a feeling of *control* (that he had the knowledge and skills to make himself feel better).[37]

Skills mastery, whether formal or not, typically involves four elements.[38] These elements are apparent in exercise therapy as well as a number of psychotherapies that emphasize cognition, behavior, and homework. I've utilized those four essential elements when prescribing exercise to depressed patients.

I begin by providing a rational structure designed to help patients believe that they could learn to control their own moods and behavior: "Exercise has been proven to be highly effective in reducing the symptoms of depression. If you were to begin to work out regularly, odds are you'll be feeling much better in a few weeks."

The second element involves teaching the skills: "Here's how you do it." The prescription is typically to walk briskly three or four days a week, first for thirty minutes, then working up to an hour. This prescription incorporates the third element: an emphasis on independent use of the skills. "You can do this on your own between our meetings, and you can use it in the future, should you encounter another period of stress and depression after treatment ends."

The final element involves attribution of the elevated mood to the use of the skills: "You're feeling much better (less depressed, enhanced self-esteem, sleeping better, etc.) because you've been exercising regularly. You've really taken charge of your life."

BIOCHEMICAL THEORIES

To explore the possibility that exercise might result in significant biochemical antidepressant effects, or even mimic the effects of antidepressant drugs, we'll begin with a look at the antidepressant drugs, how well they work, and how they work.

When depressed individuals are treated with an antidepressant for eight weeks, typically an average of 67 percent will respond with a reduction of at least 50 percent of their symptoms. If a placebo is then substituted, 50 percent of them will continue to respond and 50 percent will relapse, but if medication is continued beyond eight weeks, 90 percent of the responders will continue to respond, and only 10 to 25 percent will suffer a relapse.

In considering the above figures we should keep in mind that *respond* means a reduction of at least 50 percent of one's symptoms (an FDA standard for drug approval). Thus, the word respond does not mean that the responder is well. An individual who has *responded* and gone on to eventually become completely symptom-free has *remitted*. Unfortunately, as many as half of the responders never fully remit. While the antidepressant may have elevated their depressed mood, they may remain apathetic (have a diminished capacity for pleasure), or they may remain highly anxious. Between 20 and 30 percent of the individuals whose symptoms have fully remitted with treatment fail to maintain their response to the antidepressant during the ensuing eighteen months.[39] These numbers are not encouraging. It's past due time to search for a new kind of antidepressant that may do a better job.

To fully explain how current antidepressants work would be an enormous and unnecessary undertaking for the purposes of this book. Some readers, who have no interest in the biochemistry of depression, may choose to simply bypass this section. For others, who are curious, here are some basics.

Let's begin with an example of the least complicated synaptic event. A synapse is an extremely narrow liquid-filled gap that separates neurons (nerves). Neurons receive neurochemical messages at their dendrite end and deliver them at their axon end. When a presynaptic neuron electrically discharges, it releases neurotransmitters (chemical molecules) from its axon terminals into synapses, where they briefly occupy specific (no other kinds of neurotransmitters will fit) receptor sites on the dendrites of postsynaptic neurons. After briefly occupying receptor sites, these neurotransmitters are quickly transported back (reuptaken) into the presynaptic neuron and stored in vesicles for future use. This reasonably uncomplicated event, which attempts to pass on a message from one neuron to another, occurs in only a tiny fraction of a second.

Complicating matters is the fact that the message-receiving dendrites of a given neuron may have several kinds of receptor sites that receive messages (brief receptor site occupancies by various kinds of neurotransmitters) from a great many presynaptic neurons. Some of these neurotransmitter messengers encourage the neuron to fire and pass on a message, and others inhibit the likelihood of its doing so. With this fluctuating input, a neuron may stop and start firing many times over the course of a single second, governed by the percentage of excitatory and inhibitory messages it is receiving at a given instant.

Neurotransmission is a very sophisticated process, but the above two paragraphs provide the very simplest basic concepts that should allow interested readers to read on and have a reasonable understanding about how antidepressants work.

Since their serendipitous discovery nearly a half century ago, antidepressants have largely targeted two neurotransmitters: *norepinephrine* (NE) and 5-hydroxytryptamine (5-HT), usually referred to as *serotonin*. While the mechanisms of the various antidepressant families differ, they all have the common effect of immediately elevating the levels of these neurotransmitters in synapses, setting off a cascade of neural events, which in the course of about ten days, reregulate the neurons, boosting their activity above pretreatment levels.

Monoamine oxidase inhibitors (MAOIs), such as Nardil and Parnate, boost the levels of neurotransmitters by inhibiting the enzyme MAO, which would ordinarily destroy a small percentage of them with each firing (when they are outside their protective storage vesicles within the axon). The earliest tricyclic antidepressants, such as Tofranil and Elavil, inhibit the reuptake of both NE and 5-HT, keeping more of those neurotransmitters in synapses for longer periods of time. Other tricyclics specifically block the reuptake of either NE or 5-HT.

The tricyclics proved to be problematical because in addition to inhibiting uptake of NE or 5-HT, they also blocked three other kinds of neurotransmitter receptors, resulting in several predictable unpleasant side effects. Pharmacologists began a search for a new class of drugs that would provide only the therapeutic effects of reuptake inhibition. Thus, the selective serotonin reuptake inhibitors (SSRIs) such as Prozac, Zoloft, and Paxil arrived on the scene. Because of their reduced side effects, safety, and wide range of therapeutic applications, the SSRIs have largely replaced the MAOIs and tricyclics in this country.

Some of the very newest antidepressants include the reversible inhibitors of Type A MAO (RIMAs), which eliminate the dietary restrictions and potentially lethal effects of the original MAOIs; norepinephrine specific reuptake inhibitors (NSRIs); dual NE and 5-HT reuptake inhibitors (SNRIs); and alpha 2 (autoreceptor site) antagonists (such as mirtazapine), which effectively release the brakes and increase the activity of both NE and 5-HT.[40]

If depressed, it is wise to seek out a psychiatrist for the right prescription, since it sometimes takes considerable sophistication, as well as trial and error, to find the particular antidepressant that may work for a particular individual who often has a mixture of both depressive and anxious symptoms. Family physicians, who are typically internal medicine generalists, are not specialists in treating depression and anxiety.

Pharmacologists in the laboratories of the major pharmaceutical houses are rushing to develop new antidepressants that target neurotransmitters other than those in the monoamine family: 5-HT and NE. They're searching for a drug that will help a larger percentage of depressed people, one that has fewer side effects than those of the widely prescribed SSRIs. Although SSRI side effects typically lessen after about ten days, they can still be objectionable. While the SSRIs reregulate the 5-HT receptors that affect mood, they also affect 5-HT receptors that regulate movement, obsessions and compulsions, anxiety, appetite, sleep, sexual function, nausea and vomiting, and gastrointestinal cramps and diarrhea.

Most approved antidepressants target 5-HT and NE, and most function by inhibiting the reuptake mechanism. When we begin taking SSRIs, for example, synapses are immediately awash with higher levels of serotonin. It requires about ten days for this flood of neurotransmitters to effectively get these dysregulated neurons back up to speed: synthesizing and releasing a normal amount of serotonin. What's more, the antidepressant effect (for the 60–70 percent of patients who respond to such treatment) ranges from three to eight weeks. This suggests that the roots of depression are not simply in 5-HT or NE deficiency or in the dysregulation of their receptors. That story will not be pursued here, since our purpose is only to inquire as to whether or not exercise might have antidepressant biochemical effects or possibly even mimic those of the antidepressants: boosting brain NE and 5-HT activity.

THE BIOCHEMICAL EFFECTS OF EXERCISE

Physical activity affects an array of neurotransmitters that play roles in depression. Let's begin with a look at exercise and its impact on serotonin. Serotonin is manufactured (synthesized) in our brain's 5-HT neurons from a dietary amino acid called tryptophan. Just how much tryptophan passes through the blood-brain barrier into the brain is determined by several factors.

Diet is one factor. Carbohydrate ingestion increases, and protein ingestion decreases, the supply of tryptophan in our brains to be converted to 5-HT. The levels of 5-HT, in turn, regulate our specific appetites. For example, when our daily protein intake exceeds 10 percent of our total food intake, the carbohydrate craving that follows may trigger binging.[41]

Exercise also increases our brain's supply of tryptophan. Exercise-induced free fatty acid release has the indirect effect of significantly increasing the circulating levels of tryptophan in our bloodstream, and since tryptophan competes with several other large neutral amino acids for limited space on a common transporter (which carries them through the blood-brain barrier), the end result of exercise is that more tryptophan gets delivered to the brain.

A number of animal and human studies suggest that the increased availability of tryptophan as a consequence of exercise does result in increased brain serotonin synthesis and release. Whether the release itself is the consequence of exercise, or merely associated with it, is currently under investigation. If it turns out that exercise causes the release of serotonin in human brains, then it remains to be demonstrated that exercise's contribution is sufficiently significant to have an impact as large as that of antidepressant medications.[42]

University of Georgia exercise psychologist Rod Dishman in reviews of research on exercise and its effect on brain norepinephrine suggests that it is possible that regular exercise affects both of the human brain's NE and 5-HT systems in ways qualitatively similar to the effects of pharmacological interventions. A number of animal studies suggest that exercise many have such mediating effects. However, Dishman reports that such changes have yet to be demonstrated with humans.[43]

It's possible that exercise may exert antidepressant effects in a number of ways that differ from effects of current antidepressant medications.

For example, another brain neurotransmitter that is activated by physical activity is dopamine (DA), and it may also play a role in unipolar depression. When brain NE is depleted, DA activity appears to also be suppressed in the brain areas associated with pleasure, perhaps contributing to the anhedonia (lack of ability to experience pleasure) often associated with depression. So there is a possibility that the antidepressive effect of physical activity might be related to its capacity to elevate dopaminergic activity in the brain.

Norepinephrine's role in stress reactivity may also play a part in the antidepressive effect of exercise. One theory suggests that long-term regular, vigorous exercise thwarts depression by normalizing our body's ability to respond to chronic stress (makes it less reactive). Chronic stress, over which we have no control, can result in learned helplessness and subsequent depression. It also results in the depletion of NE and the stress hormone cortisol. Low levels of these two neurochemicals are often seen in depressed individuals.

If we look to our ancient ancestors, it's clear that those who, when faced with a novel and challenging situation, responded with a strong fight-or-flight response. Studies have shown that both high- and low-fit rats, as well as both high- and low-fit humans, do just that, responding with high NE activation. However, if exposed to the same stressful situations chronically, it is best to minimize the stress response and conserve our supply of NE for trouble down the road. Research by Rod Dishman and Mark Sothmann suggests that aerobically fit rats as well as middle-aged men have such minimal stress responses, while their sedentary counterparts do not.[44]

The longitudinal epidemiological studies reviewed earlier in this chapter also make a strong case that regular exercise and high fitness have a protective effect, reducing the likelihood of suffering a depression. The changes in our stress-response mechanisms, which result from regular exercise, might well have a role in such a protective effect.

Another theory concerning the biological basis of depression suggests that chronic stress also represses brain-derived neurotropic factor (BDNF), which normally sustains the health and growth of neurons. When BDNF is no longer produced in sufficient quantities in a subcortical brain structure called the hippocampus, its neurons atrophy and sometimes die. Neuro-imaging studies also suggest that hippocampal neurons are both decreased in size and less functional in depressed individuals. One theory suggests that perhaps a flaw in the NE or 5-HT receptor signal mechanisms is a part of the problem and that treatment with antidepressants corrects that faulty signal, causing the genes for BDNF to be reactivated so that hippocampal neurons are once again nourished.[45]

If, in fact, depression turns out to be associated with hippocampal dysfunction, the antidepressive effects of physical activity might be relevant because of its restorative effect on hippocampal health. Physical activity delivers a rich supply of oxygen and glucose to the hippocampus. It stimulates the growth of new cells and measurably prolongs the life of existing cells. Mice that are given free access to activity wheels and run at their own pace as long and often as they wish develop twice as many new hippocampal neurons as those that live in standard cages. A number of studies have confirmed that both mental stimulation and physical exercise promote the growth of new neurons in the hippocampus as well as the cortex. It remains to be seen whether such exercise-mediated changes in the hippocampus are associated with the reduction of depression.[46]

The hippocampus plays a primary role in memory. Vast neural atrophy in the hippocampus is central in Alzheimer's Disease. Aerobic exercise (especially when combined with a cognitive component as in square dancing) is only one of several interventions we can work into our daily lives in order to reduce the odds of our developing that crippling disease.

In the previous chapter, we discussed how exercise-generated beta-endorphin has been shown to be a primary biochemical agent in the anxiety reduction that predictably follows a workout. There is also a possibility that beta-endorphin may contribute to reducing depression. That possibility relates to the current search for a new class of antidepressants that are more effective and have fewer side effects than those that target the monoamines, NE and 5-HT.

One family of neurotransmitters that is currently receiving enormous attention is the neurokinen group. It contains a neurotransmitter called substance P (so named because it was first prepared in powder form in 1930). Historically, substance P was thought to be central in the pain response, but recent research has raised some questions about that assumption.[47] Nevertheless, substance P activity is involved in mood.

Substance P receptors are abundant in areas of the brain that are critical in the regulation of affective behavior and neurochemical responses to stress. Repeated administration of antidepressant drugs has the effect of reducing substance P synthesis in discrete brain regions, suggesting that reduced substance P activity may have a role in how and why antidepressant drugs work. It follows that perhaps blocking substance P receptors might have a similar antidepressant effect. The race to find such a blocker is now taking place in the laboratories of the pharmaceutical giants. The financial rewards for the winners of that race will be enormous.

For example, Merck & Company is developing MK-869, an oral medication that blocks more than an estimated 90 percent of central nervous system substance P receptors. In a human trial it was compared to the widely prescribed SSRI, Paxil, and to a placebo. MK-869 proved to be as effective as Paxil, and both drugs were found to be superior to placebo pills. In no case did MK-869 have greater adverse side effects than Paxil, but it had significantly fewer sexual dysfunction and nausea side effects.[48] Research such as this may lead to a more effective new family of antidepressants.

So what does substance P have to do with exercise? Perhaps nothing, but an interesting possibility comes to mind. If the reduction of substance P activity, by whatever means, decreases the symptoms of depression, then beta-endorphin could have a role in this drama. Beta-endorphin has been shown to block the release of substance P in spinal cord sensory nerve terminals that signal pain. In the previous chapter it was also pointed out that significantly higher concentrations of beta-endorphin are present in the cerebral spinal fluid of active rats than in those that are sedentary. If, down the line, it can be demonstrated that beta-endorphin has a similar effect on substance P neurons in the brain sites targeted by MK-869, then the antidepressant effect of exercise might in part be explained by the increased beta-endorphin activity that has been generated by physical activity. A sizable number of neurotransmitters play an interactive role in the generation and reduction of anxiety and depression, and betaendorphin may have a larger role in depression than has yet been demonstrated.

SUMMING UP

It should be noted that the American Psychiatric Association does not medically recognize exercise as treatment for depression. However, it's well to keep things in perspective. The gold standard for the psychiatric treatment of depression is the SSRIs, but unfortunately they fail to fill the pot of gold at the end of the pharmacological rainbow. They reduce symptoms in only 60 to 70 percent of patients; the placebo effect is a substantial part of their effectiveness; their beneficial effects are not permanent; and they have unpleasant side effects.

Research findings on the antidepressant effects of exercise are limited in number and vary in quality but are consistently positive. A quarter century of such research strongly suggests that regular exercise may be more than simply "associated" with the reduction of depressive symptoms. A causal relationship has been consistently demonstrated, leading to the conclusion that exercise therapy is a viable treatment for mild to moderate depression.

Therapists who "walk and talk" with patients report that such sessions are highly productive. However, few therapists are willing to get up out of their own chairs. Even those therapists who are physically active themselves are mostly unwilling to venture out of their offices with patients in an increasingly litigious society.

Psychological explanations for the antidepressive effects of regular exercise include distraction or time-out from our worries, increased self-efficacy, and the development of skills mastery.

Research also suggests that a number of exercise-mediated biochemical effects may play a role in how exercise functions to reduce the depressive symptoms. Animal research suggests that such effects may prove similar to those of antidepressant drugs, but this has yet to be demonstrated with humans.

The studies reviewed reveal that exercise therapy has a number of strengths that make it an attractive treatment alternative or adjunctive treatment for those of us who suffer from depression.

A primary strength is the *magnitude* of exercise therapy's effect. Not only does it work, but a number of studies have consistently shown that it reduces depressive symptoms as effectively as do individual and group psychotherapy. One investigation reviewed in this chapter, the first that compared the antidepressive effects of exercise with those of a proven SSRI, found the treatment effects to be equivalent.

Research has also revealed that the effects of exercise therapy appear to be unusually *durable*, typically more long-lasting than the effects of psychotherapy and drug treatment. The durability of the effects of exercise therapy does not always appear to be contingent on a continuation of regular exercise after treatment terminates. This probably reflects the fact that, at the onset of treatment, there are some individuals whose depression is reactive to an identifiable stressful circumstance and others whose depression is more of a constant companion, perhaps a biological dysregulation like a mild dysthymia. The individuals whose depressions are reactive or situational may no longer need therapy after termination, while mildly dysthymic individuals may need some form of long-term treatment. For some of them, continued regular exercise may be enough.

A third major strength of exercise therapy is that it is perhaps the only treatment that consistently offers *immediate mood-elevating and anxiolytic effects following each workout.* After a grueling psychotherapy session, patients often leave their therapist's office feeling worse than when they entered. Sometimes, for weeks on end, they leave wondering if they are making any progress. This can be discouraging and can sometimes result in premature termination of treatment. Exercise almost always offers immediate psychological rewards for our efforts.

Studies on mildly to moderately depressed outpatients suggest that both psychotherapy and exercise therapy *reduce depressive symptoms quickly.* Most patients enjoy significant symptom reduction in three to five weeks.

The antidepressant effects of regular exercise have been demonstrated in the treatment of mildly to severely depressed adult outpatients, as well as hospitalized adult patients diagnosed with very severe episodic depression, so it has a *wide range of applicability.*

Longitudinal population studies consistently suggest that physically active people are less likely to become depressed in the future than are their sedentary counterparts. Thus, exercise may well have a unique *preventative* effect.

Certainly one of exercise therapy's major strengths is the *absence of negative side effects.* Unless abused, exercise offers a vast array of beneficial effects on our physical health. (We'll examine both risks and benefits in later chapters.)

Exercise also offers a *wide variety of choices.* Our exercise can be aerobic, anaerobic, or nonaerobic. We can exercise outdoors or indoors. Our exercise can be social, solitary, competitive, easy-going, or a mixture of these activities, depending on who we are and what we need. It doesn't have to be the same old boring routine every day through every season of the year.

In comparison to other forms of treatment, exercise is remarkably *cost-effective.* Although some forms of exercise involve purchasing special equipment or membership fees, it's still remarkably cost-effective in comparison to conventional treatments. An entire month's fitness club membership fee is typically less than a single visit to a mental health professional. All that most of us need in order to get started is a pair of high-quality shoes, which also cost less than a single visit to most professional healers.

Finally, exercise is *convenient*. Some of us do all our exercise at home, perhaps watching the evening news while on an exercise machine or lifting weights in the spare room. Others of us lace up our walking/running shoes, or grab our bikes, and head for the front door.

There is cause to be very optimistic about the healing qualities of exercise and what it can do for you. Small investment. Huge payoff.[49]

7.
SUBSTANCE USE
AND OTHER
MENTAL DISORDERS

Pioneering research that examined the effects of physical activity on the many aspects of mental functioning in normal populations soon determined that its greatest effects were on mood. Consequently, the vast majority of subsequent research has concerned the effects of exercise on depression and anxiety. Relatively few studies have examined its effects on other nonpsychotic disorders.

We will begin with a look at an exploratory study that was conducted explicitly to determine whether exercise had any promise in the treatment of a wider variety of mental disorders.

Norwegian psychiatrist Egil Martinsen and his colleagues studied ninety-two patients in a hospital that specialized in the treatment of voluntarily admitted patients suffering from severe neuroses or personality disorders.[1]

The usual treatment emphasis in the clinic was psychoanalytic psychotherapy, but the patients in the study were individuals who had either not responded well to such treatment or had rejected it. Other patients in the study included those suffering from somatoform disorders (disorders that appeared to have a physical basis but could not be confirmed as such by repeated tests and examinations). This latter group had long-standing somatic complaints and had never been motivated to seek psychiatric treatment, since they did not perceive their symptoms to have psychological components.

Seventy of the patients suffered from unipolar *depressive* disorders; forty-four had *anxiety* disorders (twenty-eight diagnosed with agoraphobia with panic attacks); forty had *somatoform* disorders; and eleven were diagnosed with *alcohol* abuse or dependency. Sixty of the patients were also diagnosed as having one or another type of personality disorder.

The patients received group therapy three times a week and were medicated only when essential. Their *primary treatment* was supervised aerobic exercise for at least one hour each day (at 50–70 percent of maximum aerobic capacity). They walked, jogged, swam, cycled, skied, or worked out in aerobic classes.

The patients received eight weeks of treatment, and at discharge those in all four diagnostic categories had increased their aerobic fitness and significantly reduced their disorder symptoms. However, the greatest symptom reduction was seen in the group with alcohol dependency, followed closely by those in the depressed group.

A follow-up, one year later, revealed that the alcohol dependency and depressed groups had more than simply maintained their treatment gains. Both groups were even less symptomatic than prior to treatment (less depressed and drinking less). Within the anxiety and somatoform groups, only those diagnosed with generalized anxiety disorder, agoraphobia without panic attacks, and pain disorder maintained their treatment gains.

Sixty-six percent of the members of all four groups were still exercising at follow-up, so the persistent long-term treatment effects seen in the alcohol and depression groups were not because they continued to exercise more than those in the anxiety and somatoform groups.

This study was purely exploratory, its purpose being an attempt to determine whether certain diagnostic groups might be more or less likely to respond to exercise treatment. The short- and long-term positive effect of exercise on depressed patients was no surprise. However, the magnitude of the short- and long-term effects of exercise on members of the alcohol dependency group was so impressive that it clearly suggests that further research on this group is warranted.

SUBSTANCE-USE DISORDERS

Substance abuse and dependency disorders are the most prevalent mental disorders in America. The National Comorbidity Survey, cited in the previous two chapters, revealed that 12.5 percent of men and 6.4 percent of women had abused alcohol, and that 20.1 percent of men and 8.2 percent of women had been dependent on alcohol during their lifetime. The figures for men are worrisome, suggesting that one out of every three of this representative sample of American men had either abused or become dependent on alcohol during his lifetime. These numbers make one take a second look at the endless "fun time" beer commercials that dominate televised sporting events and are clearly aimed at young male viewers. Some of you may recall an earlier time when cigarettes were hawked on television and the percentage of us who smoked was double current rates.

Like other surveys, the NCS did not inquire about nicotine dependency disorder. The percentage of Americans who smoke cigarettes has hovered at about 25 percent for the past several years. In addition to the health problems and misery produced by those with nicotine and alcohol dependence, the two substances kill a half million American users a year. The need for interventions to help users end their dependencies is huge.

In case you are wondering just what exactly constitutes abuse and dependency, the DSM-IV criteria for both are listed below. You'll notice that the defining features of dependency, which separates it from abuse, are tolerance and withdrawal.

SUBSTANCE DEPENDENCE

Substance dependence is a maladaptive pattern of substance use, leading to clinically significant impairment or distress, as manifested by three (or more) of the following, occurring at any time in the same twelve-month period.

1. *tolerance*, as defined by either of the following:
   a. a need for markedly increased amounts of the substance to achieve intoxication or desired effect
   b. markedly diminished effect with continued use of the same amount of the substance
2. *withdrawal*, as manifested by either of the following:
   a. the characteristic withdrawal syndrome (described in sections concerned with each specific form of dependency)
   b. the same (or a closely related) substance is taken to relieve or avoid withdrawal symptoms
3. the substance is often taken in larger amounts or over a longer period than was intended

4. there is a persistent desire or unsuccessful efforts to cut down or control substance use
5. a great deal of time is spent in activities necessary to obtain the substance, to use the substance, or to recover from its effects
6. important social, occupational, or recreational activities are given up or reduced because of substance use
7. the substance use is continued despite knowledge of having a persistent or recurrent physical or psychological problem that is likely to be exacerbated by the substance.[2]

SUBSTANCE ABUSE

A. Substance abuse is a maladaptive pattern of substance use leading to clinically significant impairment or distress, as manifested by one (or more) of the following, occurring within a twelve-month period:

1. recurrent substance use resulting in a failure to fulfill major role obligations at work, school, or home (e.g., repeated absences or poor work performance related to substance use, substance-related absences, suspensions, or expulsions from school; neglect of children or household)
2. recurrent substance use in situations in which it is physically hazardous (e.g., driving an automobile or operating a machine when impaired by substance use)
3. recurrent substance-related legal problems (e.g., arrests for substance-related disorderly conduct)
4. continued substance use despite having persistent or recurrent social or interpersonal problems caused or exacerbated by the effects of the substance (e.g., arguments with spouse about consequences of intoxication, physical fights)

B. To be classified as substance abuse, the symptoms must never have met the criteria for substance dependence for this class of substance.[3]

With alcohol and nicotine dependencies being so widespread and devastating, and with early studies such as Martinsen's suggesting that exercise might hold considerable promise as a treatment for alcohol dependency, it's quite remarkable that so little research has been done. Let's look first at some studies concerning exercise and alcohol abstinence.

Three early studies examined the effects of exercise on middle-aged, hospitalized male alcoholics. These studies either lacked rigor or showed only minimal improvements in patient functioning. For example, a group of men who had been drinking an average of eighteen years jogged for an hour each day. After twenty days, they showed reduced sleep disturbances, while sedentary controls did not.[4]

A Canadian research group enlisted fifty-eight male and female alcoholic patients who lived in a group of five Quebec treatment centers to take part in an exercise program.[5] In addition to daily group therapy, the patients participated in aerobic training for one hour, five days a week for six weeks.

During the treatment period, these men and women were more responsive in group therapy and were better able to cope with stress. At the end of treatment, they had increased aerobic fitness, reduced body weight, and many were reorganizing how they utilized their leisure time. At the three-month follow-up, their abstinence rate was 69 percent, in contrast to 38 percent for patients who did not participate in the exercise program.

While the results appear very positive, the fact that patients volunteered to be a part of the exercise group is somewhat problematical. Perhaps a greater percentage of them remained abstinent because they were more highly motivated to do whatever was necessary to stop drinking (even exercise), because they exercised, or a combination of the two.

In a more recent study, sixty male college students who were heavy social drinkers were randomly assigned to a running group, a meditation group, or a control group for eight weeks of treatment. Attrition, as you might suspect among a group of habitual alcohol users, was high. About half of the sixty men dropped out. Those in the running group significantly reduced their drinking (especially weekday drinking) by about fourteen fewer drinks a week. Those in the meditation group who showed high compliance made similar gains.[6]

It is encouraging that a 1995 review of inpatient substance abuse treatment programs revealed that, following exercise programs, patients were less anxious and less depressed and had higher rates of abstinence.[7]

The research on exercise and smoking cessation is even more limited than that on exercise and alcohol abstinence. Three studies have found that exercise therapy was ineffective, or possibly even counterproductive, to smoking cessation in that it led to increased anxiety and sleep problems. However, a more recent study found that a combination of aerobic exercise and behavior counseling was more effective than behavior counseling plus nicotine gum and more effective than behavior counseling alone at the end of treatment. Unfortunately, the higher abstinence rates did not hold up at six- and twelve-month follow-ups.[8]

On a more positive note, a series of pilot investigations revealed that recruited female smokers who took part in a twelve-week exercise program were more likely to quit smoking and remain abstinent for a year than were controls.[9] These findings are open to question in that the participants who volunteered to exercise might have been more motivated to stop smoking than those who did not, so we don't know to what extent the exercise itself played a role in their greater abstinence.

While studies that have focused on alcohol abstinence and smoking cessation can be criticized by virtue of their including only volunteer participants, two of the studies that we have just discussed have demonstrated that exercise has been shown to be an *effective intervention for those who do volunteer.* If further research supports such findings—that volunteers for unconventional treatment such as exercise are helped by such treatment—what's to criticize? Let's get volunteers moving.

Unfortunately, the studies on alcohol abstinence and smoking cessation as a group don't amount to a substantial research effort when we consider the magnitude of the problems and the need for effective solutions.

Data and interviews from the three runner-motivation surveys that I carried out revealed that there are a considerable number of ex-smokers and ex-drinkers within the community of committed runners. My quarter century of experiences as a researcher—and as a member of running clubs, a competitor who interacted with countless runners at races, and a mountain trail runner who frequently met new running companions at trail heads—has reaffirmed my personal conviction that the beginning of exercise and the ending of a dependency are commonly interrelated.

The most common anecdotal stories that have been related to me by runners over the years have a predictable event sequence. The ex-smokers almost never said, "One day I decided to quit smoking and take up exercise, and I've haven't had a cigarette ever since!" What people more commonly have related is, "I started running and then I stopped smoking, or drinking, or my eating habits gradually changed."

Deciding one day to stop smoking, drinking, or overeating *and* take up exercise can be a recipe for failure. It's simply too much for most of us. But on the other hand, simply beginning to engage regularly in aerobic exercise (such as a walk/jog program) has been effective for many smokers. They commonly reported that as their fitness gradually improved, they reached a point where they were forced to make a choice: give up smoking or give up becoming more fit. Even before reaching that point, the phlegm they predictably coughed up during the early stages of each workout made them more conscious of what yesterday's cigarettes did to their lungs.

Runners who are ex-alcoholics tell similar stories that have a similar sort of sequence. They took up running and eventually were faced with a choice. They found that getting up for a morning run when dehydrated and hung over became less and less acceptable. One or the other had to go. Reflecting back over the years, it occurs to me that of the dozens of such runners whom I have encountered, not a single one has described himself as a "recovering alcoholic." To me, this suggests that they must have an internal conviction that they have taken control of their lives, conquered the problem, and are now ex-alcoholics. "I was an alcoholic. Now I am an athlete." They are now focused on staying fit and healthy, rather than on not drinking.

Finally there are the ex-overweight and ex-sedentary walk/jog/runners whom I have met. They report that as they became more fit, the nature of their diets gradually changed. Getting up to run in the morning after ingesting a sixteen-ounce steak the night before didn't feel all that great. First of all, these runners didn't sleep well. Second, they had had to ingest a huge quantity of liquids to help digest the meat, leaving them feeling like heavy water balloons when they laced up their sneakers in the morning.

Regardless of their initial weight, committed aerobic athletes almost uniformly report that as they became more fit, they began to eat less fat and meat and eat more fruit, veggies, and other carbohydrates. Constipation is no longer an issue in their lives. The evening meal is gone after morning coffee and before the morning workout. The common report is that it no longer "felt good" to eat the old way. It feels better to run feeling like a hungry antelope than a bear with a bowling ball in his belly.

The late cardiologist, philosopher, and running "guru" George Sheehan reported the same sort of anecdotal evidence, based on stories related to him by countless other runners. In his book *Running and Being: The Total Experience*, he wrote: "The athlete doesn't stop smoking and start training. He starts training and finds he has stopped smoking. The athlete doesn't go on a diet and start training. He starts training and finds he is eating the right things at the right times."[10]

This sort of knowledge constitutes common tribal wisdom among runners. So while anecdotal evidence abounds, there is a dearth of experimental evidence that exercise is a viable intervention to bring to bear on our enormous and costly national problem of substance abuse and dependencies. This is clearly an area ripe for a robust research effort.

Before leaving the topic of dependency, let's explore the neurochemical basics of substance dependency and how exercise might play a role in detoxificantion and abstinence.

Our brains produce their own cocaine and amphetamine (dopamine), nicotine (acetylcholine), morphine/heroin (beta-endorphin), and marijuana (anandamide). These are all endogenous chemicals that produce highs (brief dopamine minihighs in the case of nicotine).

Central in the reinforcement process, which is basic in virtually all substance dependencies, is the mesolimbic dopamine pathway: our brain's "pleasure center." And the messenger of pleasure is dopamine. Marvin Zuckerman, the foremost authority on sensation-seeking behavior, on the final page of one of his highly regarded books states, "Dopamine could be regarded as the substance of the 'life instinct.' Its absence results in a 'living death,' sans activity, sans desire, sans interest, sans joy, sans sensation seeking."[11]

Evidence is mounting that high sensation-seekers, such as sport parachutists and race car drivers, have a genetically determined deficiency in their dopamine pleasure systems (lazy dopamine D4 receptors), which requires that they engage in activities (which many of us consider to be very risky) in order to deliver a sufficient dopamine hit to enable them to feel excitement and intense pleasure.[12]

Those of us with normally functioning dopaminergic systems get substantial dopamine hits in our pleasure centers when we hear a live symphony, have great sex, see a scary movie, or ride a roller coaster.

Others of us have a problem with too much dopamine activity (and subsequent over arousal) in the synapses of our pleasure centers as a result of lazy dopamine reuptake mechanisms and are unwilling to take even moderate risks. Interestingly, such risk-avoidant people either don't smoke, can enjoy a cigarette now or then, or find it easy to stop smoking. They just don't need the additional dopamine activity.[13]

This fundamental personality trait (sensation seeking or openness to new experience) is 60–70 percent genetically predisposed, and dopamine dysregulation is a central determiner.[14]

Nothing compares to the dopamine hit delivered by amphetamine or cocaine. The reinforcing properties of alcohol and nicotine are less direct than those of amphetamine and cocaine, but the end result is the same: dopamine release in the mesolimbic pleasure centers. The dependency-producing opiates, such as morphine and heroin, act on another set of receptors, and as the dose increases, the effect moves from pain relief to euphoria. But the end game of opiates is also a boost in dopamine activity.

The exercise-induced elevations in dopamine and beta-endorphin activity would seem to make it a logical candidate to play at least an adjunctive role in both stimulant and opiate detox and abstinence programs. There is the possibility that they could at least partially substitute for the substances on which the patient is dependent, and the anxiolytic and antidepressant effects of exercise could also play a role in recovery.

Pavel Hoffmann, when talking about how alcohol interacts with the neurotransmitters involved in morphine abstinence, writes: "This raises the interesting and clinically important question of whether or not a program of physical activity, together with other interventions, might facilitate the conversion of the addict from dependence on alcohol or exogenous opiates to an 'endogenous endorphinist.'"[15] (Endogenous endorphinist: someone now dependent on an internally produced opioid such as beta-endorphin.)

Hoffmann also reviews studies concerning beta-endorphin and anorexia nervosa. Fasting elevates levels of opioids in rats, and excessive levels may be associated with several of the clinical symptoms of anorexia nervosa in humans. However, studies on that association are conflicting. Hoffmann points out that physical activity might counteract the effects of anorexia by restoring central opioid levels, and he further suggests that exercise might serve as a substitute for fasting as a mechanism for opioid activation.[16]

However, exercise can be a double-edged sword for anorectics. Perhaps the worst-case scenario is that an anorectic may simply add exercise to fasting to deliver an even greater opioid hit and further compromise her health. I ran into one such woman runner at a trailhead one day. She looked like a WWII concentration camp survivor—all bones. We were stretching just after each of us had finished a six-mile mountain loop. I was amazed when she told me she was about to go back out and repeat the loop.

BIPOLAR DISORDER

Once called manic-depressive disorder, bipolar disorder differs from unipolar disorders, such as major depression and dysthymia, in that is characterized by at least a single manic episode, which after a week or so usually ends in a psychotic state that requires hospitalization. It is an episodic condition that is characterized by a variety of manic and depressive patterns.

Bipolar disorder occurs in fewer than two percent of men and women. While it results in extreme dysfunctionality when untreated, a variety of drugs now allows nearly all of us with bipolar disorder to live quite normal lives (provided we stick with our medication). As was pointed out in an earlier chapter, the disorder is far more genetically predisposed than major (unipolar) depression, with identical twin concordance rates of more than 70 percent. It is treated with combinations of lithium, anticonvulsants, atypical antipsychotics, and benzodiazepines. These drugs reduce both the frequency and the intensity of episodes.

There has been no systematic research on exercise in the prevention of relapse in bipolar disorder, perhaps because the neurochemistry of the disorder would not seem to make exercise a logical candidate. However, both Egil Martinsen and I have had some limited personal anecdotal experiences with bipolar individuals who are committed athletes, and their stories seem worth sharing.

In Norway, Martinsen followed three male patients, all runners who wanted to taper off lithium to see if daily running could replace it. Within a year they had all become more fit, but all three had relapsed and were back on lithium.[17]

A dozen years ago, as a consequence of an article I wrote for *Runner's World*, I heard from several runners who had bipolar disorder. Three were women who had taken up running and subsequently had completely stopped lithium, telling me that they had never again suffered bipolar symptoms of any kind. Two were men who were able to substantially cut down their lithium dosage after beginning regular, vigorous aerobic or anaerobic exercise. There is, of course, no way to know whether the remission of symptoms among these few people was a consequence of beginning to exercise or merely incidental to it.

One man and one woman who contacted me were local, and I came to know them well. Their stories are definitely worth sharing.

The man had successfully cut down his lithium dosage after beginning to run daily. When he felt himself becoming hypomanic (highly energized but not to the degree experienced in a full manic episode), he directed that energy into increased workout intensities. He kept his car trunk full of canned vegetables and juices of various sizes, and on days when I encountered him at the parking lot preparing for a mountain run with a big can of tomato juice in each hand, I knew he was self-treating a hypomanic episode. In a decade of regular running and reduced lithium dosage, he has not experienced a full manic episode. When he feels himself falling into a depression, he enlists friends from his running club to get him up and running for a few mornings, thus avoiding serious depressive episodes.

The woman, after finally being correctly diagnosed as bipolar and medicated with lithium, had begun to function normally. However, on three occasions she had flushed her medication down the toilet and wound up hospitalized in psychotic episodes. One summer evening, she took a break from her regular bicycle ride at a high school track. Men and women of various ages were working out, and it was there that she first saw the man she would marry. He, it turned out, was an ex-drinker who had turned to running to control his dependency. In order to meet him, she figured that she would take up running.

By the time of their wedding, she was a highly fit distance runner and had totally freed herself from lithium. In the years since, she has not had another manic episode, but she has still found herself occasionally falling headlong into a depression. When that has occurred, her husband always got her out of bed, into her running outfit, and out the door. She spoke of running through the early morning darkness, and how "after the first mile I stopped crying, and by the end of the second mile I knew I was going to be all right, and by the third mile I knew that I would be going to work that day." Her normal state of being remained what people would call very "hyper," but it was an attractive feature, and she turned her abundant energy into very creative work.

When she visited my classes at the university to talk to students about her experiences with bipolar disorder and running, she related that as she looked back over the years when she was medicated, she remembered periods when she had been able to dramatically reduce her lithium intake. One was a period of six months when she rode her bicycle twenty-five-miles to and from work five days a week. Some sedentary readers might consider this long commute as hypomanic, but bicycle commutes of this distance are becoming increasingly common in the urban areas surrounding San Francisco Bay.

With bipolar disorder so firmly rooted in genetically predisposed biological dysregulation, it's unlikely that regular exercise will negate the need for medication for the vast majority of those afflicted. However, in addition to adjunctively helping to deal with bipolar depressive episodes, it has many other health benefits for those with bipolar disorder, and there have been no reports that exercise may precipitate a manic episode.

OTHER MENTAL DISORDERS

Exercise appears to have considerable positive effect when included as a component in the treatment of psychogenic *pain disorder*.[18]

The core features of this disorder are (1) severe pain, which causes significant distress and impairment and is the patient's primary focus, and (2) psychological factors have an important role in the onset, severity, exacerbation, or maintenance of the pain, but it is not intentionally produced or feigned.

Pain symptoms are sometimes perpetuated by social rewards (attention and sympathy), economic rewards, and relief from responsibility or stress when they persist beyond the normal time required for healing.[19]

Three studies have included aerobic or strength training as components in effective multicomponent behavioral treatments for pain disorder. A fourth study found exercise to be the most effective treatment component in the rapid reduction of reported pain. And a fifth study found that exercise, by itself, was ineffective in reducing pain but that it was an essential component in effective behavioral treatment program.[20]

The efficacy of exercise in the treatment of pain disorder may rest in social reinforcement and in the obvious incompatibility of regular physical activity with pain and illness.[21]

Evidence that exercise is an efficacious treatment for *schizophrenia* and other thought disorders continues to be plagued by a lack of high-quality controlled experiments. The more recent studies involving adjunctive exercise programs over the last decade suggest that exercise has some modest positive effects. However, these are pre-experimental investigations and case studies from which no firm conclusions can be drawn.[22]

SUMMING UP

While there is an absence of solid experimental evidence, there are compelling reasons that suggest that physical activity may prove to be a valuable intervention to treat substance abuse. This suggestion is based on the consistency of a number of pre-experimental studies, the anecdotal accounts of a great many athletes who are ex-smokers and ex-drinkers, and the shared neurochemical consequences of addictive drugs and physical activity.

Substance use is an enormous problem in America, and there is a need for a serious research effort to examine whether or not physical activity can be an efficacious adjunctive or primary treatment.

There is evidence that physical activity is an essential component in programs that have been shown to effectively treat pain disorder and that it may hold promise as a component in the treatment of generalized anxiety disorder as well as agoraphobia without panic attacks. Adjunctive exercise programs in the treatment of schizophrenia have resulted in reports of some positive outcomes, but there has been no high-quality controlled research that would yield any definitive conclusions.

PART 3:
EXERCISE AND PHYSICAL HEALTH

8.
THE WELLNESS
UMBRELLA

Because of running's vast array of health benefits, early California Indians, whose tribal wisdom was the product of experience rather than science, referred to running as "the Big Medicine."

The interaction between mental and physical health is a powerful one, and living a sedentary lifestyle that increases the probability of suffering years of disability and premature death does not bode well for our mental health during those later years. This chapter will outline how a failure to exercise regularly has a significant bearing on the odds of suffering encounters with insidious, lurking villains that we would all prefer to avoid: cardiovascular disease, cancer, strokes, and diabetes, to name a few. Those villains profoundly affect our mental health.

Before systematically dealing with the effects of physical activity on the many parameters of physical health, I want to share a recent personal experience that underscores the relationship between fitness and health.

A MATTER OF LIFE AND DEATH

It was only a few days after I had signed the contract to write this book that I returned from my two-and-a-half-mile morning run down the mountain to my mailbox, where I had picked up the morning paper and yesterday's mail. The run is not far but steep enough that my ears sometimes pop. After a shower and shave, I was suddenly doubled up with abdominal pain that was so excruciating that I could scarcely breathe without losing consciousness. It made no sense to me. In moments of clarity, I knew it couldn't be food poisoning, and the pain didn't seem to be focused in the appendix region. Any movement caused me to fade out of focus and functionality, but I managed to reach my two sons by phone. They dropped everything, raced up the mountain, and got me down to the valley and into an emergency room as quickly as possible. Calling that careening race down the mountain a bad trip doesn't even come close.

The emergency room doc was puzzled: dramatic acute pain onset with no nausea and no fever. He brought in a surgeon to consult. She, too, had no answer. They poked and prodded, continually asked me to rate my pain on a scale of one to ten, and requested increasingly complex diagnostic testing: blood work, ultrasounds, x-rays, and a CAT scan. Nothing. Afloat in a mind-deadening morphine lifeboat, I drifted through endless hours, while the docs waited for the emergence of any symptoms that would give them a clue as to the problem. They didn't want to undertake what might be unnecessary surgery, only to leave behind scar tissue that could spell trouble down the line. Eventually, when my kidney function was signing off, the surgeon asked my permission to have a look inside—no-brainer for me.

A week later, after getting back home, I quickly discovered that the prescription pain medications were worse than the pain, so I dumped them. At about that time, I began to be able to focus on what family and friends related to me about their experiences during my crisis. I had left a bunch of my insides, as well as fifteen pounds of body weight, at the hospital, and my memories of the whole affair were very sketchy.

My two sons and assorted family members had sweated out my operation in the surgery waiting room. After a couple of hours, my surgeon showed up. She had delayed a Friday afternoon departure for a weekend excursion to attend to me during the early evening. Exhausted after an unexpectedly long day, she told them, "Your dad is going to be fine. We found the problem, and we fixed it."

She went on to fill them in on the internal event that was my undoing, why I had experienced beyond-ten pain, and how she had fixed things. It turned out that about four feet of my small bowel had suddenly plunged through an aberrant small aperture in the fatty curtain that separates the bowels from the abdominal muscle wall. That adventurous section of bowel quickly ceased functioning, swelled up, lost blood supply, and died.

She explained to them that my operation was of such a kind that it would require about a week's stay in the hospital. After she had patiently answered all their questions, she turned to leave but paused, looked back, and added, "Oh, by the way, people who undergo this sort of procedure routinely spend a couple of days in ICU, but I'm putting your dad in a regular surgical ward room, so when you come to see him tomorrow that's where you'll find him. I'm going away for the weekend."

She was headed for the door when a family member expressed some concern as to why I wasn't headed for the added security of the ICU and why she wasn't hanging around. She stopped and thought for a moment then turned and answered, "Because your father is an unusually healthy and highly fit thirty-year-old man." I was seventy-five.

EXERCISE AND LONGEVITY

Epidemiologists are scientists who examine how we live, how long we live, and what kills us. There is now a large body of excellent research that examines the effects of regular exercise on longevity and chronic disease. As you consider these studies, it's well to keep in mind that the three leading causes of death in America, in order of incidence, are heart attacks, cancer, and strokes.

British scientist Jeremy Morris pioneered the study of the role of exercise on longevity when he examined the lives and deaths of civil servants forty years ago. His first investigation revealed that double-decker bus conductors, who spent eight hours scurrying up and down steep stairs, had significantly fewer heart attacks than did the drivers, who spent the day sitting behind the wheel.[1] His second study found that civil servants who walked to work, and those who engaged in vigorous leisure-time sports, had fewer heart attacks than those who rode to work and no longer played.[2] His two studies suggested that exercise might indeed have a role in longevity, specifically with regard to heart attack risk.

Here in America, my Fifty-Plus Advisory Board colleague Ralph Paffenbarger of Stanford University studied a group of San Francisco longshoremen over a period of twenty years.[3] The research took place at a time when dockworkers moved things around with muscles instead of machines. The workers were divided into those who expended more or less than eighty-five hundred kilocalories each week on the job. (I will, for simplicity, refer to kilocalories as calories from this point on.)

This eighty-five hundred-calorie dividing point figure represents a very large weekly energy expenditure. Most of us, even those of us in the light trades, burn about half that number of calories during our forty-hour work-weeks. Paffenbarger did not compare active and sedentary men. Instead, he compared very active men with extraordinarily active men.

Nonetheless, he found that the less active men had twice the rate of heart attacks and three times the rate of sudden-death heart attacks, as compared to the rates of the most active men. When it comes to heart attacks, very vigorous activity appears to have an even greater protective effect than does vigorous activity (if done regularly over time).

As in the case of Morris's British civil servants, exercise was found to have a *specific protective effect*, reducing heart attack, and especially sudden-death heart attack, risk (usually defined as an attack followed by death within six hours). This specificity was underscored when the four thousand longshoremen were divided into smoking and nonsmoking groups, and it was found that the smokers died more frequently from a range of heart and circulatory disorders and all forms of cancer. And when divided into hypertensive and nonhypertensive groups, those with elevated systolic blood pressure died more frequently from an assortment of heart ailments and strokes. It was clear that exercise had a specific protective consequence, one that shielded the most highly active longshoremen from the most common cause of death in America.

Paffenbarger was also a primary investigator in the landmark Harvard Alumni Study, which tracked seventeen thousand male graduates for more than thirty years in an attempt to determine the relationship between physical activity and mortality. There have been countless periodic reports of various aspects of the findings. In 1995 I-Min Lee and Paffenbarger published a report concerning exercise intensity and longevity.[4] The major conclusions of the many reports of this ongoing study are

1. Only vigorous aerobic exercise extends life.

2. The more active the men, the longer they were likely to live.

3. The increased longevity was largely the result of fewer deaths from cardiovascular disease.

4. To have a protective effect, exercise must be a lifelong component of our way of living.

5. The older we are, the more we have to gain: men in their seventies who burn two thousand calories a week in vigorous activity cut their heart attack risk by 50 percent, almost twice the risk reduction of younger active men.

6. Vigorous physical activity partially compensated for the high mortality risks of those who smoked or were significantly overweight. The mortality risk that resulted from being sedentary was the same as smoking a pack a day or weighing 20 percent more than a healthy weight.

7. Exercise begins to reduce mortality risk at five hundred calories (expended in vigorous exercise per week), and the protective effects tend to level off at about fifteen hundred calories a week, with men who burned at least that amount having a 25 percent lower death rate than those who burned less.

You're probably wondering exactly what constitutes the intensity and amount of vigorous activity that will increase your odds of greater longevity. Lee and Paffenbarger defined vigorous exercise as a physical activity that elevates metabolic rate six or more times above resting rate. In a *New York Times* interview, Lee suggested that playing one hour of singles tennis three times a week, swimming laps three hours a week, cycling for an hour four times a week, rollerblading for two and a half hours a week, jogging for three hours a week (at six to seven mph), or walking briskly for forty-five minutes five times a week (at four to five mph) are all vigorous activities that would burn about fifteen hundred calories.[5]

Since the majority of Americans get our exercise by walking, how do we figure out how much exercise results in a fifteen-hundred-calorie burn? A reasonably accurate and handy rule of thumb is that we burn an average of about *a hundred calories per mile* while walking briskly or jogging, so fifteen hundred calories translates into about fifteen miles a week.

The major factor that alters the one-hundred-calories-per-mile rule of thumb is body weight: the more we weigh, the more calories it requires for us to transport our bodies one mile. How fast we cover that mile has an insignificant effect when compared to the effects of our weight. Other factors such as air temperature, humidity, and terrain also play a role, but weight is the central determiner. The one-hundred-calories-per-mile rule of thumb is sobering when we consider that a single tablespoon of mayonnaise provides sufficient energy for us to walk an entire mile.

Two rigorous studies relating exercise and longevity, which took place at the Cooper Institute for Aerobics Research, dramatically elevated the scientific bar. The 1989 study led by Steven Blair was unique in that it was

1. the first to measure actual fitness (all participants took a maximal treadmill test as against filling out an activity questionnaire).

2. the first to include women.

3. limited to healthy individuals (who had passed an extensive health status examination and could reach 85 percent of their maximal heart rates on a treadmill stress test).

The study involved no absolute measures of fitness. Men and women were split into quintiles, from the 20 percent least fit through the 20 percent most fit as determined by the treadmill test. More than ten thousand adult men and three thousand adult women were selected for the study, of whom two hundred forty men and forty-three women died during a follow-up period, which averaged eight years.[6]

An analysis of those deaths revealed that the low-fit men had all-cause (age-adjusted) death rates 3.4 times as high as the high-fit men. All-cause death rates for the low-fit women were 4.7 times as high as for the high-fit women. These are sobering figures. We all pay an enormous price for living sedentary lives, but the cost to women may be higher.

By now it should be no surprise that cardiovascular disease was a major contributor to the follow-up deaths. Low-fit men had rates eight times as high as high-fit men, and low-fit women had rates nine times as high as high-fit women.

Cancer was also a major player, with low-fit men having four times the rate of cancer deaths as high-fit men. Low-fit women had sixteen times as high cancer death rates as high-fit women, a figure that has to be considered with caution, since the sample of women was only a third the size of that of the men. Nonetheless, a failure to exercise may present a greater cancer risk for women than for men. (We'll consider why that may be the case later in this chapter.)

The 1989 Blair study supported those of the Harvard Alumni Study in that

1. the older we are, the more we have to gain in reduced mortality risk if we are physically active.

2. vigorous physical activity reduces the risk of death from other common high-risk factors such as high cholesterol, high blood sugar, high blood pressure, smoking, being overweight, and a family history of death from coronary heart disease.

In 1996 Blair and his colleagues published a second major study that examined the influences of aerobic fitness and other precursors on cardio-vascular disease and all-cause mortality. It involved more than twenty-five thousand men and seven thousand women who completed preventive medical examinations and maximal exercise tests, but this second study, unlike the first, was *not limited to healthy individuals*. There were six hundred one male deaths and eighty-nine female deaths during the follow-up period.[7]

The significant mortality predictors for men were smoking, low fitness, an abnormal electrocardiogram, chronic illness, high cholesterol, and high blood pressure. The women had only two (equally strong) significant predictors of mortality: smoking and low fitness. Thus, men and women shared two equally strong predictors of premature death: smoking and physical inactivity. Choosing to be sedentary or to smoke is risky business. Choosing to be a sedentary smoker is extremely risky business.

The Harvard University Nurses' Health Study focused completely on the consequences of physical activity and health in women. The investigators followed 72,448 initially healthy female nurses from 1986 to 1994. They concluded that both brisk walking and more vigorous exercise, such as jogging, swimming, and aerobics, were all associated with substantial and similar reductions (30–40 percent) in the incidence of coronary heart disease. Sedentary women who became active in middle adulthood had lower risks than similar women who remained sedentary.[8]

These impressive consequences of regular exercise have consistently been the result of *vigorous aerobic activity*. It is only recently that anaerobic exercise has come under scrutiny.

The Harvard School of Public Health Study followed 44,452 male health professionals over the course of twelve years, during which time heart disease was ultimately diagnosed in seventeen hundred of them. The men who ran regularly (an hour or more a week at six mph) were 42 percent less likely to develop heart disease than the normally active men. Those who walked at a moderate pace of at least three miles per hour for at least a half hour each day were 18 percent less likely to develop heart disease, but slower walking had no protective benefit. These findings underline the protective effect of vigorous aerobic exercise.

When the investigators looked at the men who pumped iron thirty minutes or more each week, they found that these men had a 23 percent lower risk of developing heart disease than the normally active men, about half the risk reduction associated with the runners. The positive effects of weight lifting were attributed in part to reductions in body fat, but long-term weight lifting has also been shown to have moderate aerobic effects as reflected in reduced pulse rates and lower blood pressure.[9]

If we are seeking a form of exercise to protect us from the common killer diseases and extend our lives, vigorous aerobic exercise is clearly the ticket to buy.

An interesting recent study from Finland controlled for the effects of heredity and family experiences while exploring the effects of exercise on longevity. The degree of aerobic conditioning was assessed (by questionnaire) for sixteen thousand healthy same-sex twins (both identical and fraternal). Nineteen years later, there had been 286 discordant deaths (where one twin was still alive and the other was dead). The surviving twin served as a control (suggesting that the death of his or her twin was not largely the result of heredity or family experience). An examination of the exercise habits of the dead twins revealed that death rates were significantly lower for those who had exercised, and the greater the degree of physical conditioning for both sexes, the lower the death risk.[10]

There is a remarkable consistency in the findings of these investigations. There appears to be little doubt that regular vigorous exercise results in greater longevity and that the protective shield that it erects against our primary killer, heart attacks, is a primary effect.

PHYSICAL ACTIVITY AND STROKES

The effects of exercise on strokes, America's leading cause of disability and third-leading cause of death, has increasingly come under investigation. Some experts call strokes "brain attacks" because the underlying cause is essentially the same as in heart attacks—arterial blockages that cause blood circulation to fail (or bleeding to occur in the brain).

By 1996 more than a dozen studies had focused on the association between physical activity and stroke incidence. However, the mixed findings, and the strong focus on stroke incidence in males, only caused both the surgeon general and the National Institute of Health to conclude that the data were insufficient to draw meaningful conclusions at that time.[11] Since then, follow-ups of the Harvard Alumni and Nurses Studies have yielded some promising data for both sexes.

A 1998 report on the Harvard graduates found a strong association between number of calories burned in physical activity and stroke risk. Men who expended a thousand calories a week in vigorous exercise had a 24 percent reduction in stroke risk, and those who expended two thousand calories a week had a 46 percent risk reduction. Impressive numbers.

Weekly expenditures of one thousand and two thousand calories could be accomplished by five thirty-minute or five sixty-minute brisk walks, according to lead investigator I-Min Lee, who further suggested that moderately intense activities such as dancing, bicycling, stair-climbing, and gardening could also reduce stroke risk but that housekeeping activities and bowling would not.[12]

A recent analysis of data for the more than seventy thousand nurses in the second ongoing Harvard University study found that stroke incidence in women was reduced by physical activity and was related to the intensity of such activity. Brisk walking (a striding pace), for example, was associated with a lower stroke risk than was walking at an average or casual pace. The least active nurses had nearly double the stroke risk of the most active women.[13]

In March 1999, the *Journal of the American Medical Association* published the stroke prevention guidelines of the National Stroke Association's Prevention Advisory Board. One of the ten recommendations was a daily brisk walk of as little as thirty minutes.

EXERCISE AND DISABILITY

A longer life may not be all that we had hoped for if the quality of those added years is seriously impaired. So many of us endure years of disability engendered by the consequences of a stroke, a heart attack, cancer, emphysema, diabetes, obesity, or osteoporosis. These, and other unwelcome companions, can seriously impair the quality of those golden retirement years that so many of us anticipate. Or, if we intend to work for the rest of our lives, we certainly would want do so in good health.

In an earlier chapter, epidemiologist Lester Breslow found that Alameda County residents who engaged in several of what he called the lifestyle deadly sins suffered twice the rates of disability in their later years as those who avoided them. Physical inactivity was a central deadly sin.

James Fries, a Stanford University Professor of Medicine, introduced the concept "compression of morbidity." His interests were centered on how lifestyle, especially physical activity, might compress the length of disability and illness suffered prior to death. He wondered how long disability might be postponed by regular physical activity, and he has been an investigator in two large longitudinal studies that assessed the effects of healthy behaviors upon the development of disability.[14]

The first study followed a group of 1,741 University of Pennsylvania alumni, from their graduation in 1939–40 through 1994. The men and women were divided into high-, moderate-, and low-health-risk groups, prospectively defined on the basis of smoking, body mass index (an international measure that defines healthy weights), and lack of exercise risk factors. A 1998 analysis revealed that the low-risk group postponed disability by nearly nine years.

I was one of the research subjects in the second study that focused on members of our Fifty-Plus Runner's Association. Fries compared morbidity and mortality in our group of 370 active runners, who ranged from fifty to seventy-two years of age, with those of a matched control group of normally active Palo Alto never-runners.

In a paper published in 2001, Fries and his colleagues found that disability levels in the runners were initially lower than those of the never-runners, and those differences held up for the thirteen years of the investigation. The runners delayed disability by nearly nine years and were virtually disability-free through an average of seventy-two years, with female runners deriving greater disability benefits than men. However, in a presentation at the March 2002 Fifty-Plus Health Conference at Stanford, Fries told listeners that more recent data analyses revealed that our runners delayed disability an average of ten years. This is a truly remarkable figure.

The never-runners also had higher death rates in every disease category, especially cardiovascular disease and most cancers. Fries estimates that regular vigorous exercise adds about two to three years to our lives, so perhaps the more important benefit of exercise is that we are likely to remain highly functional and live fully during the last decade or more of our lives.

Finally, a recent review cited thirty investigations that reported a lack of exercise to be linked to a decline in both function and health in older adults.[15]

I've observed that the scientists who focus their efforts on examining the effects of exercise on disability and mortality are typically lean and highly fit. They take their research findings very seriously. Ralph Paffenbarger, for example, has run the Western States 100 Race many times. He has a drawer full of the gold belt buckles that are awarded to all who finish that grueling, hundred-mile mountain race in under twenty-four hours. It's appropriate that we end this section with the shared scientific tribal wisdom of those lean and fit epidemiologists who study longevity and the prevention of disease. "Exercise adds years to your life and life to your years."

THE MECHANISMS

Let's begin with a look at physiological changes that predictably follow regular aerobic training and see how these changes help explain why fit individuals enjoy a reduced risk of heart attacks.

It turns out that many of our body's systems are remarkably plastic: They gradually adjust to what we ask of them. If we ask a great deal, they increase in their capacity to deliver, and if we ask little, they shrink. Muscle mass is a good example of the "use it or lose it" dictum. Muscle cells swell or shrink, depending on what we ask of them.

The foundation of the cardiorespiratory system's reaction to aerobic training is that one critical structure in our heart becomes bigger. The left ventricle, the big pump that sends freshly oxygenated blood out to our muscle and other cells, is very responsive to the demands we place upon it. Regular aerobic training can result in an increase of as much as 40 percent in left ventricular volume, allowing it to deliver almost half again the volume of blood pumped with each stroke.[16] A power lifter who does strictly anaerobic training also shows this sort of left ventricular hypertrophy, but it reflects increased muscle wall thickness to a greater extent than it reflects increased volume. Most elite marathoners can't bench press a whole lot, and most body-builders can't run very far.

There are a host of consequences that follow an increase in our left ventricular capacity or stroke volume. If each beat of our heart pumps out far more blood, our heart will have to work less hard: fewer strokes per minute will do the job. It is the case that as our VO_{2max} increases, our resting pulse rate decreases, so resting pulse rate is one simple way for us to measure changes in our aerobic fitness.

I conducted a study of several hundred men and women in our Fifty-Plus runners group to see how their resting pulse rates were related to the number of miles they ran each week. Bear in mind that the average resting pulse rate for Americans is about seventy-four beats per minute and that the on-the-way-to-burnout, over-stressed individual might have a resting pulse rate of eighty-five or higher.

The Fifty-Plus runners who ran as little as one to ten miles a week had resting pulse rates that averaged sixty-four beats per minute. This suggests that even a little training can have a very significant effect—good news for sedentary Americans. The select few members who ran ninety to a hundred miles a week averaged thirty-nine beats per minute, and the group as a whole, who ran an average of twenty-four miles a week, had a mean pulse rate of fifty-four.

The relationship between aerobic fitness and resting pulse rate is close to being linear. During the period when I was running marathons, my pulse rate dropped into the forties but rose back up to around fifty when I cut back my weekly mileage.

When our hearts beat slowly, they also become more efficient. They have greater lag time between beats to more fully empty arterial blood, to more fully refill with venous blood, to better supply coronary arteries with fresh blood, and to rest. Heart rhythms stabilize and blood pressure reduces with aerobic training, so it has a clear place in the treatment of hypertension.

If our left ventricular volume increases by as much as 40 percent, additional blood must be manufactured to fill the system. With increased fitness, our blood volume may increase up to 15 percent above normal, resulting in 15 percent more red blood cells to carry oxygen to our working muscles. Those red blood cells don't become capable of carrying more oxygen; there are simply more of them. However, our lungs do become more proficient at transporting oxygen into blood cells (an increased ventilation-perfusion ratio).

On the other hand, when we are forced to spend several weeks in bed because of illness or injury, our blood volume will decrease, demonstrating the plasticity of the system and how it adjusts to demand.

CORONARY ARTERIES AND AEROBIC TRAINING

Our blood transport system reacts to aerobic training in other important ways. For decades, the effects of regular training on the coronary arteries of marathoners had been a matter of speculation. In 1958, "Mr. Boston Marathon," Clarence De Mar, died of cancer at age seventy. He had competed in thirty-four and won seven Boston Marathons. An autopsy revealed that his coronary arteries appeared to be two to three times normal size, suggesting that perhaps regular long-distance running caused coronary arteries to increase in diameter and explaining why marathoners have very low rates of heart attacks.

With such monster coronary arteries, even moderate blockage would not significantly reduce blood flow to the heart muscle during extreme stress. However, the case that regular running causes an increase in coronary artery diameter has never been made, since no one was able to come up with an acceptable experimental protocol.

A recent dramatic breakthrough involved several of my fellow Fifty-Plus Lifelong Fitness Advisory Board members. These ultramarathoners both conducted the study and participated as subjects. They were among eleven men who had trained an average of fifty miles a week for thirteen years. All had finished at least two marathons during the previous two years *and* had at some point finished the grueling Western States 100 Miler. Supermen all.

Exercise physiologist William Haskell, distance runner and deputy director of the Stanford Center for Research in Disease Prevention, directed the landmark study.[17] There was, of course, no way he could measure the diameter of coronary arteries while the marathoners were running, so he and his colleagues came up with a marvelously creative experimental scheme.

The eleven runners and eleven sedentary controls agreed to undergo an invasive procedure, usually done only on people suspected of having coronary disease. Coronary arteriography involves threading a tube into a leg artery and carefully guiding it upward and eventually into the coronary arteries. Injection of a dye then allows x-ray photography to measure artery diameter. These were highly motivated subjects!

When the coronary artery diameters of the runners and controls were compared, only a single runner was found to have larger coronary arteries than those of the controls. Since our hearts don't demand a large supply fresh blood when at rest, there was no reason to expect differences between the two groups.

But what happens when those hearts are stressed, as during continuous vigorous exercise? The real test would be to determine the elasticity of those arteries. Haskell did so by administering nitroglycerine to all twenty-two subjects. When patients with severely compromised coronary arteries experience angina chest pain, they take a nitroglycerine pill, which quickly causes maximum pharmacological expansion of their compromised coronary arteries, reducing their pain and anxiety.

But what about our runners and nonrunners? After being given nitroglycerine, the arteries of the eleven runners expanded more than twice as much as those of the eleven sedentary controls: 13.2 versus 6.0 square millimeters.

After all these years, this creative experiment provided the first authoritative answer to a question that has troubled exercise physiologists for a half century. It appears that the coronary arteries of marathoners respond to the regular high demands of training by becoming dramatically more flexible and capable of expanding to deliver far more blood to the overworked heart muscle during times of such stress. Mystery solved.

An accompanying editorial in the journal that published the study stated, "This study is unique in that it provides the first evidence in living humans that prolonged endurance training may substantially affect coronary artery anatomy and physiology."[18]

The chemical, which is involved in inducing arterial expansion, is nitric oxide (not the same as your dentist's nitrous oxide). Nitric oxide is a gas that has neurotransmitter functions. It is synthesized where needed on demand and is central in mediating the ability of nitroglycerin to treat cardiac angina.

Since one of nitric oxide's primary functions is to relax the walls of blood vessels, it also plays a central role in producing erections in men and in sexual lubrication and swelling in women. For those of you whose thoughts are already racing ahead, the nitric oxide dietary precursor is the amino acid L-arginine, and it can be found in foods such as tuna and almonds.

INCREASED COOLING CAPACITY

Another secondary cardiovascular adaptation to aerobic training is that additional capillaries develop that accommodate the increased blood volume and serve the increased demands of our heart and other muscles. Additional capillaries also develop near the surface of our skin, and they help stabilize our body temperature during workouts. Internal temperatures can run as high as 103 degrees Fahrenheit while we work out. Our increased blood volume, our increased number of skin capillaries, and our decreased surface fat (which typically results from fitness training) work together giving us an elevated capacity to cool our working bodies.

As we become aerobically fit, our capacity to sweat also increases (to about twice that of untrained persons), and we begin to sweat sooner (at about one degree lower body temperature than the untrained). A fit person can lose as much as a gallon of water during a vigorous two-hour workout.

There are times during competition when athletes make almost impossible demands on their highly conditioned bodies. I've lost up to fifteen pounds during marathons (which happened to fall on exceptionally hot days) despite consuming as much liquid as I could during those long hours on the road under a blistering sun. And during a thirty-mile time trial in the 2003 Tour de France, when the air temperature was nearly 100 degrees Fahrenheit (and 124 degrees down near the blacktop surface), Lance Armstrong finished in about an hour. In spite of drinking four liters of water en route, he lost nearly fourteen pounds during that one-hour, thirty-mile ride. His degree of dehydration was such that he could well have died. His ride was not just a Sunday outing.

CHANGES IN BLOOD CHEMISTRY

There is also the matter of cholesterol, an essential substance that we need for building and repairing cell membranes, manufacturing sex hormones, and helping with digestion. Since fat won't dissolve in water-based blood plasma, fat (lipids) gets packaged with proteins as lipoproteins for transport through the blood stream. Our total cholesterol (TC) is made up of very low-density lipoproteins (VLDL), low-density lipoproteins (LDL), and high-density lipoproteins (HDL).

High total cholesterol levels and high levels of low-density lipoproteins have long been associated with heart attacks and strokes. It's rare that someone with a total cholesterol count as low as 150 has a heart attack. When we overindulge in foods that contain high levels of saturated fats, trans-fatty acids, and cholesterol, our livers are unable to effectively deal with the overload, and the excessive fat, packaged as low-density lipoprotein, begins to circulate in our bloodstreams.

With each pulse beat, LDL particles bombard the walls of our blood vessels and sometimes stick, especially at flow junctions. High blood pressure is a particularly effective weapon system for imbedding LDL particles on vessel walls. If we continue to overload our bloodstream with particles of fat, plaque begins to slowly accumulate on our arterial walls. Vessels weakened by aging, high blood pressure, or smoking attract immune cells that trigger inflammation and get all tangled up with cholesterol, creating narrow, restricted blood flow points. It's an insidious process (that's why it's called a chronic disease). It is so very gradual that we seldom notice that we have a problem until our coronary arteries have lost about three-fourths of their flow capability. Eventually, critical arteries that nourish our hearts and brains totally occlude, and we suffer a heart attack or a stroke.

While TC count is one predictor of heart attack risk, experts such as William Castelli suggest that a better predictor of risk is the ratio of HDL to TC.[19] HDL is the "good cholesterol" that acts as a sort of scavenger or garbage truck, scouring our arterial walls and gathering up excessive cholesterol. With the help of VLDL carriers, it returns it to the liver for disposal. Even if we are unable to bring our total cholesterol level down as low as we would like, we can elevate our HDL levels and cut our risks of a heart attack or stroke. Next time you have a physical, be sure and ask for a printout of your lipid fractions. Divide your TC count by your HDL count. Average risk of a heart attack is about 5.0, twice-average risk is about 10.0, and half average risk is about 3.4.[20]

So how do we elevate our HDL levels? There are three major ways: (1) stop smoking, (2) lose body fat, and (3) exercise. A yearlong diet and a yearlong exercise program are equally effective in elevating HDL levels.[21] Several studies suggest that exercise-induced HDL elevations might in part be the result of weight loss and body-fat percentage adjustment.[22] But even if we engage in regular aerobic exercise without losing weight, the fat percentage decreases and muscle mass increases, resulting in LDL decreases and HDL elevations.[23]

Modest HDL increases (10–12 percent) have resulted from as few as thirteen to sixteen weeks of brisk walking or jogging,[24] but experts such as Terry Kavanagh, William Castelli, and Peter Wood suggest that substantial changes result from expending twelve hundred to fifteen hundred calories a week in such exercise for a year.[25]

We can reduce our total cholesterol levels through exercise, weight loss, and dietary change. Reducing or eliminating our saturated fat intake (red meat, butter, and very nasty tropical vegetable oils such as coconut and palm oil), and substituting polyunsaturated vegetable oils can make a difference. Canola (rape seed) oil is the best of the polyunsaturates. However, monosaturated oils such as olive and peanut oil are by far the best.

When liquid oils are heated and hydrogenated, they form semihard spreads, such as margarine, at room temperatures. However, this process has typically converted the oils into trans fats, which are at least as hazardous to our blood vessels as saturated animal fats. Some New Age margarines, which contain no trans fats, are now available, but using oils in liquid form whenever possible is a wise choice. Olive oil on popcorn just doesn't work, but it works for cooking as well as in salads, on steamed veggies, in pasta, and in many other dishes.

EXERCISE AND CANCER

There has been increasing focus on the impact of physical activity on cancer. In November 2000, the Centers for Disease Control, the American Cancer Society, the National Cancer Institute, and the American College of Sports Medicine sponsored a conference at the Cooper Institute in Dallas to review findings on the exercise-cancer relationship and determine future research directions.

The conference revealed that there is now considerable data that quite consistently finds that physically active men and women have about a 40 percent reduced risk of *colon cancer*. While overweight men are at increased risk for colon cancer, those who engage in high levels of physical activity largely cancel out that increased risk. The results of studies on *breast cancer* and *prostate cancer* were less consistent but generally positive. Lifelong physical activity (especially moderate to intense) appeared to be the best protection against breast cancer. The conference suggested that physical activity reduces risk of breast cancer by about 30 percent and prostate cancer by as much as 20 percent.[26]

A second review of the scientific literature at about the same time found that colon cancer was the most commonly investigated form of cancer and that physically active men and women experience about half of risks of their sedentary counterparts. While the results were less consistent than those found with regard to colon cancer, physical activity appeared to be again associated with about a 30 percent risk reduction for breast cancer.[27]

BREAST CANCER

A sixteen-year study of eighty-five thousand nurses found a statistically significant relationship between higher levels of physical activity and lower risk of breast cancer. Women who exercised seven or more hours a week reduced breast cancer risk by 20 percent. The investigators concluded that high levels of physical activity afforded modest protection against breast cancer.[28]

In Norway, more than twenty-five thousand women were followed for an average of fourteen years. Compared to more sedentary women, those who engaged in vigorous physical activity (enough to elevate heart rates and break a sweat) at least four hours a week had a 37 percent lower risk for developing breast cancer; the more exercise, the less risk. The effect was greatest in premenopausal women.[29]

In a study of a thousand premenopausal California women, researchers found that regular moderate exercise reduced breast cancer risk up to 60 percent. The greatest risk reduction occurred in women who exercised four hours a week, but even two or three hours of exercise per week was shown to be beneficial.[30]

A recent University of Alberta three-year investigation compared overall lifetime activity (the sum total of occupational, household, and recreational activities) of 1,233 women with breast cancer and 1,237 controls. The most active postmenopausal women reduced risk by 30 percent. Women who had been active all of their lives, such as those who worked on a job that required regular, moderately intense exercise, or those who farmed, reduced risk by 42 percent. These findings are good news for postmenopausal women and those who are normally active but don't engage in a formal exercise program. Even better news was the finding that, once inactive postmenopausal women start to become physically active, risk was reduced by 40 percent.[31]

These studies on physical activity and breast cancer are certainly promising. However, they are not definitive, since the physically active women studied in such research are all self-selected. More research is needed, but locating inactive women who are willing to become regularly active or banned from doing so for a period of ten to twenty years is probably an exercise in futility. It may be a long time before sufficient evidence is accumulated for truly definitive conclusions. However, waiting for that definitive conclusion before committing to an exercise program may be waiting too long.

Biologically it makes sense that physical activity would reduce the risk of breast cancer, since it is an estrogen-dependent disease.[32] Excess estrogen is stored in fat tissue, where it stimulates cell growth, both good and bad. It can fuel tumors.

Reduced exposure to estrogen is related to reduced breast cancer rates. For example, women who begin to menstruate late, and those who enter menopause early, have lower rates of breast cancer.

Excessive body fat also results in increased estrogen output and higher cancer risk, while exercise results in reduced estrogen output and reduced risk. When ovaries stop producing estrogen at menopause, heavy women become their own estrogen factories as the testosterone and androstenedione found in fat cells is converted into estrogen.[33]

Women who exercise regularly are typically leaner than those who do not, and this seems to be a factor in cancer statistics. A study of fifty-four hundred female college alumni (half of whom were former college athletes) found that the former athletes had 35 percent fewer instances of breast cancer and 61 percent fewer instances of reproductive cancer than the nonathletes. It was also found that the former athletes were leaner in every age group, from ages twenty to eighty. A fifteen-year follow up of 3,940 women found the former athletes to have a 17 percent reduced risk of breast cancer.[34]

Since estrogen fuels breast cell growth, and because fat cells continue to produce estrogen after menopause, women who are at high risk for breast cancer should make a serious effort to make regular exercise a part of their lives.

COLON CANCER

The logical mechanism to explain the reduced rates of colon cancer in physically active people is reduced stool transit time. Physically inactive people, especially those who consume prodigious quantities of meat, often suffer from constipation wherein the colon might be irritated and have prolonged contact with carcinogens that are contained in stubborn, hard stools.

There is considerable evidence that men and women who take up regular exercise soon change their diets to foods that are fibrous, easily digested, and quickly eliminated: here today, gone tomorrow. One survey of seven hundred runners revealed that after beginning to run, two-thirds of them reported that they began to eat more chicken and fish, more fruits and veggies, more whole grain and bran cereals, and less food that contained high saturated fat.[35] A similar recent survey of senior athletes found essentially the same thing.[36] Thus, one way you might possibly alter your eating habits and cut your risk of colon cancer is to make a habit of exercise. Dietary change will often follow.

OTHER FORMS OF CANCER

Steven Blair is currently investigating the association between exercise and lung cancer. His preliminary findings are that unfit men are twice as likely to die from lung cancer as those who are fit: moderately fit men had a 20 percent reduced risk, and highly fit men had a 60 percent reduced risk. He attributes the effect to exercise-induced heightened immune function.[37]

Prostate cancer is a leading cause of cancer deaths among American men, second only to lung cancer. There is evidence that exercise may reduce the risk of such cancer by 20 percent. And now there is some good news for men who have prostate cancer, men whose cancer may not have responded well to radiation or surgery, or those who have chosen "watchful waiting." At UCLA's Jonsson Cancer Center, William Aronson has found that a low-fat, high-fiber diet plus regular exercise can slow prostate cancer cell growth by up to 30 percent.[38]

There is also limited evidence that exercise might reduce the risk of endometrial and testicular cancer.

Kathryn Schmitz of the University of Minnesota—an expert on exercise and cancer—has listed some of the ways in which exercise might reduce the risk of developing cancers of all kinds.[39]

1. It helps maintain a healthy body weight.
2. It helps maintain healthy amounts of overall body fat.
3. It helps maintain low levels of fat in and around the abdomen.
4. It helps maintain the biological system that regulates blood sugar levels.
5. Its control of some tumor factors.
6. It helps suppress prostaglandins (hormone-like substances that are released in greater quantities by tumor cells).
7. It improves immune function, including increased levels of natural killer cells.
8. It reduces symptoms of mild to moderate anxiety and depression (which may improve immune function and overall physiologic functioning).
9. It increases levels of free radical scavengers to assist the body in preventing DNA damage.

EXERCISE AND DIABETES

Type 1 diabetes is often called juvenile diabetes, since it typically strikes during childhood. It is the consequence of a misguided immune system attack on our insulin-producing cells. Left with too few insulin-producing cells, individuals suffering from type 1 diabetes must inject insulin daily throughout life. Insulin is the hormone that transports glucose from the bloodstream into cells where it can be converted to energy.

Type 2 diabetes does have genetic predisposition, but it is largely the result of obesity and inactivity. The consequences of overeating and unrelenting demand are that the cells in our organs become resistant to the action of insulin, and the overworked insulin-producing cells on the pancreas begin to self-destruct.

Whether the result of insulin-insufficiency, resistant cells, or both, glucose that cannot find its way into cells of diabetics continues to circulate in the bloodstream, where it contributes to the thickening of arterial walls, the reduction of arterial diameters, and the gradual restriction of blood flow. There are very predictable consequences of untreated diabetes—heart attacks, strokes, kidney failure, blindness, inability to perform sexually, and eventually lower-limb gangrene that may require amputations.

However, the disease is highly treatable, and even preventable, if detected early. Experts agree that the fundamental causes of type 2 diabetes are (1) overeating and (2) physical inactivity, and the routine prescription for high-risk people has been diet and exercise.

One recent study of people at high risk for developing diabetes (high blood sugar levels, overweight, sedentary, and averaging fifty-one years of age) compared lifestyle interventions with conventional drug therapy (850 mg metformin twice daily). Goals of the lifestyle modification group were to lose at least 7 percent of their weight and to exercise for at least one hundred fifty minutes weekly. A follow up (average 2.8 years later) assessed how many in each group had developed diabetes. It was found that the lifestyle intervention reduced the incidence of diabetes 58 percent, and the drug therapy reduced incidence 31 percent, as compared to a third placebo group.[40]

A second study found that adults who had lived with diabetes for an average of eleven years reduced their risk of all-cause death by 39 percent by walking as little as two hours a week. Those who walked three to four hours a week reduced risk by 54 percent.[41] Small effort, huge payoff.

Studies such as these illustrate the importance of lifestyle change in both the prevention and treatment of type 2 diabetes. Exercise, which has long been known to normalize fat and carbohydrate metabolism (reduce insulin resistance), as well as contribute to weight loss, is an essential component in a treatment program.

EXERCISE AND OSTEOARTHRITIS

At last year's Fifty-Plus health conference, arthritis expert Kate Lorig, director of the Patient Education Research Center at the Stanford University

School of Medicine, presented a paper on her area of expertise: physical activity and arthritis. After she finished her formal presentation, the first question from the audience was, "What's the most dangerous exercise for people with arthritis?" Without missing a beat, she responded, "No exercise."

Osteoarthritis is a degeneration of the cartilage that cushions our joints, sometimes progressing to the point where bones are rubbing against one another. The pain that results, and the fear of doing more harm to ourselves, typically causes us to reduce our physical activity, leaving us deconditioned, weaker, less flexible, and experiencing more pain than is necessary. Proper exercise will increase flexibility and muscle strength, which, in turn, will lessen the load placed on the afflicted joint or joints and reduce the pain.

A review of the scientific literature indicated that osteoarthritis is caused by genetic predisposition, obesity, trauma, and anatomical abnormalities of weight-bearing joints. It is more related to age and heredity than to overdoing exercise.[42] One excellent study found that long-distance running by seniors was associated with increased bone density but not with clinical osteoarthritis.[43]

Some years ago my colleague, cardiac expert Peter Wood, related that he had run in excess of 110,000 miles. He continues to run on joints that work just fine, as do I and other Fifty-Plus members who have logged twenty-five thousand to seventy-five thousand miles. Besides having the good fortune of inheriting the right genes, most of us carry a minimum of body fat.

There is some very good news for less active ordinary folks. Men and women in the Framingham Osteoarthritis Study who lost ten pounds over the course of ten years reduced their risk of developing osteoarthritis of the knee by 50 percent. Extra pounds are tough on weight-bearing joints, and even modest weight loss can have a very significant preventive effect.

A growing body of research now confirms that aerobic and resistance exercise programs are both highly effective interventions: reducing pain, increasing strength, and increasing flexibility, which together add up to increased functionality and longer life. Because of such evidence, the high cost of drugs, and the problems of adverse drug effects, the American College of Rheumatology recommends that treatment of osteoarthritis should begin with nondrug interventions. Exercise is central, and working with qualified experts is essential.[44]

EXERCISE AND OSTEOPOROSIS

Let's begin with three true stories that illustrate some critical points concerning osteoporosis. The first is drawn from a recent *San Jose Mercury News* account of a remarkable local woman.[45]

At age ninety-five, Mildred Snitzer lived alone in a walk-up apartment. She had become increasingly active when she came west to retire in California. She began to teach line dancing to non-English-speaking Chinese immigrants shortly after her arrival. Before long, she began to teach ballroom dancing, and she led flexibility and strengthening classes for seniors at a community center in Mountain View. Then, after a quarter century of teaching seniors, many of them decades younger than herself, one day she slipped on a pebble, fell, and fractured her hip.

After surgery, she spent some time in a nursing home, and what she witnessed there dramatically increased her motivation to get back on her feet and regain her functionality. Three months after her fall, she was back at the community center, dancing to the big band beat—this at a time when about one-fourth of the elderly who fall die within a year—with falls being a leading cause of death among those over the age of seventy-five.

At age ninety-four, while not as physically active as Mildred, my mother was living alone in her home and still driving in a small midwestern community. However, she was increasingly unable to keep up her house, her diet was inadequate, and her steep basement stairs were highly hazardous. Had she fallen, she might not have been found for days on end. It was a painful experience when my brothers and I moved her a few blocks away into a nice assisted-living facility, where she already had many younger friends.

At age ninety-six, she fell and fractured her hip. Her postsurgery experience in a nursing home, like Mildred's, speeded her efforts at recovery. My mother's ancestors included Chief Joseph Brant, and she always attributed her many independent and courageous acts to her "Mohawk blood." Three months after her fall, she was moving well with a walker and back in her room at the living center.

However, during the course of the next six months, she had two more falls. She survived both without physical injury, but the terror of falling again resulted in her gradually giving up walking. She took to a wheelchair, where she very rapidly lost strength and functionality. She was unwilling to take part in the physical strengthening sessions offered at the living center, so when her arms could no longer propel her to the dining area, she was forced to return to the nursing home, where she would die from a massive stroke at age ninety-eight.

Continuing physical activity is critical for our functionality, especially as we grow older. My mother was always more active than most of her younger friends. In her late eighties, she drove about with her ukulele, entertaining younger folks in various senior facilities. Mildred took up a lifetime of dancing in her early seventies.

My colleague Paul Spangler died of a heart attack while on a run at age ninety-four. He was training for yet another marathon. Paul had taken up distance running when he retired from his medical practice at age sixty-five, and at the time of his death he held countless world age-group race records. While most Americans become increasingly inactive and disabled as they age, these stories suggest that there is an alternative way to grow older.

Let's turn now to how physical activity is associated with bone mass and vulnerability to osteoporosis. During adolescence most of us begin to accumulate bone mass at a high rate, and the more active we are, the greater our increase in bone density. Maximum mass is typically achieved by our midtwenties, after which bone resorption gradually exceeds rebuilding.

Following menopause, if estrogen is not replaced, women's bone loss accelerates markedly for six or more years, leaving their bones more susceptible to developing osteoporosis (weakened, porous bones). Women constitute 80 percent of Americans with osteoporosis, and as they age, they have two to three times the risk of hip fractures as a result of falls as do men. When the upper end of our femoral (thigh) bones breaks, we have sustained a hip fracture. Such fractures are easily repaired, but the fear of falling again and engendering a second break typically causes older women, like my mother, to become increasingly less active and less self-sufficient.

The density of our bones is dictated in part by the "use it or lose it" principle. Many studies have found that bone loss can not only be stopped but actually can be reversed through exercise. One such study of a group of more than forty senior male and female long-distance runners found that their femoral bones were 40 percent more dense than those of matched nonactive controls.[46]

However, we don't have to become distance runners to benefit from weight-bearing exercise to reduce bone loss and cut our risk of hip fractures. A recent study followed more than sixty-one thousand healthy nurses for a period of twelve years and analyzed the relationship between physical activity and the 415 hip fractures that occurred in the group over that time period. Even more time spent simply standing was associated with lower risks. Active women who exercised the equivalent of walking eight hours a week reduced risk by 55 percent, and those who engaged in no other exercise except walking four hours a week reduced risk by 41 percent.[47]

On the other hand, when it comes to our bone health, too much exercise can also be hazardous. Athletes who run in excess of forty to fifty miles a weeks risk decalcified bones, decreased bone mass, stress fractures, and scoliosis. And young women who semistarve themselves, whether anorectic or in pursuit of athletic glory, delay puberty. Dancers and gymnasts who retain little girl bodies and squeaky voices well into their teens are examples. Sexually mature women who overtrain often suffer irregular periods or stop having periods altogether.

When body fat falls below about 10 percent, amenorrhea (the absence of menstrual periods) will likely result. When there is not enough fat available to convert androgen into estrogen, less estrogen is produced. This has ramifications beyond reproduction. Estrogen helps recalcify bones, and too little estrogen can result in osteoporosis.[48]

Nations such as the United States and New Zealand whose citizens consume unusually large quantities of meat, have among the world's highest rates of osteoporosis and hip fractures. The more protein we eat, the more calcium our kidneys excrete. When we double our protein intake, we double our calcium loss.

The National Osteoporosis Foundation tells us that there are four steps to prevent osteoporosis and that no single step is sufficient, but all four may be. They are (1) a balanced diet rich in calcium and vitamin D, (2) no smoking or excessive alcohol use, (3) weight-bearing and resistance exercise, and (4) bone density testing and medication when appropriate. Those of us with osteoporosis should work with a specialist in designing a safe and effective treatment program. The American College of Sports Medicine has also published recommendations concerning exercise and osteoporosis.[49]

EXERCISE AND IMMUNE FUNCTION

David Nieman of Appalachian State University, an authority on exercise and immune system function, points out that high-quality epidemiological and laboratory studies have demonstrated that moderate exercise is associated with reduced disease incidence (such as heart disease, strokes, and cancer), as well as heightened or improved immune function. He further points out that studies have also found that the benefits of exercise can be reversed with immoderate (excessive) exercise.[50] When we consider the risks associated with exercise in a later chapter, you'll learn that "immoderate" exercise doesn't have to be very vigorous to be extremely hazardous for individuals whose coronary arteries are constricted by accumulated plaque, the result of genetic misfortune, or years of sedentary life fueled by unhealthy diets.

What Nieman is suggesting is that, as in the case of our bone health, moderate physical activity can elevate our capacity to resist illness, but excessive or "immoderate" exercise can depress our immune function.

Upper respiratory tract infections (URTIs) have been the focus of many investigations, because common colds usually come and go rather quickly and make a good real-life laboratory. Such investigations give us a clue as to what moderate and immoderate exercise might mean.

Running a twenty-six-mile marathon is clearly immoderate exercise, and the hundreds of miles of training prior to the race can also be immoderate. Studies in South Africa and California have shown that marathoners have far more URTIs during the two weeks following a race than do sedentary controls or recreational runners. And during the two months of training prior to the race, there was a clear positive relationship between miles of training per week and incidence of URTIs.[51]

However, moderate exercise is a whole different story. One study demonstrated that women (who averaged thirty-five years of age) who walked forty-five minutes five days a week, over the course of fifteen weeks, had fewer than half the rate of URTIs than similar sedentary women.[52]

A study of elderly women compared URTI rates for three groups. Fifty percent of the sedentary women had URTIs during the twelve-week study period, but only 20 percent of the women who walked forty minutes five times a week had URTIs during the same time frame. The third group was a remarkable one, composed of women who averaged seventy-three years of age who had been exercising moderately for about an hour a day for eleven years. Only 8 percent of them had URTIs during the twelve-week study. The author of the study related that these last women had the hearts and lungs of women in their forties, were remarkably free of depression and anxiety, weighed an average of twenty-three pounds less than the sedentary women, and consumed more healthy foods.[53]

There is a clear dose-relationship here. The more days per week the women engaged in moderate exercise, the fewer colds they suffered. On the other hand, when training miles per week become immoderate, marathoners suffered more colds. The marathon itself negatively impacts the immune systems of the participants, who suffered a high rate of postrace colds.

We all must, through trial and error, determine what constitutes moderate exercise that heightens our immune function and what is immoderate exercise that reduces our immune function. If our exercise program is making us "sick and tired," it's clearly time to cut back.

When we do suffer a cold, it's also a good idea to stop or minimize exercise during its acute phase. We don't want to unnecessarily prolong our illness. It's not a good idea to exercise at all if we are feverish, since there is always a slight chance that the invading pathogen might have found its way to our heart, where it could cause serious problems if great demands are placed on those infected muscles. When we have a cold, our resting pulse rate is typically elevated: a signal that our immune system is hard at work dealing with the invading virus and doesn't want deal with any further demands that might be imposed by vigorous exercise.

Exercise has very significant short- and long-term effects on our immune systems. Let's begin with a look at its short-term effects.

If we examine a sample of our blood immediately following a vigorous workout, it will reveal that our total leukocyte (white blood cell) count is 50–100 percent above normal. This increase is largely the result of the elevations of two lymphocytes (a subfamily of leukocytes). Natural killer (NK) cells elevate 150–300 percent, and T (cytotoxic suppresser) cells elevate 50–100 percent. The activity of both NK and T cells is enhanced during both moderate and intense activity. These white cells are frontline defenders against bacteria, as well as against viral and tumor cells. While we engage in exercise, and for a short time following, these lymphocytes do a general housecleaning. Together with an elevated core temperature, they make our bodies a hostile environment for unwelcome invaders.

About thirty minutes postexercise, our lymphocyte count drops below normal (baseline) for two or more hours. Duration depends on the length and intensity of our exercise. Very intense exercise leaves considerable damaged tissue debris that needs to be cleaned up by white blood cells. During such extended cleanups, our bodies are left relatively unprotected from invading pathogens, such as cold viruses. Moderate exercise reduces that vulnerable period.[54]

So much for the immediate effects of a bout of exercise on immune function. What effect do weeks or months of regular exercise have on our immune systems? When concentration levels of circulating *total* leukocytes or lymphocytes are compared in athletes and sedentary people, or between sedentary people before and after a training period, most studies fail to show significant differences between the groups.

However, a large number of studies deliver good news in that they have shown improvements in the *activity of white cells* in response to a program of regular physical activity. Both NK cytotoxic activity and T cell ability to proliferate increase following training. For example, increases of 57 percent have been demonstrated by women who walked five days a week for fifteen weeks, and natural killer cell cytotoxic activity was found to be 47 percent higher in a group of active Japanese men than in a group of similar sedentary men.[55]

Of the many immune system components, T cells are most affected by aging, with the elderly showing decreases of 45 to 65 percent in T cell ability to proliferate in response to invaders. However, highly conditioned elderly women have been shown to have 56 percent higher proliferation levels than sedentary women and nearly as high as college-age sedentary women.[56]

Thus, with regard to immune function, exercise can be for better or for worse: moderation for better, and immoderation for worse. We each must discover how much is good for bad for ourselves.

BACK TO THE SURGERY WARD

I'll close this chapter with a second story about my recent hospital stay. It delivers a message that has to do with fitness, an unexpected tribal encounter, intimacy, recovery, and that powerful and essential aspect of life we refer to as hope.

Picture this. I'm several days post-op. I have a tube shoved up through my very sore nose and down into my stomach; another ("this may hurt a little") into my bladder; IV tubes connected to assorted drips, including morphine; and thankfully one from my nostrils to the oxygen tank. I wasn't very clean; I was sprouting a gray beard; and my hair was plastered down and greasy. My pallor was grey, and I was mostly sleeping, too often lost in frightening opiate-induced paranoid dreams. I had no energy to watch TV or read. People were waking me up every couple of hours to check vitals, draw blood, and replace IVs that plugged up now and then. I just wanted to be left alone. I hadn't been in a hospital since I was a nineteen-year-old armored car commander with the Third Cavalry and wasn't prepared for such helpless dependence.

The nurses who attended me were varied, often moving from one hospital to another, doing short shifts. There was only one whom I saw with any regularity. The rest were transients. I was impressed that those typically twenty-something health professionals who poked at my body during that week were, almost without exception, significantly overweight. One was morbidly obese.

Then one day I had a single visit by a first-class, no-nonsense senior nurse. She was a tall and lean black woman of about forty whose uniform wore an assortment of small badges that suggested that she had been through the wars and was to be taken seriously. I wasn't looking or feeling very good, nor was I feeling very good about myself the day when she awakened me and announced that she was going to check my vitals. My first thought was relief. She wasn't here to stick yet one more needle into me. She made routine inquiries and bland professional small talk while she read my signs, never making eye contact with me.

Then she noticed that my lower right leg was tangled in the sheets. She reached down to get me untangled and back under the blanket. When she grasped my right calf, she froze, and softly uttered, "Oh, my!" She was neither looking at nor speaking to me. After a moment, she lifted the blanket and tucked my leg back in. Only then did she slowly turn to me and make eye contact for the first time, suddenly perceiving me as an individual with a life and a history, as against just one more of the fading old geezers who populated the ward. She said, "You work out." It was not a question.

I struggled for a breath, experienced my first post-op semismile, and in a whisper I croaked, "Distance runner." She continued to silently look me in the eyes, slowly nodding her head. I felt my eyes begin to tear up. This totally unexpected instant moment of intimacy struck deep. Quality time.

I suddenly felt no longer alone. Attempting to take the focus off me and discourage my tears, I dug deep for another usable breath and whispered, "It takes one to know one." She smiled and nodded, saying, "Cardio and yoga."

Her work with me was complete, but she stayed for a few minutes, and we talked like old friends. She told me that she'd been unexpectedly called to work on this, her day off, had slept for only four hours but had set her alarm to spend an hour at the gym before arriving at the hospital. She mused, "If I couldn't work out, there's no way that I could function on this job." We shared common hard-earned wisdom such as how, on the days when we least feel like working out, the payoff is always the greatest and how it takes a while to learn that working out actually delivers energy.

There were some comfortable silences, and a little more quiet talk, then it seemed like we were done. Then she reached out and put her hand on mine for what seemed like a very long time, looked me in the eyes, and said, "You know, you're going to be just fine." I smiled and whispered, "I know."

9.
AN EXERCISE FORMULA FOR WEIGHT LOSS

HOW DO WE KNOW IF WE'RE OVERWEIGHT?

If we think that we just might possibly be carrying a few extra pounds, one way to seek an answer is to set aside a few minutes each day, stand naked before a full-length mirror, and examine ourselves from all angles: painful moments set aside in a struggle for increased objectivity. No question that we look better with clothes on.

If we *look overweight*, we probably are (since there is considerable fat stored around internal organs, only minimally reflected by our more obvious beer bellies and saddle bags). Having little muscle definition can signal a lack of fitness, but it might also reflect a layer of external fat that smoothes out everything.

If the technician at the lab has to play a sometimes long and painful guessing game when trying to locate a vein from which to draw blood, we could well be overweight. Skinny people with veins not obscured by a smooth layer of fat only have to deal with a single right-on puncture.

There's also the simple the *back of the hand test*. It involves pinching the skin on the back of our hand and pulling it away from the tendons and bones. If we're holding anything more than two very thin layers of skin, we're carrying excessive fat.

We need a cloth or plastic tape measure to assess our *waist-to-hip ratio*. We measure the narrowest part of our waist and the widest part of our hips. We then divide our waist inches into those of our hips. The American College of Sports Medicine tells us that a woman's ratio should be no more than 0.85 and a man's no more than 0.95. Higher figures signal an increased risk of a heart attack.

It was perhaps no accident that a British scientist whose surname was Lean took an interest in the waist circumferences of his countrymen and women. He and a colleague measured the waists of more than twelve thousand adults and related waist size to a number of health measures. Women with waists in excess of 34.6 inches and men whose waists were in excess of 40.1 inches were far more likely to have high cholesterol, high blood pressure, diabetes, and certain forms of cancer. Women with waists in excess of 32 inches and men whose waists were in excess of 37.5 inches had double the risk of heart attacks than those with waist sizes below those figures.[1]

We can rationalize these simple estimates of healthy weights by telling ourselves that such arbitrary figures don't account for the fact that we have big builds and so on, but heart attacks are serious matters not to be rationalized.

A lot of us guys have no idea what our waist size actually is. We don't want to know. Many of us continue to wear our size thirty-four jeans and belts when our waist size is actually up in the forties or fifties. We hang our distressed leather belts over our hipbones, and use it as a sling to hold up our pregnant-like bellies. Paunch denial.

As today's women become progressively chunkier, many dressmakers have helped their denial process by downsizing size standards. We're more likely to buy brands that enhance our self-esteem rather than those that make us feel bad about ourselves. As I passed a group of three thirty-something women in an upscale shopping mall the other day, I overheard one say, "Marsha, can you believe I'm still only a size ten?" It was one of those "we haven't changed since our college days" conversations, but all three were chunky.

Becoming overweight is typically an insidious process, and we are often blind to our transformation. Beginning in 1990, we Americans steadily put on an average of a pound a year. It was easy to ignore our own increasing girth, especially when just about everyone else around us was doing the same thing. We didn't look fat compared to our friends.

Our body images can be almost unbelievably out of sorts with reality. Anorectics see excess fat in their mirrors, and muscle-bound body builders obsess over what they perceive as the underdevelopment of certain muscles in theirs. No surprises there. What is frightening is that the majority of us are now overweight or obese, and we commonly see reasonably normal and healthy images in our mirrors.

The international standard for assessing healthy body weights is the *body mass index (BMI)*, computed by multiplying our weight (in pounds) by 703 and then dividing that figure by our height (in inches) squared. The upper limit for healthy weight is a BMI of 25. BMIs from 25.1 through 29.9 are classified as overweight; those of 30 through 44.9 are classified as obese; and those of 45 and over are considered severely obese. Some experts argue that the upper limit of healthy weight for women should be 24, and for men 27 to 28, because of the gender differential in bone and muscle mass. However, the international standards are uniformly applied in research on weight and health. Normal weight ends at twenty-five, and obesity begins at thirty.

There are three ways to have our body fat percentage estimated by professionals. Least accurate are electrical conductance tests. The skin fold test, when measured by a first rate technician, can be reasonably accurate. The most accurate estimate involves underwater weighing in a physiology laboratory.

Reasonably healthy levels are 14–20 percent body fat for men and 17–25 percent for women. Body fat percentages essential for normal functioning are 3–5 percent for men and 11–14 percent for women. Obesity begins at 25 percent for men and 30 percent for women. Today's average adult American could walk half way across the continent, powered only by the energy provided in his or her store of fat.

JUST HOW DANGEROUS ARE THOSE EXTRA POUNDS?

Those of us who are overweight and obese die sooner from nearly everything. A recent study, which followed a group of Americans from 1948 to 1990, found that obese nonsmoking men and women lost an average of 5.8 and 7.1 years of their lives. Obese female smokers lost 7.2 years when compared to thinner smokers and 13.3 years when compared to thinner nonsmokers. Obese male smokers lost 6.7 years compared to thinner smokers and 13.7 years compared to normal weight nonsmokers. The men and women studied were classified according to BMI standards. This study found that if we are carrying excess pounds during the period from our midthirties to our midforties, even if we lose weight later on, we still carry a higher risk of early death.[2]

A second study focused on life expectancies of severely obese twenty-year-olds (those with BMIs of at least forty-five). Maximum years of life lost due to severe obesity was estimated to be thirteen for white men, twenty for black men, eight for white women, and five years for black women. The investigators suggested that obese young people are especially vulnerable because they have more years to live in obesity and to increase their risks of heart disease, strokes, cancer, and diabetes.[3]

In April 2003, the American Cancer Society completed a sixteen-year study of nine hundred thousand people across the nation. It provided the first truly definitive understanding of the role of obesity as a cause of cancer. Being overweight increases the risk of nearly every form of cancer, and risk increases with each added pound. Obesity is responsible for 14 percent of cancers in men and 20 percent of those in women.

Men and women in the heaviest weight groups were at very serious risk. Those men were 52 percent more likely to die of cancer than normal weight men. Deaths from gallbladder, stomach, and colorectal cancer were 75 percent more common; deaths from liver cancer were six times as common; and those from pancreatic cancer were more than twice as common.

Women in the heaviest weight groups had cancer death rates 60 percent higher than normal weight women. Deaths from uterine cancer were six times as common; those from kidney cancer were five times as common; those from cervical cancer were three times as common; and those from gallbladder, breast, pancreatic, and esophageal cancers were more than twice as common.[4]

Obesity is clearly implicated as a major cause of type 2 diabetes. As obesity has become epidemic, so has type 2 diabetes, which is commonly referred to as adult-onset diabetes, because it has typically struck men and women after the age of fifty. No more. Increasing numbers of children and adolescents are now afflicted.

In 1990, only four percent of men and fewer than six percent of American women had type 2 diabetes. But at the June 2002 meetings of the American Diabetes Association, Venkat Narayan of the Centers for Disease Control and Prevention presented a terrifying picture of the future for America's children. Of those born in 2000, 27 percent of white boys and 31 percent of white girls, 40 percent of black boys and 45 percent of black girls, and 45 percent of Hispanic boys and 53 percent of Hispanic girls will develop type 2 diabetes in their lifetimes. (The grim consequences of untreated diabetes were spelled out earlier.)

Increased rates of vascular disease also go hand in hand with rising rates of obesity. Rates of hypertension began a steady rise during the 1990s, and there is no reason to believe that they will level off soon.[5] High blood pressure is linked to kidney disease, stroke, heart failure, and blindness. Obesity, a sedentary lifestyle, and an aging population all play a role. Two-thirds of Americans sixty and older now suffer from hypertension.

Obesity has long been linked to heart failure, and a recent study has revealed that being even slightly over a healthy weight (as little as four pounds) increases that risk, quite apart from the added risks associated with excess fat's effect on diabetes and hypertension. Being overweight by itself is the cause of 11 percent of heart failures in men and 14 percent of those in women, according to a recent fifteen-year study of six thousand Americans.[6]

These are sobering figures. However, we humans often tend to dismiss such risk odds, thinking that they apply to other people. We figure that we're special or different. But then one day, like the soldier who hears an explosion and is surprised to find that one of his legs is missing, we are surprised when the doc tells us that we have cancer or diabetes, or that we urgently need bypass surgery.

What is so very disturbing about the epidemic of obesity here in America is that our scientists have found that *underfeeding* may be the most critical key to robust health and great longevity.

For more than a half century, experiments have demonstrated that mice and rats that are fed 30–40 percent fewer calories than they would normally eat live 30–40 percent longer than usual. These slender animals retain robust health and youthfulness until death. A long-term ongoing experiment suggests that the same may be true for primates, but we cannot ethically carry out such research on humans. However, the biological markers that occur in long-lived, underfed rodents (lower body temperature, lower insulin levels, and a steady level of a particular steroid hormone), have all been found in particularly long-lived men.[7]

A second study that compared gene change in normally fed and underfed rats found that by slowing metabolism, low-calorie diets reduced harmful oxygen free radicals and other metabolic byproducts that damage cells. For that reason, one of the authors of this study, who had relied on distance running (which elevates metabolism) to maintain a healthy weight, has begun to rely as much on dietary restriction as exercise.[8]

LIFE JUST ISN'T FAIR

Many studies have demonstrated that heredity plays a very significant role in our personal battle of the bulge. One outstanding study analyzed the adult weights of four adult groups: identical and fraternal twins, reared apart or reared together. The correlations between the BMIs of the male and female identical twins reared apart were 0.70 and 0.66—amazingly high but only slightly lower than the correlation coefficients of those the identical twins reared together. Childhood environment was found to have little or no influence on the adult weights of the twins. The fact that these identical twins seemed to end up with very similar adults weights whether they are reared together or apart underlines the major influence of genetic predisposition.[9]

This suggests that some of us can eat with considerable gusto and gain little or no weight, while others of us inherit mechanisms that seem to turn virtually all of our excess dietary calories into fat. Definitely not fair.

To test this notion, a group of Canadian investigators selected twelve pairs of young male identical twins and systematically overfed them: an extra thousand calories a day, six days a week, for a total of eighty-four days. This amounted to an excess of eighty-four thousand calories over the course of one hundred days. Most men gained an average of about eighteen pounds, but the range was from nine to twenty-nine pounds, making it clear that the men had widely differing genetic predispositions to turn excess calories into fat. The weight gains were very similar between pairs of twins, which further suggested a very strong genetic component in determination of body weight. While heredity is not destiny, such studies make it clear that some of us must be very careful of our caloric intake.[10]

What's also not fair is that if we are overfed, or overfeed ourselves when we are children, we develop far too many fat cells, which can result in life-long weight problems. We are all born with a given number of fat cells that, if we maintain healthy weights, attain adult size at around puberty. However, when the fat cells in overfed kids fill up, they produce additional cells. Up until early adolescence, we can add to the number of our fat cells without limit, but we can never get rid of them, short of surgery. Thus, those of us who were plumped up in childhood carry an excess number of fat cells that, throughout our lives, are going to be sending our brain commands to eat whenever they become less than full.[11] Overfed, fat, and happy kids are likely to smile less in adulthood.

Finally, it's just not fair that those of us who are overweight and obese cannot put the blame our low metabolic rates.

DIETS, EXERCISE, AND METABOLIC RATES

Rockefeller University researchers suggest that we all have a "set point," a weight to which we naturally gravitate by virtue of adjustments in our metabolic rates. Our set point might vary as much as ten or more pounds over our adult lives, determined largely by our diets and physical activity. As our weight elevates upward above our current set point, our metabolic rates increase, and when we manage, through extended caloric restriction, to bring our weight down below our current set point, our metabolic rates reduce.[12]

Thus, if we are overweight, our body is doing the best it can to compensate for those extra pounds by burning energy at a higher rate. On the other hand, when we restrict our food intake, our metabolic rate decreases in an attempt to conserve energy. So, in a sense, dieting is its own worst enemy. The more we restrict our diet, the more our bodies resist weight loss.

There are television advertisements extolling exercise devices, which, if used a few times a week, will so elevate our metabolic rates that we will burn extra calories even as we sleep. These caloric "afterburn" claims are exaggerated. When exercise is very strenuous (resulting in exhaustion), resting metabolic rates remain significantly elevated for only about fifteen minutes.[13] Prolonged or very strenuous exercise can cause resting metabolic rates to remain somewhat elevated for as long as twenty-four to forty-eight hours.[14]

Studies at Laval University in Quebec found that both normal weight and moderately overweight women who did aerobic training five days a week for eleven weeks elevated their resting metabolic rates by only about 8 percent. Thus, after all that work over all those weeks, these women burned only an extra hundred or so calories each day (while not vigorously exercising). So much for the magic shedding pounds while we sleep. Dream on. A second Laval University study found that highly conditioned distance runners who refrained from exercise for only three days suffered a 7 percent reduction in resting metabolic rate.[15]

These are not encouraging findings, and they seem to reflect an obvious catch-22. Those of us who are unfit and overweight, and would most benefit from the caloric afterburn produced by very strenuous exercise, are unable to carry it out. However, on the bright side, such findings suggest that a program of regular aerobic exercise does very modestly elevate our resting metabolic rates. More importantly, later in this chapter, we will learn that such an exercise program for unfit and overweight individuals can substantially help reduce weight as a result of other mechanisms. Metabolic rate a minor player in the weight-loss game.

The best predictor of resting metabolic rate is our lean body mass. However, we can roughly estimate our resting metabolic rate by dividing our weight in pounds by 2.2 and multiplying that number by 24. The resulting figure is an estimate of the number of calories we need each day to do the things we do. About two-thirds of those calories fuel our vital functions (simply keep us alive), about 10 percent are required to digest food, and 20–25 percent power our physical movement.

There is, of course, a bottom line. Whether we had the misfortune of inheriting a fat-predisposing genetic package or were overfed as kids, that bottom line is that we cannot be overweight unless we regularly consume more calories than we expend: calories in, minus calories out, equals calories stored as fat. Energy cannot be created or destroyed. It can only be transformed. Life can be neither easy nor fair, but it is precious and time limited, and we do have choices about what passes through our mouths.

THE SOLUTIONS

The people in third world countries, who sometimes deal with starvation, are not likely to feel sympathy for fat Americans who spend in excess of 130 billion dollars each year on diet plans and products.

Diets are big business, and they can help us lose weight. However, their effects are not long lasting for many of us. *Consumer Reports* magazine in June 1993 published the results of a poll of ninety-five thousand readers who had tried to lose weight during the previous three years. Readers who dieted independently lost an average of 10 pounds, while those enrolled in commercial diet programs for as long as six months did better, losing about fifteen to twenty pounds. Unfortunately, those who lost weight typically gained back half of the lost pounds in six months and two-thirds in two years. Joel Gurin, the science editor, concluded that to lose weight, people should set reasonable goals, exercise, and rely on a low-fat diet rather than counting calories.

High-carbohydrate and low-carbohydrate diets are the teeter-totter of weight loss hope in America. Every decade or so, one predictably rises in popularity while the other drops out of favor, only to resurface in a decade or so with new zingy names and explanatory mechanisms such as ketones, eicosanoids, insulin surges, and so on. Currently, carbohydrates are once again considered to be the villains.

The entire April 2003 issue of the *Journal of the American Medical*

Association (JAMA) was devoted to America's obesity epidemic and possible solutions. They concluded that people can reduce weight by dieting on their own, but joining a structured program was more effective. Their findings echoed those of *Consumer Reports.*

With regard to exercise, JAMA reported the results of a Harvard University study of fifty thousand women, which revealed a 23 percent increased risk of obesity and a 14 increased percent risk of diabetes for every two hours of TV watched daily. Watching ten or fewer hours of TV weekly, and walking at least thirty minutes daily, reduced obesity and diabetes risks by 30 and 43 percent.

The JAMA review concluded that weight loss that occurs as a result of currently fashionable low-carbohydrate diets was attributable to reduced calories rather than the elimination of carbohydrates. They concluded that evidence on the safety and efficacy of low-carbohydrate diets was insufficient to recommend them, especially for longer than three months, or for people over the age of fifty.

There are some problems with attempting to lose weight by dieting alone. The first is that the genetically programmed wisdom of our bodies reacts to food deprivation by dialing down our metabolic rate as a conservation measure. Second, even sensible long-term diets result in a loss of muscle mass, which is also self-defeating, since our muscles burn the majority of our stored fat. A third problem is that diets are too often thought of as time-limited tasks, rather than permanent changes in lifestyle. We want to lose so many pounds before the reunion, swimsuit season, or the holidays (when we plan to seriously overindulge). Finally, we too often tend to think of weight loss in terms of appearance rather than health and survival.

Because diets have several weaknesses and do not have a record of long-term success, and because 90 percent of our stored fat calories are burned in our muscles, it makes sense to look to physical activity as a central component in weight loss and in permanent lifestyle change.

FIT AND FAT

Some of us work hard at becoming more aerobically fit, but we are unwilling to stop overeating. Is there any point to staying fit if we continue to be overweight or obese?

Carolyn Barlow headed a team of researchers at the Cooper Institute for Aerobics Research that addressed this question. Their task was to follow more than twenty-five thousand healthy men for more than eight years to see whether exercise could reduce death risk in those who were overweight or obese and had failed to lose significant weight through regular exercise.

The men were divided into three groups according to body mass index: (1) healthy weight (BMI of less than twenty-seven), (2) overweight (BMI of twenty-seven to thirty), and (3) obese (BMI of greater than thirty). The men averaged five feet, ten inches, in height, and their initial average weights were 170, 199, and 232 pounds. During the follow-up period, there were 673 deaths.

When the all-cause, age-adjusted death rates for the men in the three groups were converted to relative risk factors, the men in the healthy weight and overweight groups had death risks 81 percent and 72 percent lower than the obese men.

The men in the three groups, on the basis of treadmill tests, were then classified into low-, moderate-, and high-fitness groups. The high-fit healthy weight men had death risks 66 percent lower than low-fit men in the same group, and the high-fit overweight men had risks 60 percent lower than low-fit overweight men. The restricted size of the obese group (three thousand) required that the moderate- and high-fit men be combined for comparison with the unfit men. The combined more fit group had death risks 71 percent lower than the unfit obese men.

The investigators discovered that each additional minute the men spent on the treadmill during a maximal aerobic fitness test reduced death risk by 9.5 percent. The men in the three groups spent an average of nineteen, sixteen, and thirteen minutes on the treadmill.

This high-quality investigation made it clear that no matter how much we weigh, increased aerobic fitness can dramatically reduce death risk.[16]

THE FAT-BURNING MANTRA

Let's turn now to the business of how exercise can be best utilized to help us control our weight.

Our physical activity is fueled by two major sources: carbohydrates and fat. Carbohydrate fuel consists of glucose that either circulates in our bloodstream or is stored in the form of glycogen in our muscles (with a big reserve stored in our liver).

Because carbohydrates are so readily available to the energy furnaces (mitochondria) in our muscles, they fuel the vast majority of our daily activities. Fat is our second major fuel source, and it is stored as triglyceride in our fat cells. In order to be utilized as an energy source, it first must be released from those cells by hormonal action, and the enzymes that convert them into burnable free fatty acids must be activated. Fat fuel becomes a more significant fuel source when we engage in prolonged vigorous physical activity. But most of the day, and on most days, we're fueled by carbohydrates.

We have a limited capacity to store carbohydrates, but our capacity to store fat has no limits, so when we engage in extended physical activity, our carbohydrate fuel supply gradually diminishes, and we must then turn increasingly to fat for fuel.

This primary-secondary fuel utilization formula was not a problem for the health of our lean and physically active ancestors, but for the vast majority of us who now work with our heads instead of our bodies, it has become an enormous problem. One of the reasons that so many of us are overweight and obese is because our daily activities are now largely powered by sugar while we conserve our fat.

Certain of our ancestors, by virtue of genetic accident, had a greater tendency to conserve fat, increasing the probability that they would leave their genes in the human gene pool. There was an increased likelihood that these fat conservers would survive periods of famine, had sufficient fat stores to bear and care for their young, and could engage in the prolonged vigorous physical activities that were often demanded for their survival. Nowadays, with food as close as our refrigerator, and physical activity virtually unnecessary for survival, our inherited capacity to store unlimited amounts of fat has dramatically subtracted from our capacity to survive.

If we are overweight or obese and unfit, we must make a special effort to access that stored fat for removal, and an essential intervention is *prolonged physical activity* during each of our workouts, especially during the early months of our exercise program.

Exercise physiologist David Costill of Ball State University measured the relative contributions of carbohydrate and fat fuels as fit male runners worked out at a consistent 65 percent VO_{2max} for an extended period on a treadmill. At the onset of exercise, 80 percent of his runner's energy was provided by carbohydrate fuel and 20 percent provided by fat fuel. After seventy-five minutes of sustained running, those values had completely reversed, with fat providing 80 percent of the runner's fuel. The relative contributions of the two fuel sources were equal at thirty minutes.[17]

Running at 65 percent VO_{2max} is a medium-intensity aerobic workout, in the 70–75 percent range of our HR_{max}. But, what happens if we go out for a long hike in the hills and exercise at a lesser intensity? The same sort of reversal can occur, but it will take longer. The fuel sources are likely to equalize after a couple of hours and totally reverse after about four hours.[18]

The basic point here is that if our primary goal is to rid ourselves of fat, the exercise of choice is prolonged exercise. Even if our workout fails to attain aerobic training intensity, every minute we add results in greater fat utilization. When I start an overweight sedentary person on a walking program, I always suggest that, when walking, they remember my fat-removal mantra: *"Long and slow is the way to go."*

Costill's research has also revealed that there is a sneaky way to trick our muscles into burning even greater quantities of fat during each workout. He has found that drinking two cups of caffeinated coffee an hour before exercising can double the amount of fat we burn, as well as increase our endurance.[19]

Caffeine stimulates the release of dopamine and norepinephrine, which in turn release fat from storage so that more fatty acids are available to be utilized as fuel earlier in the workout. If we utilize the caffeine strategy, we should remember that coffee dehydrates us, so it's especially important for us to drink considerable water before and during our workouts.

CONVERTING OUR MUSCLES INTO FAT BURNERS

An advantage to becoming aerobically fit is that as our fitness increases, our ability to utilize fat fuel increases.

While an *acute effect* of a single session of prolonged aerobic exercise is to burn a greater percentage of fat calories, the important positive *chronic effect* of regular prolonged sessions is to convert our muscles into more efficient fat-burners.

The calf muscles of a trained marathoner have seven times the capacity to burn fat than those of untrained normal adults. The consequences of continuous endurance training are (1) an increase in the number and size of the mitochondria in the involved muscles and (2) an increase of up to three times in the activity of the enzymes that convert stored fat into burnable free fatty acids.[20]

What this translates into is that as we increase our aerobic fitness (and reconfigure our muscles), we can work out at very high intensities for shorter periods of time because of our increased capacity to utilize fat fuel. So when you watch a group of highly fit aerobic dancers work out at an unbelievably high intensity for an hour, their increased capacity to burn fat is an important part of the explanation. Thus, as our fitness increases, we can work out more intensely for briefer time periods to control our weight and maintain our fitness. Our choice.

How we exercise depends on our goals, our needs, and what we can work in to our schedules. A quarter century, and thirty-two thousand miles ago, I started running nearly every day. Regular exercise had a very significant impact on my eating habits: what I ate and how much I ate. I shed sixty pounds, dropping my BMI from a borderline obese 29.0 to a healthy 22.0. During the early years, a new self-image and a search for personal bests kept me motivated to stay thin and to actively race. Now I run mainly for mental and physical health, preferring easy runs in my mountains in the company of coyotes.

HOW DO WE DECIDE WHAT TO EAT?

For starters, it's wise to treat diet plans and products with caution. Whether it's a new revolutionary diet plan book, a program, pills, or food products, the seller is usually in business and looking to make a profit. The product may or may not be both effective and safe in the long run. For objective answers, you should rely on reports from professional scientific journals by researchers (who are typically associated with universities) and reports from government agencies that are concerned with health. Important new findings from both sources are routinely summarized in newspapers.

There is a very strong case to be made for a high proportion of complex carbohydrates in our diets. Carbohydrates are not our enemies. Nutritionist Sharon Bortz, while with the Stanford Center for Research in Disease Prevention, wrote an article concerning our predictable cyclical diet fad frenzies. She ended it with, "In the meantime, there's always the Food Pyramid, as unsexy and unprofitable as it is, it's what works in the long run."

The FDA Food Pyramid is the end product of decades of research by objective scientists, and its broad base is composed of complex carbohydrates. Bortz correctly suggests that our ancestors were more gatherers than they were hunters, and carbohydrates historically have been our major food source.[21] Spectacular as a mammoth kill might be, the meat soon rotted, and our ancestors went back to more reliable vegetable food sources. Eventually we killed all the mammoths and turned to farming. Carbohydrates have always been are our primary fuel source.

It's no secret that those of us who eat a high proportion of fat in our diets tend to carry more body fat than those of us who eat a larger proportion of carbohydrates. This would be expected, since a pound of dietary fat contains forty-eight hundred calories (a pound of our fat tissue contains thirty-five hundred calories), and a pound of glucose contains 1,920 calories. However, even when we carefully hold the number of daily dietary calories constant, people who eat a greater percentage of carbohydrates and a smaller percentage of fat weigh less after a year than those who consume the same number of calories but whose diets contain a greater percentage of fat. Bortz explains the reasons:

1. More energy is required to convert excess dietary carbohydrate calories into body fat (30 percent of excess ingested carbohydrate calories) than to convert dietary fat into stored fat (about 5 percent of excess ingested fat). In other words, if we overdo our carbohydrate intake, less of it will be converted to fat than if we overdo our fat intake.

2. There is a limit to the amount of glucose that can be converted to glycogen and stored in our bodies (an average of about sixteen hundred calories), but we have an unlimited capacity to store fat.

3. Only after our glycogen storehouse is filled are excess dietary carbohydrates converted to fat, but there is no such regulator to govern our storage of excess fat calories.

4. It's very hard to keep our glycogen storehouse full, since we're constantly drawing on it to fuel our daily activities. It's like trying to fill a bathtub with a leaky drain plug. The result is that typically only 1–10 percent of our ingested carbohydrate calories get stored as fat. However, a large percentage of excessive fat calories find their way into our fat cells.[22]

When we think about choosing a diet for lifelong health, it makes sense to listen to the unbiased scientists who recommend the food pyramid. It's also wise to listen to the unbiased epidemiologists who tell us about the diets of unusually long-lived groups such as the adherent Adventists, who live an average of a dozen years longer than most of us, and the farmers of rural Bama province in China, who have the world's largest population of centenarians and who subsist on a diet made up largely of rice and beans.

We don't have to go to such dietary extremes, but if we want enhance our chances of a long life, we might want to at least attempt to emulate the common lifestyle denominators of the groups of people who tend to enjoy unusually long and disability-free lives: a diet low in calories, protein, and fat; no tobacco; little alcohol; and regular vigorous physical activity.

SOME THOUGHTS ON WEIGHT-LOSS STRATEGIES

One of the most authoritative sources for good information on weight control and body composition is the American College of Sports Medicine.[23] After reviewing countless dozens of relevant studies, their conclusions are

1. Physical exercise alone, without dieting, has only a modest effect in reducing fat mass.
2. Diets produce greater weight loss because it's easier to induce an energy deficit by caloric restriction than by exercising.
3. The most successful programs (weight loss and maintenance of loss) have been a combination of diet and exercise.
4. For sedentary individuals who are beginning a weight-loss exercise program, exercise should be frequent, of considerable duration, and moderate in intensity.

An extensive ACSM position statement on exercise and weight loss programs was published in 1983.[24]

If you've found a formula to lose weight, and keep that weight off permanently, you're indeed fortunate, provided that formula is a not a dietary trade-off that carries serious long-term health risks. If your attempts to reduce weight have been unsuccessful, I would like to suggest an alternative strategy.

After nearly a half century of treating depressed and/or overweight patients and interacting with countless lean athletes who were once fat or depressed, I'm left with several conclusions, the most important one being, *if we can begin and sustain a program of moderate regular physical activity, good things will follow.*

I've encountered very many people who began to exercise regularly and *subsequently* changed their eating habits and lost weight. Exercise is not an end in itself. It is often a beginning, a springboard for significant lifestyle changes that may have been resistant to other more direct interventions.

A second conclusion is that *moderation is the key to change*. What most of us truly desire is a permanent lifestyle change. We don't just want to fit into a smaller dress size for the family reunion. We would like to carry an attractive and healthy body weight and configuration for the rest of our lives. We'd also like that life to be long and disability-free. For most of us, significantly changing the set pattern of our lives is not something that can be accomplished overnight. It is seldom the result of a crash diet.

The increased physical activity and dietary changes that result in permanent weight loss are most commonly a very gradual process. Fat cells slowly shrink and muscle cells slowly enlarge. These changes result in gradual weight loss punctuated by plateau periods where we don't lose weight at all. While our weight may remain constant, our body's composition and configuration slowly alter during such plateau periods: less fat—more muscle.

Moderation also involves modest goals. It's a mistake to ask so much of ourselves that we are likely to get discouraged and fail. For example, deciding to exercise *and* drastically reduce our caloric intake may be asking too much. One problem with packaging the two together is that if we one day decide that we are simply unwilling go on depriving ourselves of food, we may also stop exercising. This was demonstrated in a Baylor University study.[25]

Men and women who averaged thirty or more pounds overweight took part in weight-loss programs that lasted a year and were followed up at the end of a second year.

At the end of the first year, when supervision and support ended, a diet-only group and a diet-plus-exercise group had both lost more weight than an exercise-only group (an average of fifteen, nineteen, and six pounds, respectively). However, at the end of the second (unsupervised) year, the diet-only group weighed an average of two pounds above their *pretreatment* weights, while the exercise-plus-diet and exercise-only groups weighed an average of five and six pounds below their pretreatment weights.

The investigators concluded that dieting alone was associated with weight loss followed by weight gain when treatment ends, while exercise alone produced smaller weight loss but better maintenance. Interviews with the diet-plus-exercise group members who regained a substantial part of their lost weight during the second unsupervised year revealed that when they gave up their restrictive diets they also stopped walking. For them, giving up was a package deal.[25]

Finally, *it may be unwise to focus too heavily on food*, to count calories, and to have obsessive internal conversations such as, "When am I going to eat? How long since I last ate? What am I allowed to eat? How much am I allowed to eat? How many calories are there in this or that? How am I going to cook for the family and myself?" *Counting calories is a most unnatural activity for human animals.* Walking is not.

My almost universal weight-loss prescription for sedentary overweight patients has been that they slowly work up to walking for an hour five days a week and cut down on the amount of fat in their diets. No mention of how far or how fast they should walk. No mention of caloric counting or restriction, no mention of how many grams of fat they are allowed each day. Just walk and cut back on the fat.

If months of following the prescription haven't led to spontaneous dietary changes and weight loss, I then suggest other changes in the kind and amount of food patients consume and changes in their exercise programs.

10.
THE RISKS

The risks associated with exercise and sports fall into three major categories: injury, physical and psychosocial risks associated with exercise abuse and dependency, and death.

High-risk sports, such as climbing, aerobatics, parachuting, and auto racing, all involve high speeds and/or very difficult interactions with forces of nature. In such sports, a momentary lapse in attention, or just plain bad luck, can result in serious injury or death. Some high-risk sports don't require a high degree of fitness.

Medium-risk sports, where aggressive and violent physical contact is normal, would include sports such as ice hockey, boxing, football, and rugby. Medium-risk sports predictably result in injuries but rarely in death. The focus of the participants is usually centered on competition, especially as the caliber of play escalates. Fitness may be a necessary but secondary goal for professional athletes. On the other hand, fitness may be far more important to amateurs, who can find motivation for physical activity only in competitive sports. Soccer is one of the very best choices for people who place a high priority on aerobic fitness, but, like other medium-risk sports, it carries a substantial risk of injury.

Low-risk sports, such as running, track and field, tennis, and rowing, do not involve violent physical contact and take place in relatively safe environments where an error in judgment that could lead to a fatality is highly unlikely.

But even in low-risk sports, we always run the risk of injury or perhaps even permanent disability. Bicycling, for example, can carry a wide range of risks. It can be a safe, blissful, and anxiety-free ride in the park. However, sharing the roads with automobiles or engaging in extreme mountain biking can be fatal. And while rowing is a low-risk sport, rowing above Niagara Falls may be an exception.

Those of us whose primary goal is to become more fit typically choose low-risk physical activities or only moderately competitive team sports. But no matter how we exercise, we run the risk of injuries.

Those of us who are very unfit, and especially those of us who are unfit and older, also must be concerned about the risk of exercise-related death.

EXERCISE AND SUDDEN DEATH

Fortunately, *exercise-related deaths are rare*. For example, of 2,606 sudden cardiac deaths analyzed in Finland, only twenty-two (less than 1 percent) were exercise induced. To put that risk in perspective, 33 percent of those 2,606 sudden deaths in Finland occurred in sauna baths, where the stress of attempting to compensate for excessive heat was sufficient to stop problematical Finnish hearts from beating further.[1]

It's also the case that *exercise-induced sudden deaths are rarely the result of exercise itself*. Exercise is most often a triggering event, with the root cause of the death being one or another existing physiological problem.

Olympic track and field champion Florence Griffith Joyner and Russian Olympic skating champion Sergei Grinkov are only two of many elite athletes who have suddenly died from cardiovascular disease or heart failure. The list includes high school, college, and professional athletes who appeared to be in robust good health. Such young people typically die because of one or another congenital cardiac or coronary artery malformation that was discovered only after their deaths.

AGE AND ATHEROSCLEROSIS

Among older athletes, the most common cause of sudden cardiac and stroke deaths is atherosclerosis (a narrowing and final closing of the arteries that supply our heart muscles or brains with blood). Well-known marathoner and author Jim Fixx was a young man who chose to ignore his very pronounced symptoms of coronary artery disease. Despite his symptoms and a family history of heart disease, he continued to run until he dropped dead on a Vermont roadside.

However, most exercise-induced sudden deaths occur among atherosclerotic, hypertensive older men. During an eighty-eight-month period, there were eighty-one such deaths in Rhode Island, most occurring in men aged fifty to fifty-nine and next most in men aged forty to forty-nine. Advanced atherosclerosis accounted for seventy-one of those eighty-one exercise-triggered sudden deaths. If our coronary arteries are seriously compromised, it doesn't take much stress to cause heart failure. The greatest number of those Rhode Island sudden deaths occurred on golf courses, and the fourth most common venue was bowling alleys.[2]

Three decades ago, when a larger percentage of us smoked, two studies found that 70 percent of exercise-induced sudden deaths were suffered by heavy smokers.[3] While fewer of us now smoke, for those of us who still do, tobacco escalates our risk. Those of us who are sedentary smokers (especially if we are older and overweight) should engage in any exercise program only after consultation with a physician.

CATCH-22

Whether we are elite athletes or confirmed couch potatoes, our risk of death is greater while we are exercising, especially during the thirty minutes that follow a workout. None of us is immune. However, the more aerobically fit we are, the less likely that we will suffer an exercise-induced sudden death. Sounds like a classical catch-22, but this dilemma has a solution.

Infrequency of exercise is clearly related to sudden death risk. Older joggers have sudden death rates of one per fifteen thousand, but older, more highly fit marathoners have rates of only one per fifty thousand. The American Heart Association has found sudden death rates among normally inactive men aged forty-five to fifty-four to be about 124 per hundred thousand.[4]

A University of Washington research group found that men who spent 140 minutes or more a week in a variety of strenuous aerobic and anaerobic activities, such as jogging, swimming, singles tennis, and chopping wood, were five times as likely to suffer a sudden cardiac death while exercising than at other times. That doesn't sound good. However, those who exercised less faced far more serious odds of exercise-induced sudden death. Men who engaged in such exercise at least twenty minutes a week were thirteen times as likely to die while exercising. Finally, those who exercised less than twenty minutes a week were fifty-six times as likely to die while exercising, ten times the risk of the most active men.[5]

A paper read by Barry Franklin of Wayne State University at the 2000 meeting of the American Heart Association underlined (1) how rarely exercise-induced sudden deaths occur and (2) how those deaths are related to exercise infrequency.

The researchers surveyed three million members of a chain of 320 American health and fitness centers. During 182 million workouts, only seventy-one fatal heart attacks or strokes occurred. Three deaths occurred among those who worked out five or more times a week, sixteen deaths among those who worked out three or four times a week, and an additional sixteen deaths among those who worked out one to two times a week. However, thirty-four deaths occurred among those who worked out less than once a week. While the huge risk reduction came with five or more workouts a week, *working out as little as once or twice a week reduced death risk by half. It doesn't take much.*

The research findings are quite consistent. While we are more likely to die while exercising or shortly thereafter, such deaths are very rare, and the less fit we are, the greater the risk. These findings suggest that those of us who are unfit have two choices. We may remain unfit, but be very careful about infrequent bouts of even moderately intense exercise that may be more strenuous than our systems can handle, or we may cautiously become more fit, reducing the odds of untimely death and opening the door to fuller lives. While we can rationalize and minimize our risks, the choice can be a life-or-death matter.

Those of us who are unfit and over the age of thirty and those of us who are in high-risk groups—such as those of us with family histories of heart attacks or strokes; those who are diabetic, overweight, or obese; and those with high blood pressure—should begin to exercise only after an appropriate physical examination (perhaps including a treadmill stress test) and the advice and supervision of appropriate medical specialists.

INJURIES

The Stanford University osteoarthritis studies, which followed several hundred long-term senior distance runners and several hundred normally active control subjects for varying numbers of years, shed light on several aspects of running and injuries.

The runners visited physicians less often than the nonrunners, but one-third of their visits were for running-related injuries.

The runners had more fractures (mostly lower extremity) than the non-runners. However, only eight members of the running group stopped running because of musculoskeletal injuries, while during the same time period, one-third of the nonrunners had stopped performing other preferred forms of exercise because of musculoskeletal injuries.

Both runners and nonrunners showed age-related progressive osteoarthritis, but the runners' rate of progression was no different than that of the nonrunners. That is, regularly running long distances didn't speed up the degenerative process. The runners had stronger bones, delayed disability, and missed an average of only one and a half days of work a year.[6] Thus, while regular distance running carries the risk of injury, the many other payoffs are enormous.

Those of us who take up other low-risk activities, such as regular walking or swimming, will also run the risk of sport-specific injuries, but in general, the benefits will far outweigh the risks. Most often our injuries will heal, and we can get back to our chosen form of exercise. And it is usually the case that, while that healing process is taking place, we can substitute another form of exercise that does not interfere with the healing process. For example, when a weight-bearing joint or muscle is injured, we can often substitute a non-weight-bearing activity, such as swimming, rowing, or riding a stationary bicycle.

Problems arise when we are unwilling to give up training in our chosen form of exercise and don't allow our injuries the necessary time to heal. This is can be a signal that we may be abusing exercise.

With regard to risk of injury, the American College of Sports Medicine tells us that the frequency of injuries is greatest among women and overweight men.[7]

EXERCISE ABUSE AND DEPENDENCY

In 1976, William Glasser wrote a book called *Positive Addiction*, in which he contended that running and various other activities, while addictive, added positive mental health benefits to our lives.[8] Three years later, William Morgan published a professional journal article titled, "Negative Addiction in Runners." The debate had thus begun.

Morgan chronicled eight cases in which addiction to running had resulted in irreparable physical injuries, damaged interpersonal relationships, lost jobs, and even death.[9] In a subsequent paper, Morgan pointed out that some runners, like those with chemical dependencies, become habituated and require greater amounts of exercise to experience the equivalent psychological effects.[10]

I recall one of my students, a bodybuilder, who often stopped to chat during my office hours. He was obsessed with his regimens, the potential harmful effects of the expensive chemicals he injected, his perceived less-than-perfect body configuration, and his predominant social life at the gym (time spent discussing his obsessions with other similarly obsessed men and women). During that semester, his wife finally gave him an ultimatum: build a life with our little girl and me, or build it at the gym. He chose life at the gym. She chose to continue her studies and became a physician.

The word "dependency" has long since replaced "addiction" in professional lexicon. But whatever the terminology, there is now convincing evidence that athletes can become dependent on exercise.

In researching the effects of exercise deprivation, scientists have had a very difficult time recruiting athletes who are willing to stop exercising long enough to determine whether symptoms of withdrawal become apparent. Most athletes who work out with regularity are simply unwilling to do so, probably because (1) they will miss the psychological and physiological hits that the exercise provides, and (2) they know very well the negative mood consequences that predictably will follow.

One investigator succeeded in convincing a group of college students who exercised "only three or four days a week" to give up exercise for an entire month. Nocturnal EEG records revealed that the students suffered significant sleep disturbances after they stopped exercising: deep, relaxing slow-wave sleep diminished and REM sleep (which signaled dream activity) increased.[11]

A second study found that men and women who had been running five days a week for at least a year reacted to even a single day of deprivation. Psychological and physiological tests revealed that depression scores and tension levels rose.[12]

Other investigations have quite consistently found that exercise deprivation elevates both depression and anxiety and interferes with sleep. Other withdrawal symptoms commonly reported are restlessness, frustration, and irritability.[13] One of my running friends once commented to me that "when I'm injured and can't run, my husband says being around me is like living with a bear!"

These studies have found that many of the behaviors exhibited by normal committed athletes parallel some of those that define substance use and dependence (as listed in chapter 7). Using bad judgment about injuries and experiencing withdrawal are not uncommon, especially in the early stages of our athletic lives. But most of us do not exhibit the systematic pattern of pathological behavior that characterizes those who abuse and depend on exercise.

Exercise-abusive or exercise-dependent athletes sometimes fail to fulfill major role obligations at work, school, or home and continue to engage in excessive exercise despite recurrent social or interpersonal problems that it creates with spouses, families, and friends. They continue to exercise in spite of physical injuries that (1) were caused by the exercise, (2) were exacerbated by continued exercise, and (3) could turn into permanent disability with continued exercise. Some exhibit the symptoms of both tolerance and withdrawal. There is no question that some men and women abuse and become dependent on exercise, and in such cases there is absolutely nothing positive about the role of exercise in their lives.

Probably all of us who are committed athletes with a long history of exercising most days of the week are to some extent exercise dependent. However, the vast majority of us neither abuse exercise nor pathologically depend on it. We don't allow exercise to rain misery down upon ourselves or upon those around us.

Psychologist Rod Dishman views such healthy dependence as an intrinsic and integrative motivational process that keeps us exercising and helps us get past the common compliance barriers that seem to intimidate or overwhelm less active people.[14]

Exercise is only one of many potentially abusive roads that we can choose to follow when we urgently need to distract and medicate ourselves. Nonetheless, most of us can drink without becoming alcoholics, study without becoming bookworms, work without becoming workaholics, and enjoy sex without becoming compulsive sexualizers. Exercise can be beneficial and healthy, or it can be abused and destructive.

CONFESSIONS OF A BORN-AGAIN RUNNER

I entered the San Francisco Marathon six months after I began running, at the age of fifty. Not smart. Since I almost never visited doctors, a couple of weeks before the race I thought it might be prudent to go for a physical exam and stress test. A local community college had an excellent exercise physiology laboratory. It turned out I had 20 percent body fat (acceptable, but high for a marathoner), a VO_{2max} of fifty-five (sufficient to finish the race), but a far too-high percentage of fast-twitch muscle cells in my legs (the expert said my ideal racing distance was the mile and that my legs would make me pay if I ran the marathon).

The expert was right. When I reached mile twenty (considered by many runners to be the true halfway point in a 26.2-mile marathon), I was seriously dehydrated, and my leg muscles were experiencing painful lactic acid baths. They began to cramp up, forcing me to periodically stop, stretch, and walk. During those excruciatingly painful last six miles, I swore I would finish but never run another marathon. The second vow was immediately voided by the high I experienced when I crossed the finish line at Polo Field. That night I was scouring the race schedules for the next local marathon. Insane.

I ran a dozen marathons over the next couple of years, during which time I gradually came to realize that I was always running on some sort of edge, risking illness and injury in the name of personal best performances. I had to log very high training mileages to run faster (and less painful) marathons, but the higher my training mileage, the more often I would be suffering upper respiratory infections or balancing on the edge of an overuse injury when race days finally arrived. I recall beginning one marathon while running a mild fever, unwilling to set aside all those miles and months of careful training. Because of bad judgment and overuse, I also blew out a knee ligament and a plantar muscle during that period.

No one knew much about exercise and immune function at that time, so I was exploring unknown territory. Also, since that time experts have found that it is possible to run marathons with considerably less training mileage. Still, looking back, I find that my near-obsessive focus on running during that period to be forgivable, since I was going through a tough time in my life. I needed distraction and something to fill the voids.

My knee injury was the result of too many premarathon training miles, exacerbated by being born a male. I was splendidly prepared for the Livermore Marathon, healthy and ready to set a personal record, knowing for certain that I could, for the first time, average eight-minute miles over the distance. But early that morning I fell in love in the prerace staging area, struck dumb by a woman I had never met: My heart raced, I became short of breath, and my knees became weak when I so much as glanced at her. I realized that feelings of this magnitude didn't happen more than once in a blue moon, so I played it very cool.

When the race began, I followed her, determined that she was running alone, and didn't speak to her until I drew up beside her at about mile three.

I suggested that since we seemed to be running about the same speed, why didn't we pace one another for a while. Super cool dude!

What was surprising was that it turned out that we hit it off big time. Clearly we were meant for each other. Then about mile ten, my right knee began sending me some brief, blinding flashes of pain, so powerful that my brain began to periodically head north and reoccupy my head. I finally checked my stopwatch, and realized we had been cruising along at a seven-minute-per-mile-pace—fine for her but suicidal for me.

Over the next couple of miles, the pain got progressively more frequent and intense, and just before mile thirteen, I was forced to bail out. She stopped and asked if she should send help, told me her phone number, and asked me to repeat it and promise to call. Then she took off. What was so agonizing about this story is that, in dealing with the trauma of stupidly ruining a race in which I had invested months of hard training, I forgot her phone number.

One last "born-again" abuse tale. Our plantar muscle attaches to our heel bone and fans out across the bottom of our foot to hook up with the toe area. When it tears a hunk of bone loose from the heel, we have what's called a heel spur. I ruptured my plantar muscle at about the midway point under the arch. The injury was strictly the result of overuse: running up to sixty miles a week in marathon training. A man possessed.

I wouldn't stop running, in spite of severe pain during the early stages of each run. The rupture slowly swelled, first to marble size, and then progressively larger. I continued to run. Marathon on the horizon. Finally, I visited a podiatrist, who taught me how to wrap it and ice it. He suggested cortisol injections. I continued to run, and the injury continued to worsen. Finally, when I could no longer bear the pain, I went to see our local Olympic sports medicine orthopedist.

He examined me and asked about my running habits and treatment histories. He made no response when I complained that I could now only manage to run twenty miles a week. He measured my thighs and told me that they were no longer even close to being the same size: the muscles on my noninjured side having compensated by becoming much larger. That was sobering. Finally, he looked me in the eye and told me that I had a choice. Unless I stopped running entirely for six months, I might never run again. He mentioned alternative exercise. As I was walking to the door, he quietly inquired, "What's the matter with running only twenty miles a week?"

One morning, five months later, I walked down the hillside with my Alaskan malamute to get the paper. As I turned to head back up to the house, she ran ahead, turned to face me, and dropped her front quarters onto the road: an ancient wolf invitation to play tag. Without thinking, I sprinted up the driveway chasing her. After a few yards I stopped, bent over, and began to sob. Oh, how I had missed playing wolf games with Tasha, and how I had missed running.

After running a dozen marathons, I accepted the fact that I could no longer improve my best time and that my physiology was simply not designed for such long races. However, I continued to run shorter races for all sorts of reasons. They kept me motivated to keep running and fit, gave me precious time with my running son, provided affirmation and fellowship with other members of the running tribe, and occasionally provided quite lovely age-group medals for a display in a nook of my bedroom wall, reminding me some mornings, while shaving, that I could still be my own hero. Running also made depression a stranger, got me through tough times, and kept off the pounds I had shed in a previous life.

I survived that "born-again" period of my life and never again abused exercise. Moreover, those experiences made it clear that regular exercise was profoundly important to me and that I could no longer take my health and functionality for granted. I became increasingly unwilling to engage in pleasurable and thrilling activities that might break my body and jeopardize my morning runs. During my early sixties, as I became aware of slowing reflexes and impaired balance, I stopped riding my beloved old motorcycles, jumping out of airplanes, and climbing high mountains. Running only twenty miles a week turned out to be just fine.

PART 4:
THE ART OF
EMBRACING SWEAT

11.
HOW CAN I
MAKE MYSELF DO IT?

This is always the bottom-line question. Whether I'm talking with students, patients, or other professionals in training seminars, this is what it always boils down to: "How can I make myself stop eating?" and "How can I make myself exercise?"

The most straightforward answer, of course, is that *maybe you can't.* The odds are stacked against you. At least two-thirds of us, here in the land of plenty, have failed to find the answer and are living lives out of control.

We live in a highly seductive and thinly veiled evil empire, surrounded by powerful forces that conspire to keep us unfit, fat, and stupid. Here we will attempt to identify your enemies, alter your odds of success, and plot your escape from the great mass of sedentary and overweight Americans.

REALISTIC GOALS

First off, it's wise avoid being overly ambitious. A guaranteed recipe for failure is trying to do too much at once. Going on a restrictive diet *and* beginning an exercise program at the same time may work for a short while, but the odds of sticking with such a massive lifestyle change are slim. The same goes for starting to exercise and stopping smoking or drinking.

Your single goal should be to begin to exercise. If you can do that and are able to continue to exercise most days of the week for several months, there is a good chance that *exercise will no longer be something you have to do but something you are unwilling to do without.*

THE CHUNKY MASSES ARE NOT OUR FRIENDS

Only a decade or two ago, very few of us were overweight or obese. Think back to your grade school class pictures. How many of your classmates were obese or overweight? The older we are, the leaner were our classmates. Today's grade school children don't look the same. Some are even showing up with fat-induced adult-onset diabetes before they reach middle school, and some are getting their stomachs stapled. Almost overnight, we find ourselves surrounded by great masses of chunky people of all ages, and they have completely redefined normalcy standards. We're not so fat compared with everyone else is our common form of denial, reinforced by the fact that nearly one in three people we see around us is obese. We can now be overweight, headed for premature disability and death, and feel quite normal. We need to plot our escape from normalcy.

TELEVISION AND VIDEO GAMES ARE NOT OUR FRIENDS

One of the fundamental truths I learned over a nearly a half century of practicing psychotherapy was that *if you want to do something very important and very difficult, the first step is to stop doing the something else(s) that get(s) in the way.*

In a clinical setting, this involves convincing a patient to stop his predictable defensive behaviors (which interfere with good interpersonal relationships and lead to isolation and depression). Defensive behaviors, such as rationalization, denial, or guilt-provoking passive aggressiveness, always distance us from others. They reduce our anxiety and make us feel safe, but such unconscious protective behaviors can constitute a lifelong barrier to self-awareness and satisfying relationships with others. It's no easy task for the patient to give up these defenses, for each time he avoids such behavior, he is left in a terrifying sort of identity purgatory, knowing what not to do but having no idea of *what to do.*

I suggest that *if you want to make physical activity a part of your life, a primary intervention is to stop doing the something else(s) that pre-*

dictably get in your way of doing so. While there are all sorts of something else(s) in our individual lives, there are a couple of major villains.

During class at the university one day, a student surprised me by asking, "If you were God, how would you make people in America more physically active?" In my years of teaching, no one had ever asked that question, and I surprised myself when I answered without hesitation, "For starters I'd ban video games, television, and professional sports." I later amended that statement, adding all high school and college athletic team sports.

I explained to the student that there actually was *life before television* and that we Americans (even adults) used to actually get outdoors and be physically active before *we gave away our play and our games to the talented few:* the varsity high school and college athletes and the superelite professionals. *Once active participants, we have now become a nation of sedentary observers.*

We wear our heroes' jerseys while we sit in front of our televisions, in arenas, or in coliseums, where we passively eat, drink, and watch. Senior writer Frank Deford, in a recent *Sports Illustrated* piece on the rise and fall of yet another of our athletic legends, wrote, "Athletes are romantic idols, worshipped by innocent children and stunted adults." I agree with Deford and told the student that I have always encouraged everyone, of all ages, to attempt be his or her own hero. I commented that, in my mind, struggling to be a good parent was a particularly heroic act.

It was great fun being a university professor, challenging sacred icons, and igniting spirited discussions. I invited that student and his classmates to play collective God and devise a master plan to get sedentary Americans moving again.

Over the course of two class meetings, they decided that our government should get serious about a big preventative health budget rather than spending most of its dollars on repair work.

They also thought it would be a good idea to have all public schools, from elementary through college, open their physical education facilities to the people in the communities (who pay for them). This would mean cost-free facilities for all of us to exercise during nonclass hours, six in the morning to midnight: facilities staffed with people to provide equipment, instruct, and organize games and local amateur leagues for people of all ages and skill levels.

I told the students about the fine soccer field at the Norwegian National University of Sport in Oslo, where there were *no spectator seats.* Can you even imagine an American high school or university without a football stadium? In Oslo, a few scattered spectators sometimes sat on a hillside above, but nearly all of the people at the field were playing, had finished playing, or were warming up to play. About a third of adult Norwegians were playing in amateur sport leagues of one sort or another at the time I lived at the university.

I first visited Oslo one January, when daylight was gray and short. I lived in a small room above the university soccer field, which was surrounded by huge piles of snow. Snow removal equipment often kept me awake from midnight to six in the morning, at which time soccer play began under the lights in typically below-freezing weather. In addition to the soccer stadium, 125 miles of cross-country ski trails were lighted and maintained in Oslo. This, of course, was at a time when Norway had only a single government-controlled television station.

Back in my California classroom, my students decided that video games should be made illegal and that television stations should be allowed to broadcast only from eight in the evening until midnight. They figured that such limits would add to children's literacy, reduce their aggressiveness, get them outside playing after school, and would allow families to join together at least once a day to have an evening meal—where people could make eye contact—and talk to one another.

This student grand plan to get people moving here in America is, of course, the stuff of dreams. It isn't going to happen. This a consumer culture than runs on money. However, this radical plan was the work of highly intelligent, informed, and open-minded women and men. Can you imagine Americans of any age getting up in the freezing morning darkness to go out and play soccer on an icy, rock-hard playing field?

But each of us individually has the power to make positive changes for ourselves and our families. Playing video games, watching daytime television, and spending time watching others engage in sports are the major *something else(s)* here in sedentary America. It's clear that television and video games can be hazardous to the mental and physical health of children and adults. As the number of hours we spend in front of the tube increases, so do the risks of depression, aggressiveness, obesity, and heart attacks.

There actually are some families here in America who choose not to own television sets or video games. In my volunteer work as a nature docent, leading families on mountain hikes and hosting a skyline nature center, I run across such families on occasion. They are typically foreign-born, coming from countries where weekend physical activity is a part of the culture. Besides being physically fit at very early ages, the children are polite, responsible, and highly literate. Their eye-hand coordination may not quite match those of the expert video gamers, but they can read and write.

I had a recent encounter with a not-quite-five-year-old boy from such a family. He had run ahead of his parents at the end of a four-mile mountain hike to rush into the front door of our nature center. I was sitting alone facing the door, the only volunteer on duty that day. There was just the two of us. He walked directly up to me, looked me squarely in the eyes, and said, "I'm interested in anthropology." Showing respect, I responded with, "What kind?" He answered, "Physical. May I touch those skulls over there?"

We all have choices about how we live. If we want to free up some time and enhance the odds of becoming physically active, the most obvious something else(s) most of us can choose to give up or restrict are television and video games. We don't need to make a lifetime commitment, but we might try a month-long experiment, knowing we can always return to our more passive gluttonous and slothful ways down the line. It might seem heretical to unplug the TV for a month, but that would be the most powerful medicine.

If life without TV is no life at all, perhaps we could at least give up daytime television and attempt to follow the recommendations of my students. No television before eight in the evening, seven days a week. We can always record daytime and evening news, sporting events, or other special interest programs and watch them at night, skipping the commercials and shortening our exposure to the tube's numbing opiate aura. We might also experiment with no TV whenever there are guests in our house.

Going without television for a month will leave us with time on our hands, and a large measure of TV detox restlessness. When feeling restless, we might consider going for a walk and thinking about what we'll do with our free time and, for that matter, our lives. We can get acquainted with the outdoors and our bodies. See what it feels like to walk in the rain. Maybe take along a family member and get acquainted. Perhaps play some outdoor games. Toss the football around, or shoot some hoops.

A PERSONAL ODYSSEY

You should be prepared to travel the road to fitness alone. Don't embark with an expectation that you will receive a great deal of support or understanding along the way.

Significant changes in our behavior, such as beginning to exercise several times a week, can often upset people close to us. "Is she building a life of her own and leaving me?" "Doesn't he care about me or want to be with me anymore?" Important people in our lives, whom we assume would support our struggle for increased fitness and slimmer bodies (and who on the surface may verbalize support), often have enormous unconscious investments in keeping us just the way we are. Consciously or unconsciously, they often engage in sabotage.

"I think it's great that you're going walking every day before dinner, but our kids see so little of you as it is." "How can you justify stopping at the gym on your way home from work every night? What about your family?" "I think you looked better carrying a little more weight." Many couples have relationships based on unspoken ground rules such as, "I won't talk about how fat you're getting if you don't talk about how fat I'm getting."

If one member of a couple begins to exercise, loses weight, becomes more attractive, and leaves depression behind, this can cause considerable anxiety and apprehension in the unfit partner, whose role of understanding caretaker no longer works within the dynamics of the evolving relationship.

Charting our own course and reestablishing our personal identity and space can be tough after years of an entangled relationship, one that often involves at least partially enmeshed personal boundaries. "We" has long been a major part of the equation, so when one member becomes more fit, emotionally stable, and independent, serious relationship problems may follow (or long-existent problems may surface). Dealing with these problems may lead, on the one hand, to increased richness and intimacy or, on the other hand, to tough choices.

All things considered, the mental health benefits of increased fitness—reduced depression and anxiety, increased self-esteem, and a sense of increased self-efficacy and empowerment—are substantial rewards for the individual. They may or may not be wonderful for a relationship. The road to fitness is often a solitary odyssey, which can generate resistance or support, and which can significantly alter one's life.

TOO MANY RESPONSIBILITIES, TOO LITTLE TIME

When those of us who are sedentary are asked why we aren't exercising, the predictable response goes something like, "Yeah, I know it's good for me, but *I just don't have the time*." There's a great deal of truth such testimonials. We live in busy times, with responsibilities to and expectations from bosses, teachers, lovers, spouses, parents, kids, and friends. Sometimes it seems as though everyone is clamoring for a piece of us.

Being a parent has suddenly become very demanding: we have to be everything to our spouses and kids. There was a time when parental roles were simpler and the expectations fewer. Husbands and wives weren't expected to have such multidimensional roles in one another's lives or those of their children. Adults spent most of their social time with adults, and kids spent theirs with kids. Kids invented, played, and refereed their own neighborhood games. Many moms now spend a great deal of their time hauling kids to and from school, to the after-school organized sport leagues, and to day camps. Mom, Dad, and the kids used to have more time to do as they pleased.

There is also pressure on parents to schedule "quality time" with all other family members, leaving Mom and Dad with little time or no time to be with themselves. True quality time, of course, cannot be scheduled. It comes at totally unpredictable odd moments, when the moods and needs of the people involved converge.

The search for personal "time-out" space becomes even more difficult in families where both parents work and in split families where kids are traded off, sometimes between Dad and his new wife and Mom and her new husband. In such families, where guilt is a big player, kids are given an inordinate amount of power, further draining parental time resources.

But even among families with enormous time constraints, some parents make time to exercise. It's a matter of their priorities. Some are unwilling to put years of their lives and their own personal needs "on hold" while largely devoting themselves to satisfying the needs of others. Some parents realize that living for others, at some level, results in their resenting those others and that if they give their own personal needs a fair share of time, they will be more loving spouses and parents. This sort of behavior represents mentally healthy selfishness and not narcissism. Selflessness is not healthy and often is associated with depression.

Freud once wrote, "The price of consciousness is guilt." He believed that much of our important behavior was unconsciously driven and that to become more fully conscious, we had to admit some painful things to ourselves and subsequently begin to act in ways that reflected those admissions. For those of us who need to carve out a fair slice of time for ourselves, this often means saying no to some important people. We don't have to think very hard to identify those people in our lives. I used to tell my patients that the ticket to freedom—to truly be themselves—was to embrace their guilt.

GETTING OUR PRIORITIES STRAIGHT

Sometimes it's helpful to make lists. I suggest that you make a list of your responsibilities. This would at the very least include your responsibilities to lovers, spouses, kids, bosses, parents, and friends, as well as household responsibilities. Be specific, including items like "Driving Nancy to and from her dance lessons." When you've completed the list, carefully prioritize those responsibilities from most to least important. Where will you put "my fair share of my time" and "my present and future health?"

THE POWER OF KNOWLEDGE

Finally, there is the matter of this book. My primary purpose in writing it is to motivate sedentary readers to get moving by informing them about the benefits of active lives and the risks of inactive ones. For more than a dozen years, I taught a course at the university that focused on how exercise affects mental and physical health, and I was amazed at how the course content appeared to have an immediate impact on the lifestyles of many students. Often at each semester's end, a few reported that they had begun to exercise early on and how it had helped them end a depressive period or shed a substantial number of pounds. This book contains the essence of that semester-long course. If you're a reader who is ready for change, knowledge can sometimes provide ample motivation.

So when you're having a conversation in the mirror each day, talk about what you've learned. This book provides explicit risk numbers for specific physical disorders associated with being overweight, obese, a smoker, or sedentary. Look yourself in the eyes. Talk about those risks, how they can be reduced by physical activity, and what you plan on doing or not doing about yourself.

I have also provided specific information on how you can use exercise to deal with your depression and anxiety. Talk to yourself about what a single session or many sessions of exercise can do for your mental health, and talk about whether or not you are ready to take some responsibility for how you feel.

12.
DOING IT

In the world of exercise, nothing can compare to what walking has to offer those of us who are struggling to leave a sedentary life behind. If we seek fitness and better mental and physical health, *it may simply boil down to whether or not we are willing to walk in a society where walking is no longer required.*

There are a host of reasons why walking has become the most common form of exercise engaged in by active Americans. For starters, the kinds of physical activity that are most likely to become permanent fixtures are those that we can *easily integrate into a part of our everyday lives.* Some of us may be able to commute to work on a bicycle, but for the great majority of us, only walking fills the bill.

It's not too difficult to reprogram our lives and those of our children so that we walk more and ride less. If we cannot walk to work or to the stores where we shop, we can certainly park as far away as possible and work in some walking. While parking lots at shopping malls present some traffic hazards, such lots are typically enormous and offer us substantial walking distances if we resist the urge to compete for spots as close as possible to our target stores. This strategy also helps reduce the number of door dings on the side of your car, always a bonus.

Instead of meeting friends for lunch, a healthy alternative is meeting them for a long walk. When on the job, a brisk walk during the noon lunch hour can usually be worked into the schedule.

Walking can do more than just get us from one place to another. It can help us get work done at home, and it can be a part of our recreation. We can say goodbye to all of the hired services that tend to our lawn, garden, house-cleaning, and swimming pool. These tasks all involve being on our feet, moving around, elevating our heart rates, and burning calories. Some, like mowing the lawn, clearly offer a great aerobic workout. Taking over these tasks will save us money as well.

Walking can be a significant part of our recreation. During low-demand hours, we can walk the golf course instead of using a cart. Weekend outdoor hikes can become an activity to which we look forward.

Walking is convenient. Since we take our legs with us wherever we go, they are there for us to use whether we are in a strange city or country or between planes at an airport. Brisk walking between plane connections is marvelous for reducing tension and working the kinks out of our backs. When the weather is freezing or blistering hot, huge heated or air-conditioned indoor shopping malls make great walking venues. If we arrive about opening time, we are likely to find a number of walkers who have already discovered this option. We might find companions. However, for a great many of us, walking is as close as our front door.

Walking is economical. Our only investment is a high-quality pair of running shoes. Even if our intentions to exercise fade, we are left with a pair of the most comfortable shoes we've ever owned.

Another strong point (in contrast to many other activities such as biking, swimming, or rowing) is that *walking keeps our weight-bearing bones dense and strong.* This becomes increasingly critical as we age and face increased risks of falls and broken hips.

Walking is very easy to monitor. Time, distance, and pulse rates are easy to keep track of as we walk along in a safe environment. It's tougher to monitor our pulse rates when we are moving swiftly in circumstances that are sometimes hazardous (as on a bike when sharing roads with cars). One of the advantages of moving through the world slowly is that we are typically safer.

Because walking is relatively safe and easily monitored, it *allows us to progressively move through stages*, from slow to fast, or even on to jogging and running, depending on our goals. As in the case of lap swimming, time and distance are very easy to keep track of.

Walking allows us to satisfy many goals. We can (1) improve our moods, (2) shed pounds, and (3) reap a vast array of physical health benefits that follow when we enhance our cardio-respiratory fitness. Even long, slow walks will shed pounds. We know that walking at most intensities will improve our moods and that most of us can achieve aerobic training intensities while walking.

For example, in one study, several hundred men and women aged thirty to sixty-nine, were asked simply to "walk as fast as possible" for a measured mile. Overall, 67 percent of the men and 91 percent of the women were able to attain a mid-range aerobic training intensity of 70 percent HR_{max}. The lower percentage of men attaining the target intensity is explained by the fact that many of the men were highly fit prior to the test.

In the older (fifty to sixty-nine) group, 83 percent of the men and 91 percent of the women attained the target intensity while walking. Even the most highly fit younger men who were unable to attain the target intensity when simply asked to "walk as fast as possible" were able to do so when provided with pulse rate feedback monitors.[1]

If the target intensity had been set at 55 percent HR_{max} (which is appropriate for unfit and sedentary people who are just beginning an exercise program), it is likely that almost all of the participants would have attained that intensity when simply walking "as fast as possible."

What's so encouraging about the above findings is that virtually all of us can satisfy most psychological and physiological health goals through walking. What's even more encouraging is that the more out of shape we are and the older we are, the easier it is to attain an aerobic intensity.

Perhaps more than any other form of exercise, *walking offers us an ideal venue for socializing and companionship*. Even when we're walking briskly, it's easy to carry on a conversation with a friend.

I've been a morning runner for a very long time and have had occasion to observe fellow exercisers in both urban and rural mountain settings. I don't see men walking (or running) with other men anywhere nearly as often as I see pairs of women. I do see groups of men on racing bikes or mountain bikes silently following one another on roads and trails. During their rest stops, they seem to chat mostly about their bikes and rides. The guy thing.

On the other hand, women seem to walk or run in pairs very often, and they're always busy talking to each other. In my old urban neighborhood, almost every weekday morning, rain or shine, I ran into the same group of three women and their kids in strollers. They hustled along less-traveled urban byways, constantly chatting. I watched their kids eventually outgrow their strollers over the course of a few years, then the moms walked while the kids were in kindergarten.

Walking outdoors seems to have a healing effect. We typically enjoy a larger mood elevation when we exercise outside. Walking in the woods, in a park, or on the beach is not the same as working out on a treadmill in the spare room. Exposure to sunlight adds to the effects of exercise when days are short and so many of us are prone to suffer a seasonal affective disorder brand of mild depression. Walking or running in the rain, or in a soft snow-fall, is sometimes best of all: experiencing ourselves as a part of nature—the smells, the silence, the wind, the rain, or the touch of melting snowflakes on our faces.

For many of us, adults and children alike, riding a bicycle can also serve as a substitute for the SUV and can supplement walking when time and distance become significant factors. Some people who begin riding bicycles to and from work to solve traffic and parking problems discover that biking has other payoffs, and they continue to ride for the weight- and mood-control benefits that they only incidentally discover as the months pass.

Dozens of surveys have attempted to identify specific factors that will best predict sticking with exercise (adherence). The two most consistently powerful predictive factors turn out to be *convenience* and *social support*.[2]

The greater the distance from our homes to our exercise facilities, the less likely we are going to stick with our program. The three walking women with strollers knew what they were doing. They chose walking from their homes with neighborhood friends. Feeling like you might be coming down with a cold or not feeling like you wanted to walk in the rain don't hold up as excuses when friends, who are already all pumped up and ready to go, come knocking insistently on your door.

So you may be thinking that exercising at home is the way to go. It may or may not be. A residence can certainly satisfy the convenience criterion when it serves as home base for walking, running, or bicycling, even though we don't actually carry out those activities indoors. Those of us who exercise within our homes sometimes do aerobic dance with video music and instructors, use free weights, or utilize one or another kind of exercise machine.

Some of us take to the machines very well and systematically use them at home to accommodate our busy schedules. But there are others of us who can only work out on a machine in the social atmosphere of a fitness center and still others who can do so only when taking a supportive, trainer-led social fitness class at the facility.

On television there are very seductive advertisements that urge us to buy high-tech exercise machines (no money down and easy monthly installments). They typically feature ripped, closely shaved, and well-oiled handsome male and female models who demonstrate the machine while a voiceover suggests that with workouts of only twenty minutes three times a week we can soon look as good. Yeah, right.

Many of us discover that we are so very boredom-prone that our expensive new exercise machines quickly wind up in the closet or basement even before we've made our second paid installment.

Before investing in a machine, it's wise try it (them) out for a while. Perhaps you can borrow one from a friend who is no longer using it. Have her dig it out of her closet. If you like it, she may be willing to sell it cheaply. You can also invest in trial membership in a fitness club and try several machines over the course of a month or two. See whether any of them work well for you, or whether you find yourself resisting a workout on them. Consider whether your potential marriage to a machine will work in the solitude of your home, as against the social and supportive atmosphere of the club.

The slick television advertisements make it seem like the machines will almost magically do the work for us or will at least help us do the work. They won't. We may come to despise them. No matter how high-tech or zippy the design, machines won't motivate us to work up a sweat. It's up to us to provide the motivation, and that means we had better take a close look at who we are, what we can tolerate, and what our needs are when it comes to selecting a form of exercise or combination of exercises with which we can live.

WHO WE ARE AND WHAT WE NEED

Exercise can offer the "time-out" that so many of us need in our demanding lives. For those of us whose personal boundaries are constantly battered by the demands of others on the job or at home, peace of mind may come only in the form of solitary exercise in a distraction-free and safe environment, a place where we aren't obligated to even talk with any one. This could be an hour with our weights in the garage, a ride along a bike trail, laps in a nearby pool, or a walk or run in the park. Cell phones not allowed.

Others of us may find such solitary activities boring and insufficient when it comes to taking our minds off our worries. We may require social activities or the challenge of competition to distract ourselves and hold our interest enough to keep us working out. Commercial fitness centers, the YMCA, and adult sport leagues offer all sorts of options for organized play.

Another solution for those of us who are easily bored and need more external stimulation is to mix up our physical activities and change our surroundings. We may do aerobic dance three days a week for cardio-respiratory fitness and take some long walks or bicycle rides a couple days a week for working off pounds. We can mix social with solitary, aerobic with anaerobic, and competitive with noncompetitive.

Where we live can also be an important factor in choosing a kind of exercise that we can easily work into our lives. Living close to a fitness center, a high school or community college track, a YMCA, a swimming pool, a mountain fire trail, the beach, a cross-country ski area, a park, or a nature preserve can importantly influence what we will do and how long we are likely to stick with it. Close is good.

Sometimes when getting started, we might consider paying a visit to an old, neglected friend—a sport we once loved. Most of us have a sport history with particular physical activities or games that were our favorites when we were kids, in high school, or in college. Our old favorites might still kindle our athletic fires and make sweating a pleasure. Or maybe something new has come along that looks good to us. Even at my age, with reflexes and balance heading south, I still find myself very tempted to take snowboard lessons. I haven't yet done so because the possibility of injuring myself and being unable to run every day is unacceptable.

Sometimes a friend can help us get started. Maybe we know someone who is regularly doing aerobic dance or some other physical activity that looks inviting to us. Getting started with a supportive friend is a fine alternative to starting off alone.

In the world of sports, there is something or some things for everyone. Finding the right niche is essential.

AVOIDING PROBLEMS

First off, it's prudent to *check with our physician* to determine whether it is safe for us to begin to exercise. This is especially important if we are routinely taking medications of any kind or if we belong to a high-risk group. Examples of a few such groups would be the overweight, the obese, the hypertensive, those who have high blood sugar levels or are diabetic, those with a family history of heart attacks or strokes, and smokers. Our physician may recommend that we take a maximal treadmill stress test before embarking on an athletic journey or that we begin to exercise only in an approved group under close supervision.

Second, *moderation should be the rule* in all things related to exercise. We are most likely to stick with exercise, avoid injuries, and realize the many benefits of regular physical activity if we consistently set modest goals.

Basic to avoiding problems when we take up physical activity is using *the right equipment*. Here are some tips for those of you who are considering taking up walking.

Even if you think you'll never move from walking to jogging or running, buying a pair of "walkers" may not be the best choice. It's wiser to invest in a pair of high-quality running shoes or cross trainers. Today's running shoes represent decades of development and are something quite special. They are light, cooler than leather, and they offer the kind of firm heel support and cushioning that allows us to exercise on all kinds of surfaces. Most of the name brand companies make both economy and high-quality models.

You can currently get into a high-quality pair of running shoes or cross trainers for about $75 to $100. You should avoid the most expensive new models. They can cost well over $100, and their styling pluses sometimes subtract from their functionality. Too much high-style, unventilated surface area can turn your feet into furnaces. Seek out a pair with areas of open mesh that will allow your feet to breathe and stay cool. You're not buying shoes to make a fashion statement, so ugly is just fine, and hot is not.

Quality shoes flex in only one place (at the ball of the foot), are well cushioned, and have a very firm heel cup. Trail running shoes (not hiking shoes) tend to have a broader, more stable heel and more corrugated tread patterns that reduce the risk of slipping and falling on loose dirt and gravel surfaces. Many regular running shoe models also have this desirable broad heel footprint. Look for it, and be sure to buy your shoes larger than you may be accustomed to. While standing up, allow a full thumb width distance between the end of your longest toe and the front of the shoe's toe cavity. Having shoes that are too short can quickly make walking or running downhill a nightmare.

Some outdoor equipment stores that sell a variety of hiking boots in addition to running shoes provide a steep surface in the shoe section, where you can check out toe box room when you're facing or walking downhill. Try it. Sometimes satisfying this generous but necessary thumb width criterion is problematical for women, in that they may find the heel cup too large. Two pair of socks is the usual solution.

Since all name brand manufacturers make high-quality shoes, buy the pair that feels best. Rely on your feet rather than the salesperson. *Your feet will let you know when you find the right pair*. If you can't find them in one store, try another that may offer additional brands. Most stores will let you give the shoes a try and invite you to walk or jog around in the store or even outside. Do it. If you find the right pair, you'll probably never again be without running shoes in your lifetime. They are sweet for our feet.

STRETCHING, WARM-UP, AND COOL-DOWN

Most experts agree that we are inviting injury if we launch into high-intensity exercise without a warm-up period to prepare our muscles for the demands we will make on them. In most cases, the warm-up can be accomplished by beginning our chosen brand of exercise at a very moderate intensity: a slow walk before we begin to lengthen our stride and pick up our pace, an easy jog before we begin running, running before we begin periodic sprints, working from light weights on up to heavier ones, or starting our bike ride at an easy pace. Warming up, by engaging in our target exercise at a moderate intensity, prepares the specific muscle groups that we will be stressing during our workout, whether we're swimming, bicycling, or lifting weights.

It's also important to cool down if our exercise has been very intense, essentially reversing the warm-up procedure. For example, if you have been running at a moderately intense pace, a block or so before your stopping point, slow to a jog, move into a brisk walk, and finally slow to a walk. This progression translates easily into other forms of aerobic exercise. The cool down gives our circulatory systems and muscles a chance to readjust slowly and safely to the changes in demands.

While stretching is essential prior to some forms of exercise, it can open the door for injury in others. The hundreds of walkers and runners I have known quite universally stretch only after finishing their workouts, when their muscles are warm and flexible. Many had learned the hard way that attempting to stretch cold muscles prior to running could lead to tissue damage.

INJURIES

No matter how careful we are, injuries are going to happen. As pointed out in chapter 10, women and overweight men run the highest risks of injury, and many of us who experience an early "born-again" phase in our exercise history can unknowingly fall into exercise abuse. Overuse and bad judgment can play a large role in our injuries. The very motives that cause us to overdo exercise make it hard for us to stop when we injure ourselves through overuse or misfortune.

Many of us go from one doctor to another, hoping that one will give us the pill, the shots, the bandage, the ultrasound, or other special magic intervention that will make it possible for us to continue to engage in our preferred form of exercise while our injuries heal. If we survive this perilous journey without doing irreparable damage, and if we learn from it, we may be able to continue our favorite form of exercise for life.

"If it hurts, don't use it," should become our own personal guideline.

Often there are alternative forms of exercise that will allow us to stay fit while we heal. It's no fun to leave our first love behind for a while and settle for a second best, but the alternative of no exercise at all is a grim one.

If we are taking up walking or running, spending too much time on hills can cause problems for many of us. Specifically, going downhill presents hazards. There is the matter of loose gravel and other slippery surfaces such as mud, snow, or ice that can suddenly slam us to the ground and sometimes create larger problems than just abrasions and a headache. Walking and running downhill create large G-forces on our lower extremities, especially on our knee joints. Fortunately, our knees will let us know if we are doing too much downhill walking or running, and those pain signals offer us the option of either doing it less frequently or at more moderate speeds. If your knees are talking to you, you'd better listen.

A WALKING PROGRAM

We can walk on a treadmill, in the neighborhood, or in a nearby park. For maximal mood benefits, it's essential to walk in an environment where only minimal attention is required to keep us safe from traffic or other threats.

Monitoring the time we spend walking, rather than how fast or how far we walk, is the best strategy because it encourages moderation. Most of us can initially manage to walk for twenty to thirty minutes. Walking ten or fifteen minutes out from our starting point, turning around, and heading back is an easy plan, and something we can work into our lives, a minimum of three times a week.

Our pace should be modest. Our only concern should be to avoid exceeding a sensible pulse rate. Those of us who are very unfit, sedentary, and overweight should start walking within the 55–65 percent HR_{max} range. Even this very modest beginning pace will burn calories, elevate our moods, and gradually build aerobic fitness. It's also not likely to result in injuries, and it's not so demanding that we are likely to give up and return to the couch full-time.

When our increased fitness tells us that we are ready, we can increase our walking time, our speed, or the number of days we walk during each week. We can monitor our aerobic fitness by checking our resting pulse rate once a week. Count heartbeats for a full minute when totally relaxed and lying down. Sometimes the second minute is a more accurate reading. As we get in shape, our pulse rates will gradually decrease.

If we check our pulse rates each morning before getting out of bed and find one day that it is five or ten beats above our usual reading, this may be a signal that our body is busy contending with an invading virus. Might be a time to go easy or take the day off from exercise.

If our main concern is weight loss, over the course of weeks or month we can gradually move toward *walking for an entire hour at an easy pace* and eventually consider walking more than three days a week. My routine prescription for overweight patients has been that they work up to a one-hour daily walk. Those who were able to do so lost weight, elevated their moods, enhanced their feelings of control, and boosted their self-esteem. Some, who chose to become more aerobically fit, moved from walking to jogging, then on to running. This increased fat-burning capacity allowed them to decrease their exercise time and still get the weight-control benefits.

If our main concern is for increased aerobic fitness, we can choose to stay within a thirty-minute time frame and move from brisk walking into a walk/jog regimen. After walking to warm up, we jog until we need to ease off, then walk to regain our breath, then jog, and so on. As the weeks go by, we will be able to jog more and more of the time, until we can do so for an entire half hour.

Jogging for half an hour three or four days a week is enough for us to maintain minimal aerobic fitness. Of course, the ability to jog for thirty minutes can be a springboard to run farther, faster, or more frequently (depending on our goals).

It's important to keep in mind that our primary goal is simply to become more physically active. Our initial main focus should not be on our stopwatch, mileage, pulse rate, or caloric burn. It should be on getting moving and keeping moving. The psychological benefits will be invaluable to us and to others who are important in our lives.

Whether we are beginners or experienced athletes, the problem often comes down to taking that first step each day. There are all sorts of excuses and reasons that we shouldn't do so: not feeling just right, too much to do, the weather, not enough time, and on and on. Taking that first step is critical, no matter what confronts us. Even what seems to be impossible can only be accomplished if we begin. If we can just lean forward and take that first step, the remaining steps will fall into place, and so, very often, will our lives.

EPILOGUE
A BRIDGE OVER TROUBLE WATERS

USING EXERCISE TO COPE WITH STRESS

Friedrich Nietzsche once wrote: "A man's stride betrays whether he has found his way. . . . I love to run swiftly, and though there are swamps and thick melancholy on earth, whoever has light feet runs even over mud and dances as on swept ice."[1]

Nietzsche, of course, was not the first to have arrived at the personal conviction that exercise can importantly influence how we feel and that it can also help us make it through tough times.

Several hundred years before the time of Jesus, the Greeks were similarly convinced of this mind-body connection. Greeks of all ages routinely exercised for many hours each day during those golden years. It was apparently Homer who coined the phrase *Mens sana in corpore sano*, which translates to "Healthy mind in a healthy body." Over the centuries, it has been simplified into "Sound mind, sound body."[2]

Conviction on the order of Nietzsche's comes about only after months and years of regular vigorous exercise. Something so precious does not come cheap, nor can it be purchased with traditional currency. Dues are payable only in the form of sweat. Once acquired, this knowledge is deep: a credo of faith, a hard-earned conviction, proven over and over again without exception. Experienced endurance athletes simply take this knowledge for granted. Exercise can make them feel better and get them through tough times. It constitutes matter-of-fact tribal wisdom.

Nietzsche advised us that aerobic fitness, this ability to run swiftly on light feet, can carry us safely through the mud, swamps, and thick melancholy that we inevitably encounter on our journeys through life. His message is important. He's suggesting that fitness not only can affect how we feel, but it may also have a preventative effect: It may help us avoid falling into the depression and despair that frequently occur during times of prolonged stress.

Nietzsche speaks powerfully in metaphors. I want to end this book by sharing with you (in real-life terms) how exercise helped me survive a truly awful extended period of stress in my own life. Those months were so very difficult that I was later compelled to record the experience on paper. The result was the nonfiction short story that follows. Read on.

THE TRUTH COOKIES

It was a relief when Bill Fujima finally sold his family's old Japan Town café, the Mandarin. On those rare occasions when the stakes were enormous, when all the cards were on the table, and when all the chips were down, his fortune cookies invariably spoke the pure truth.

My first such experience was on a terrible December night many years ago. That afternoon, the sky had turned black early on as a winter storm front came surging in from the south. It carried wind, rain, and a PSA jet that delivered a woman who was central in my life. Our difficult two-year relationship was now further strained by professional decisions that had separated us by five hundred miles a few months earlier. This weekend we would decide if the future held any hope of our remaining a pair.

We left the airport as night descended and headed toward the warmth and security of a private booth next to Bill's steaming kitchen. At closing time, except for the two us, the place was empty. So were we. Hours of talk had resolved nothing. I finally thought to check out my fortune cookie to see what our future held in store. It held a blank slip of paper: the first blank slip in more than twenty years of reading weekly "benign fortunes" at the Mandarin. I felt like throwing up.

My next big-stakes encounter with Bill's fortune cookies came eight or so years later. I had left the university one warm summer day for an appointment with my urologist. Two weeks before, he had said not to worry, but I might have cancer. Odds only about one in three. Not to worry he said. Our secret. Today I would find out for sure. I intended to head straight to Los Gatos and the clinic, but my aged pickup truck, with a loving set of the most nurturing maneuvers, parked me right in front of the Mandarin. What the hell, I had a little time.

The place was empty at midafternoon, and for a half hour I was warmed by a big steaming bowl of mushroom beef noodles and the full attention of the Fujimas. I was about to leave when Bill's wife, Sue, laid a fortune cookie in front of me. My heart stopped. It was as if she had upended a gunnysack and dumped a rattlesnake on the table. I could neither open it nor leave it. After a brief moment of paralysis, I stuck it into my shirt pocket and split for the doctor's office.

It had been the worst six months of my life—one of those periods where the hammer just kept on falling. There had been signs that the coming year would be a tough one, so to care for myself I had begun to train seriously, slowly increasing my mileage, adding a weekly long run, aiming for two marathons.

On New Year's Day, the dark clouds that had lingered on the horizon for months finally arrived, and a seven-year relationship ended. She moved out that day. With son Mark and daughter Paula long since departed, I was left with our old Irish setter and my last resident son, Kris, who was off skiing for the holidays. Not the greatest opening act for the New Year.

However, one nice thing about a long run on a winter holiday is that the roads are empty of everything, save dead leaves shuffling along before you on the wind. Soon I settled into a fifteen-miles-every-other-day routine, and, in late January, I lowered my personal best time by more than half an hour when I ran the Paul Masson Champagne Marathon in Saratoga. I would never run a faster time.

Not long after, my son moved out to set up housekeeping with his future wife, and my dreams reminded me that I had completed yet another passage.

I began to concentrate on my form and breathing, aiming for the the San Francisco Marathon. Then one spring morning as I was leaving for an early training run, I was puzzled to discover that my back door appeared to be jammed. I looked down and saw our old setter lying there. He was very still. My two sons, Mark and Kris, came over later with a twelve-pack of beer and a young peach tree from the nursery. We drank beer and reminisced while we dug his grave, shed our tears, said our good-byes, and buried our friend in our backyard, where his remains would nourish his memorial peach tree.

Meanwhile, my urologist kept me waiting. He was very relaxed when he finally greeted me. It wasn't his biopsy. He smiled and reminded me that he had told me that I probably had nothing to worry about. What a guy.

When I got home, I uncorked a chilled bottle of my best white wine and poured a generous glass. Time to celebrate life. But as I raised the glass I remembered the fortune cookie. I set the glass down and retrieved Bill's fortune cookie from my pocket, figuring it was now safe to see what it had to say. I shuddered when I read, "Among the chosen few, you are the lucky one."

Once again I reached for the glass. This time the phone interrupted. I thought at first that the caller was either drunk and had a wrong number, or was a child playing a prank. Sounded like a sobbing little girl, and I nearly hung up. Then, when I finally made out the words, "Your father is dead," I knew that little girl was my mother.

After a long, tortured talk I put down the phone, dumped the wine, put on my running gear, and headed for the foothills. The day had become more than I could handle. I needed to leave it behind. Not easy.

As I ran, I discovered that I needed a mantra to escape from my internal conversations and grief. With each footfall I uttered, "con-cen-trate, con-cen-trate." Breathe in every four strides on the downhills, every third on the flats, and every two on the uphills. Remember to pump your arms and use your upper body strength on the hills. Stay off your heels. Imagine that a powerful elastic cord is raising your knees up toward your chest and that a great ski lift is magically pulling you up the hills. Let nothing into your mind. If your mind begins to wander, you must chant and go faster. Con-cen-trate, con-cen-trate.

When the hills had done their work, it was cold and nearly dark. I felt like an exhausted child, a long way from home. I glanced at my watch and found three hours had passed.

Shivering and dehydrated, I stuck out my thumb, and eventually got a ride toward home. The next day my bicycle's odometer told me that the route I had taken the afternoon before was nearly twenty-five miles. I had run the race of my life. Never again would I run so far so fast. A week later I hit the wall at mile seventeen in the San Francisco Marathon. I had nothing left.

I went home and bought a puppy. The act of loving had, over the past six months, become almost impossibly hazardous. I figured that I had to start somewhere. She was an Alaskan malamute whom I selected from the litter because of her social forwardness, her self-assurance, and her markings, which were those of a timber wolf. I named her Tasha, the Arapaho

Indian word for that sacred animal. Perhaps she could one day penetrate the shroud of numbness that had mercifully descended.

There are times when no matter how hard we try, we just can't seem to get the wine to our lips. When loss and grief come rolling in like successive great gray winter storm waves, we must find an occasional harbor or simply perish on the rocks. Grieving takes a year or two, no matter how we cut it. It has got to get spaced out. We must sleep. We must function. There are many ways to distract or self-medicate ourselves. Some eventually add to our misery, some are dangerous, and others are lethal. None can match the beneficence of physical activity.

NOTES

Chapter 1

1. J. McGinnis and W. Foege, "Actual Causes of Death in the United States," *Journal of the American Medical Association* 18 (1993): 2207–12.

2. M. Brunet and M.P.F.T., "A New Hominid from the Upper Miocene of Chad," *Nature* (July 2002).

3. L. Cavalli-Sforza and M. Feldman, "The Application of Molecular Genetic Approaches to the Study of Human Evolution," *Nature Genetics* 23 (1999): 266–75.

4. L. Quintana-Murci et al., "Genetic Evidence of an Early Exit of *Homo Sapiens Sapiens* from Africa Through Eastern Africa," *Nature Genetics* 23 (1999): 437–41.

5. P. Underhill et al., "Y Chromosome Sequence Variation and the History of Human Population," *Nature Genetics* 26 (2000): 358–61.

6. Robert Hotz, "Intriguing Clues to First Americans," *San Jose Mercury News* (March 28, 1998).

7. D. Keefer et al., "Early Maritime Economy and El Niño Events at Quebrada Tacahuay, Peru," *Science* 281 (1998): 1833.

8. Hotz, "Intriguing Clues to First Americans."

9. A. Leaf, "Unusual Longevity: The Common Denominator," *Hospital Practice* 8 (1973): 75–78.

10. "Rural Corner of China Boasts Long-Lived Farmers," *San Jose Mercury News* (November 16, 1997).

11. J. Brody, "Adventists Are Gold Mine of Data on Diet and Longevity," *San Jose Mercury News* (November 29, 1986).

12. J. Enstrom, "Health Practices and Cancer Mortality among Active California Mormons," *Journal of the National Cancer Institute* 81 (1989): 1807–14.

13. L. Breslow and J. Enstrom, "Persistence of Health Habits and Their Relationship to Mortality," *Preventive Medicine* 9 (1980): 469–83; J. Brody, "The Seven Unhealthy Sins and How They're Growing: The More of Them You Practice Now, the Sooner You Face Disability or Death," *San Jose Mercury News* (June 23, 1993).

14. J. Fries and L. Crapo, *Vitality and Aging* (San Francisco: Freeman, 1981).

15. Ibid.

16. McGinnis and Foege, "Actual Causes of Death," pp. 2207–12.

17. K. Flegal et al., "Prevalence and Trends in Obesity among U.S. Adults," *Journal of the American Medical Association* 288 (2002): 1723–27.

18. D. Kirschenbaum, "Toward the Prevention of Sedentary Lifestyles," in *Exercise and Mental Health*, ed. W. Morgan and S. Goldston (Washington, DC: Hemisphere, 1987), pp. 17–35.

19. K. Johnsgard and B. Ogilvie, "The Competition Driver: A Preliminary Report," *Journal of Sports Medicine and Physical Fitness* 8 (1968): 87–95; K. Johnsgard, B. Ogilvie, and K. Merritt, "The Stress-Seekers: A Psychological Study of Sports Parachutists, Racing Drivers, and Football Players," *Journal of Sports Medicine and Physical Fitness* 15 (1975): 158–69; K. Johnsgard, "Personality and Performance: A Psychological Study of Amateur Sports Car Drivers," *Journal of Sports Medicine and Physical Fitness* 17 (1977): 97–104.

20. J. Bule, "'Me' Decades Generate Depression," *APA Monitor* (October 1983); J. Myers et al., "Six-Month Prevalence of Psychiatric Disorders in Three Communities," *Archives of General Psychiatry* 41 (1984): 959–67; D. Regier et al., "The NIMH Epidemiologic Catchment Area Program," *Archives of General Psychiatry* 41 (1984): 934–41; L. Robins et al., "Lifetime Prevalence of Specific Psychiatric Disorders in Three Sites," *Archives of General Psychiatry* 41 (1984): 949–58.

21. Bule, "'Me' Decades Generate Depression."

22. Myers et al., "Six-Month Prevalence of Psychiatric Disorders," pp. 959–67; Regier et al., "NIMH Epidemiologic Catchment Area Program," pp. 934–41; Robins et al., "Lifetime Prevalence," pp. 949–58.

23. R. Kessler et al., "Lifetime and 12-Month Prevalence of DSM-III-R Psychiatric Disorders in the United States," *Archives of General Psychiatry* 51 (1994): 8–19.

24. J. A. Egeland, D. S. Gerhard et al. "Bipolar Affective Disorders Linked to DNA Markers on Chromosome 11," *Nature* 325 (1987): 783–87.

25. M. G. Allen, "Twin Studies in Affective Illness," *Archives of General Psychiatry* 33 (1976): 1476–78.

26. J. Murphy et al., "Stability of Prevalence: Depression and Anxiety Disorders," *Archives of General Psychiatry* 41 (1984): 990–97.

27. Kessler et al., "Lifetime and 12-Month Prevalence," pp. 8–19.

28. Steve Johnson, "Immigrants' Family Health Sinks," *San Jose Mercury News* (September 10, 1998).

29. W. Vega, "Lifetime Prevalence of DSM-III-R Psychiatric Disorders among Urban and Rural Mexican Americans in California," *Archives of General Psychiatry* 55 (1998): 771–78.

Chapter 2

1. E. McClam, "Americans Need More Exercise," *San Jose Mercury News* (April 7, 2002).

2. Department of Health and Human Services, *Physical Activity and Health: A Report of the Surgeon General* (Atlanta: U.S. Department of Health and Human Services, 1996).

3. E. Hsiao and R. Thayer, "Exercising for Mood Regulation: The Importance of Experience," *Journal of Personality and Individual Differences* 24 (1998): 829–36.

4. K. Johnsgard, "You're Never Too Old," *Runner's World* (July 1981).

5. K. Johnsgard and E. Suggs, "Why We Do It: A Psychological Study of *Running Times* Readers," *Running Times* (May 1985); K. Johnsgard, "The Motivation of the Long-Distance Runner: I," *Journal of Sports Medicine and Physical Fitness* 25 (1985): 135–39.

6. B. Edmiston, "The Motivation of Women Distance Runners and Aerobic Dancers" (senior thesis, San Jose State University, 1984).

7. Johnsgard and Suggs, "Why We Do It"; Johnsgard, "Motivation of the Long-Distance Runner: I," pp. 135–39.

8. Johnsgard, "You're Never Too Old."

9. K. Johnsgard, "The Motivation of the Long-Distance Runner: II," *Journal of Sports Medicine and Physical Fitness* 25 (1985): 140–43.

10. K. Johnsgard, *The Exercise Prescription for Depression and Anxiety* (New York: Plenum, 1989).

11. Hsiao and Thayer, "Exercising for Mood Regulation," pp. 829–36.

12. Johnsgard and Suggs, "Why We Do It."

13. P. Hoffman, "The Endorphin Hypothesis," in *Physical Activity and Mental Health*, ed. W. Morgan (Washington, DC: Taylor & Francis, 1997), pp. 163–77.

14. M. Csikszentmihalyi, "If We Are So Rich, Why Aren't We Happy?" *American Psychologist* (October 1999): 821–27.

15. M. Carmack and R. Martens, "Measuring Commitment to Running: A Survey of Runner's Attitudes and Mental States," *Journal of Sports Psychology* 1 (1979): 25–42; Hsiao and Thayer, "Exercising for Mood Regulation," pp. 829–36; W. Vitulli, "Manifest Reasons for Jogging," *Perceptual and Motor Skills* 64 (1987): 650.

16. H. Eysenck and M. Eysenck, *Personality and Individual Differences: A Natural Science Approach* (New York: Plenum, 1985).

17. M. Zuckerman, *The Psychobiology of Personality* (New York: Cambridge University Press, 1991), p. 27.

18. P. Costa and R. Macrae, *The NEO PI:FFI Manual Supplement* (Odessa, FL: Psychological Assessment Resources, 1989).

19. Hsiao and Thayer, "Exercising for Mood Regulation," pp. 829–36.

Chapter 3

1. American College of Sports Medicine, "Position Stand: The Recommended Quantity and Quality of Exercise for Developing and Maintaining Cardiorespiratory and Muscular Fitness, and Flexibility in Healthy Adults," *Medicine and Science in Sports and Exercise* 30, no. 6 (1998): 975–91.

2. V. Foster et al., "Endurance Training for Elderly Women: Moderate versus Low Intensity," *Journal of Gerontology* 44 (1989): 184–88.

3. R. Debusk et al., "Training Effects of Long versus Short Bouts of Exercise in Healthy Subjects," *American Journal of Cardiology* 65 (1990): 1010–13.

Chapter 4

1. M. Zuckerman, *The Psychobiology of Personality* (New York: Cambridge University Press, 1991), p. 27.

2. W. Sime, "Exercise in the Prevention and Treatment of Depression," in *Exercise and Mental Health*, ed. W. Morgan and S. Goldston (Washington, DC: Hemisphere, 1987), pp. 146–48.

3. D. Lobstein et al., "Depression as a Powerful Discriminator Between Physically Active and Sedentary Middle-Aged Men," *Journal of Psychosomatic Medicine* 27 (1983): 69–76.

4. D. McNair et al., *Profile of Mood States Manual* (San Diego: Educational and Industrial Testing Service, 1971).

5. W. Morgan, "Test of Champions: The Iceberg Profile," *Psychology Today* (July 1980): 92–99.

6. B. Berger and D. Owen, "Mood Alteration with Swimming: Swimmers Really Do 'Feel Better,'" *Psychosomatic Medicine* 45 (1983): 425–31.

7. B. Berger and D. Owen, "Stress Reduction and Mood Enhancement in Four Exercise Modes: Swimming, Body Conditioning, Hatha Yoga, and Fencing," *International Journal of Sport Psychology* 18 (1987): 431–37.

8. D. Harris, "Comparative Effectiveness of Running Therapy and Psychotherapy," in *Exercise and Mental Health*, ed. W. Morgan and S. Goldston (Washington, DC: Hemisphere, 1987), pp. 126–28.

9. R. Brown et al., "The Prescription of Exercise for Depression," *Physician and Sportsmedicine* 6 (1978): 34–49.

10. W. Zung, "Self-Rating Depression Scale," *Archives of General Psychiatry* 12 (1965): 63–70.

11. W. Morgan and M. Pollock, "Physical Activity and Cardiovascular Health: Psychological Aspects," in *Physical Activity and Human Well-Being*, ed. F. Laundry and W. Orban (Miami: Symposia Specialists, 1978), pp. 163–81.

12. Ibid.

13. W. Morgan et al., "Psychological Effect of Acute Physical Activity," *Archives of Physical Medicine and Rehabilitation* 52 (1971): 422–25.

14. T. Nelson and W. Morgan, "Acute Effects of Exercise on Mood in Depressed Female Students," *Medicine and Science in Sports and Exercise* 26 (supplement 1994): 156.

15. L. Leith, *Foundations of Exercise and Mental Health* (Morgantown, WV: Fitness Information Technology, 1994), pp. 151–55.

16. Ibid.

17. S. Biddle et al., *Physical Activity and Psychological Well-Being* (London: Routledge, 2000), pp. 77–80.

18. T. Stephens, "Physical Activity and Mental Health in the United States and Canada: Evidence from Four Population Surveys," *Preventive Medicine* 17 (1988): 35–47.

19. P. O'Connor, "Overtraining and Staleness," in *Physical Activity and Mental Health*, ed. W. Morgan (Washington, DC: Taylor & Francis, 1997), pp. 145–59.

20. W. Morgan et al., "Psychological Monitoring of Overtraining and Staleness," *British Journal of Sports Medicine* 17 (1987): 107–14.

21. O'Connor, "Overtraining and Staleness," pp. 145–59.

22. J. Raglin et al., "Changes in Mood State During Training in Female and Male College Swimmers," *International Journal of Sports Medicine* 12 (1991): 146–59.

23. O'Connor, "Overtraining and Staleness," pp. 145–59.

24. R. Sonstroem, "Physical Activity and Self-Esteem," in *Physical Activity and Mental Health*, ed. W. Morgan (Washington, DC: Taylor & Francis, 1997), pp. 127–44.

25. Ibid.; Leith, *Foundations of Exercise and Mental Health*, pp. 151–55.

26. Leith, *Foundations of Exercise and Mental Health*, pp. 151–55.

27. Ibid.; Sonstroem, "Physical Activity and Self-Esteem," pp. 127–44.

28. A. King et al., "Influence of Regular Aerobic Exercise on Psychological Health: A Randomized, Controlled Trial of Healthy Middle-Aged Adults," *Health Psychology* 8 (1989): 305–24.

29. D. Ossip-Klein et al., "Effects of Running or Weight-Lifting on Self-Concept in Clinically Depressed Women," *Journal of Consulting and Clinical Psychology* 57 (1989): 158–61.

30. H. Marsh, "A Multidimensional Self-Concept: A Social Psychological Perspective," *Annual Review of Psychology* 38 (1990): 299–337.

31. Sonstroem, "Physical Activity and Self-Esteem," pp. 127–44.

32. Leith, *Foundations of Exercise and Mental Health*, pp. 151–55.

33. A. Bandura, "Self-Efficacy: Toward a Unifying Theory of Behavior Change," *Psychological Review* 84 (1977): 191–215.

Chapter 5

1. R. Kessler et al., "Lifetime and 12-Month Prevalence of DSM-III-R Psychiatric Disorders in America: Results from the National Comorbidity Survey," *Archives of General Psychiatry* 51, no. 1 (1994): 8–19.

2. S. Stahl, *Essential Psychopharmacology: Neuroscientific Basis and Practical Implications* (Cambridge: Cambridge University Press, 2000), p. 298.

3. American Psychiatric Association, *Diagnostic and Statistical Manual of Mental Disorders* (Washington, DC: American Psychiatric Association, 1994).

4. C. Spielberger, *Manual for the State-Trait Anxiety Inventory* (Palo Alto, CA: Consulting Psychologists Press, 1983).

5. Ibid.

6. L. Leith, *Foundations of Exercise and Mental Health* (Morgantown, WV: Fitness Information Technology, 1994), pp. 69–74.

7. J. Raglin, "Anxiolytic Effects of Physical Activity," in *Physical Activity and Mental Health*, ed. W. Morgan (Washington, DC: Taylor & Francis, 1997), p. 113.

8. J. Raglin et al., "State Anxiety and Blood Pressure Following 30 Minutes of Leg Ergometry or Weight Training," *Medicine and Science in Sports and Exercise* 28 (1993): 372–77.

9. K. Koltyn et al., "Influence of Weight Training on State Anxiety, Body Awareness, and Blood Pressure," *Medicine and Science in Sports and Exercise* 16 (1993): 266–69.

10. Raglin et al., "State Anxiety and Blood Pressure," pp. 372–77.

11. Leith, *Foundations of Exercise and Mental Health*, p. 53.

12. J. Taylor, "A Personality Scale of Manifest Anxiety," *Journal of Abnormal and Social Psychology* 48 (1953): 285–90.

13. Leith, *Foundations of Exercise and Mental Health*, p. 61.

14. Raglin, "Anxiolytic Effects of Physical Activity," p. 113.

15. J. Moses et al., "The Effects of Exercise Training on Mental Well-Being in the Normal Population," *Journal of Psychosomatic Research* 33 (1989): 47–61.

16. M. Barkhe and W. Morgan, "Anxiety Reduction Following Exercise and Meditation," *Cognitive Therapy and Research* 2 (1978): 323–34.

17. J. Raglin and W. Morgan, "Influence of Exercise and Quiet Rest on State Anxiety and Blood Pressure," *Medicine and Science in Sports and Exercise* 19 (1987): 456–63.

18. M. J. Breus and P. J. O'Conner, "Exercise-Induced Anxiolysis: A Test of the 'Time-Out' Hypothesis in High Anxious Females," *Medicine and Science in Sports and Exercise* 30, no. 7 (1998): 1107–12.

19. H. de Vries, "Tranquilizer Effect of Exercise: A Critical Review," *Physician and Sportsmedicine* 9 (1981): 46–55.

20. Ibid.

21. K. Koltyn, "The Thermogenic Hypothesis," in *Physical Activity and Mental Health*, ed. W. Morgan (Washington, DC: Taylor & Francis, 1997), p. 113.

22. J. Buckworth and R. Dishman, *Exercise Psychology* (Champaign, IL: Human Kinetics, 2000), p. 129; P. Hoffman, "The Endorphin Hypothesis," in *Physical Activity and Mental Health*, ed. W. Morgan (Washington, DC: Taylor & Francis, 1997), p. 173.

23. Hoffman, "Endorphin Hypothesis," p. 171.

24. Ibid., p. 175.

25. O. Appenzeller and D. Shade, "Neurology of Endurance Training: 3. Sympathetic Activity During a Marathon Race [Abstract]," *Neurology* 29 (1979): 542.

26. R. Dishman, "The Norepinephrine Hypothesis," in *Physical Activity and Mental Health*, ed. W. Morgan (Washington, DC: Taylor & Francis, 1997), p. 203.

27. Stahl, *Essential Psychopharmacology*, pp. 306–23.

28. Buckworth and Dishman, *Exercise Psychology*, p. 129.

29. E. Martinsen et al., "Aerobic Exercise in the Treatment of Non-Psychotic Mental Disorders: An Exploratory Study," *Nordic Journal of Psychiatry* 43 (1989): 411–15.

30. E. Martinsen et al., "Aerobic and Non-Aerobic Forms of Exercise in the Treatment of Anxiety Disorders," *Stress Medicine* 5 (1989): 115–20.

31. H. Sexton et al., "Exercise Intensity and Reduction of Neurotic Symptoms: A Controlled Follow-Up Study," *Acta Psychiatrica Scandinavia* 80 (1989): 231–35.

32. Kessler et al., "Lifetime and 12-Month Prevalence," pp. 8–19.

33. Stahl, *Essential Pharmacology*, p. 347.

34. Ibid., pp. 352–54.

35. D. Barlow and J. Cerny, *Psychological Treatment of Panic Disorder* (New York: Guilford Press, 1988).

36. F. Pitts and J. McClure, "Lactate Metabolism in Anxiety Neurosis," *New England Journal of Medicine* 277: 1329–36.

37. P. O'Connor, "Anxiety Disorders and Physical Activity," *Exercise & Sport Psychology News: APA Division 47* (fall 2000).

38. A. Broocks et al., "Comparison of Aerobic Exercise, Clomipramine, and Placebo in the Treatment of Panic Disorder," *American Journal of Psychiatry* 155 (1998): 603–609.

39. Kessler et al., "Lifetime and 12-Month Prevalence," pp. 8–19.

40. Stahl, *Essential Psychopharmacology*, pp. 352–54.

41. A. Orwin, "Running Treatment: A Preliminary Communication on a New Use of an Old Therapy (Physical Activity) in the Agoraphobic Syndrome," *British Journal of Psychiatry* 122 (1973): 175–79; Orwin, "Treatment of a Situational Phobia: A Case for Running," *British Journal of Psychiatry* 125 (1974): 95–98.

42. Other references pertinent to this chapter include P. Crocker and C. Grozelle, "Reducing State Anxiety: Effects of Acute Aerobic Exercise and Autogenic Relaxation," *Journal of Sports Medicine and Physical Fitness* 31 (1991): 277–82; and J. Raglin and M. Wilson., "State Anxiety Following 20 Minutes of Leg Ergometry at Differing Intensities," *International Journal of Sports Medicine* 17 (1996): 467–71.

Chapter 6

1. R. Kessler et al., "Lifetime and 12-Month Prevalence of DSM-III-R Psychiatric Disorders in America: Results from the National Comorbidity Survey," *Archives of General Psychiatry* 51 (1994): 8–19.

2. American Psychiatric Association, *Diagnostic and Statistical Manual of Mental Disorders-IV* (Washington, DC: American Psychiatric Association, 1994).

3. L. Judd et al., "Socioeconomic Burden of Subsyndromal Depressive Symptoms and Major Depression in a Sample of the General Population," *American Journal of Psychiatry* 153 (1996): 1411–17.

4. L. Derogatis et al., "SCL-90: An Outpatient Psychiatric Rating Scale (Preliminary Report)," *Psychopharmacology Bulletin* 9 (1973): 13–27.

5. R. Spitzer et al., "Research Diagnostic Criteria," *Archives of General Psychiatry* 35 (1978): 773–82.

6. W. Zung, "Self-Rating Depression Scale," *Archives of General Psychiatry* 12 (1965): 63–70.

7. A. Beck et al., "An Inventory for Measuring Depression," *Archives of General Psychiatry* 4 (1961): 561–71.

8. T. North et al., "Effects of Exercise on Depression," *Exercise and Sport Sciences Reviews* 18 (1990): 379–415.

9. D. McDonald and J. Hodgdon, *The Psychological Effects of Aerobic Fitness Training: Research and Theory* (New York: Springer-Verlag, 1991).

10. R. Dishman, "Physical Activity and Mental Health," *Quest* 47 (1993): 362–85.

11. L. Craft and D. Landers, "The Effect of Exercise on Clinical Depression and Depression Resulting from Mental Illness: A Meta-Analysis," *Journal of Sport and Exercise Psychology* 20 (1998): 339–57.

12. M. Farmer et al., "Physical Activity and Depressive Symptoms: The NHANES I Epidemiologic Follow-Up Study," *American Journal of Epidemiology* 128 (1988): 1340–51.

13. T. Camacho et al., "Physical Activity and Depression: Evidence from the Alameda County Study," *American Journal of Epidemiology* 134 (1991): 220–31.

14. R. Paffenbarger, I. Lee, and R. Leung, "Physical Activity and Personal Characteristics Associated with Depression and Suicide in American College Men," *Acta Psychiatrica Scandinavia* 89 (1994): 16–22.

15. S. Weyerer, "Physical Inactivity and Depression in the Community: Evidence from the Upper Bavarian Field Study," *International Journal of Sports Medicine* 13 (1992): 492–96.

16. K. Gøtestam and T. Stiles, "Physical Exercise and Cognitive Vulnerability: A Longitudinal Study" (paper presented at the annual meeting of the Association for the Advancement of Behavior Therapy, San Francisco, 1990).

17. E. Martinsen, L. Sandvik, and O. Kolbjomsrud, "Aerobic Exercise in the Treatment of Nonpsychotic Mental Disorders," *Nordic Journal of Psychiatry* 43 (1989): 411–15.

18. J. Greist et al., "Running as a Treatment for Depression," *Comprehensive Psychiatry* 20 (1979): 41–54.

19. M. Klein et al., "A Comparative Outcome Study of Group Psychotherapy vs. Exercise Treatments for Depression," *International Journal of Mental Health* 13 (1985): 148–77.

20. J. Freemont and L. Craighead, "Aerobic Exercise and Cognitive Therapy in the Treatment of Dysphoric Moods," *Cognitive Therapy and Research* 2 (1987): 241–51.

22. I. McCann and D. Holmes, "Influence of Aerobic Exercise on Depression," *Journal of Personality and Social Psychology* 46 (1984): 1142–47.

23. E. Doyne, D. Chambless, and L. Beutler, "Aerobic Exercise as a Treatment for Depression in Women," *Behavioral Therapy* 14 (1983): 434–40.

24. W. Sime, "Exercise in the Treatment and Prevention of Depression," in *Exercise and Mental Health*, ed. W. Morgan and S. Goldston (Washington, DC: Hemisphere, 1987), pp. 145–52.

25. E. Doyne et al., "Running versus Weight-Lifting in the Treatment of Depression," *Journal of Consulting and Clinical Psychology* 55 (1987): 748–54.

26. Ibid.

27. N. Mutrie, "Exercise as a Treatment for Moderate Depression in the UK National Health Service," in *Sport, Health, Psychology, and Exercise Symposium Proceedings* (London: Sports Council and Health Education Authority, 1988): 96–105.

28. E. Martinsen et al., "Effects of Aerobic Exercise on Depression: A Controlled Trial," *British Medical Journal* 291 (1985): 109.

29. E. Martinsen et al., "Comparing Aerobic and Non-Aerobic Forms of Exercise in the Treatment of Clinical Depression: A Randomized Trial," *Comprehensive Psychiatry* 30 (1989): 324–31.

30. M. Babyak et al., "Exercise Treatment for Major Depression: Maintenance of Therapeutic Effect at 10 Months," *Psychosomatic Medicine* 62 (2000): 633–38.

31. K. Hays, *Working It Out: Using Exercise in Psychotherapy* (Washington, DC: American Psychological Association, 2002).

32. L. Heinisch, "Working It Out: Using Exercise to Fight Depression," *City Sports* (June 1993).

33. Sime, "Exercise in the Treatment and Prevention of Depression," pp. 145–52.

34. National Institute of Mental Health, *Electroconvulsive Therapy: A Consensus Statement* (Bethesda, MD: U.S. Department of Health and Human Services, 1985).

35. J. K. McNeil, E. M. LeBlanc, and M. Joyner, "The Effect of Exercise on Depressive Symptoms in the Moderately Depressed Elderly," *Psychology and Aging* 6 (1991): 487–88.

36. Ibid.

37. Greist, "Running as a Treatment," pp. 41–54.

38. L. Zeiss and R. Munoz, "Nonspecific Improvement Effects in Depression Using Interpersonal Skills Training, Pleasant Activities Schedules, or Cognitive Training," *Journal of Consulting and Clinical Psychology* 47 (1979): 427–39.

39. S. Stahl, *Essential Psychopharmacology: Neuroscientific Basis and Practical Implications* (Cambridge: Cambridge University Press, 2000), pp. 147–53.

40. Ibid., pp. 245–95.

41. R. Wurtman, "Nutrients That Modify Brain Function," *Scientific American* (April 1982): 50–59.

42. F. Chaouloff, "The Serotonin Hypothesis," in *Physical Activity and Mental Health*, ed. W. Morgan (Washington, DC: Taylor & Francis, 1997), pp. 179–98.

43. J. Buckworth and R. Dishman, *Exercise Psychology* (Champaign, IL: Human Kinetics, 2000), p. 150.

44. B. Azar, "Exercise Fuels the Brain's Stress Buffers," *American Psychological Association Monitor* (July 1996).

45. S. Stahl, *Essential Psychopharmacology*, p. 187.

46. E. Gould et al., "Learning Enhances Adult Neurogenesis in the Hippocampal Formation," *Nature Neuroscience* 2 (1999): 859–61; H. van Praag, G. Kempermann, and F. Gage, "Running Increases Cell Proliferation and Neurogenesis in the Adult Mouse Dentate Gyrus," *Nature Neuroscience* 2 (1999): 266–70.

47. Stahl, *Essential Psychopharmacology*, p. 187.

48. M. Kramer et al., "Distinct Mechanism for Antidepressant Activity by Blockade of Central Substance P Receptors," *Science* 286 (1998): 1640–45.

49. Other references pertinent to this chapter include R. Dishman, "The Norepinephrine Hypothesis," in *Physical Activity and Mental Health*, ed. W. Morgan (Washington, DC: Taylor & Francis, 1997), p. 210; H. O'Neal, A. Dunn, and E. Martinsen, "Depression and Exercise," *International Journal of Sport Psychology* 31 (2000): 110–35.

Chapter 7

1. E. Martinsen, L. Sandvik, and O. Kolbjomsrud, "Aerobic Exercise in the Treatment of Nonpsychotic Mental Disorders," *Nordic Journal of Psychiatry* 43 (1989): 411–15.

2. American Psychiatric Association, *Diagnostic and Statistical Manual of Mental Disorders* (Washington, DC: American Psychiatric Association, 1994).

3. Ibid.

4. A. Frankel and J. Murphy, "Physical Fitness and Personality in Alcoholism," *Quarterly Journal of Studies on Alcoholism* 35 (1974): 1272–78; V. Gary and D. Guthrie, "The Effect of Jogging on Physical Fitness and Self-Concept in Hospitalized Alcoholics," *Quarterly Journal of Studies on Alcoholism* 33 (1972): 1073–78; J. Murphy et al., "Some Suggestive Data Regarding the Relationship of Physical Fitness to Emotional Difficulties," *Newsletter for Research in Psychology* 14 (1972): 15–17.

5. R. Sinyor et al., "The Role of a Physical Fitness Program in the Treatment of Alcoholism," *Journal of Studies on Alcohol* 43 (1982): 380–86.

6. T. Murphy, R. Pagano, and G. Martlatt, "Lifestyle Modifications with Heavy Alcohol Drinkers: Effects of Aerobic Exercise and Meditation," *Addictive Behaviors* 11 (1986): 175–86.

7. D. Kremer, M. Malkin, and J. Benshoff, "Physical Activity Programs Offered in Substance Abuse Treatment Facilities," *Journal of Substance Abuse Treatment* 12 (1995): 327–33.

8. G. Tkachuk and G. Martin, "Exercise Therapy for Patients with Psychiatric Disorders: Research and Clinical Implications," *Professional Psychology: Research and Practice* 30 (1999): 275–82.

9. B. Marcus et al., "Exercise Enhances the Maintenance of Smoking Cessation in Women," *Addictive Behaviors* 20 (1995): 87–92.

10. G. Sheehan, *Running and Being: The Total Experience* (New York: Warner Books, 1979).

11. M. Zuckerman, *Behavioral Expressions and Biosocial Bases of Sensation Seeking* (New York: Cambridge University Press, 1994), p. 387.

12. J. Benjamin et al., "Population and Familial Association Between the D4 Dopamine Receptor Gene and Measures of Novelty Seeking," *Nature Genetics* 12 (1996): 81–84; R. Ebstein et al., "Dopamine D4 Receptor (D4DR) Exon III Polymorphism Associated with the Human Personality Trait of Sensation Seeking," *Nature Genetics* 12 (1996): 78–80.

13. C. Lerman et al. "Evidence Suggesting the Role of Specific Genetic Factors in Cigarette Smoking," *Health Psychology* 18 (1999): 14–20; S. Sabol et al., "A Genetic Association for Cigarette Smoking Behavior," *Health Psychology* 18 (1999): 7–13.

14. M. Zuckerman, *The Psychobiology of Personality* (New York: Cambridge University Press, 1991), p. 98.

15. P. Hoffman, "The Endorphin Hypothesis," in *Physical Activity and Mental Health*, ed. W. Morgan (Washington, DC: Taylor & Francis, 1997), pp. 173–74.

16. Ibid.

17. E. Martinsen and R. Dishman, "Antidepressant Effects of Physical Activity," in *Physical Activity and Mental Health*, ed. W. Morgan (Washington, DC: Taylor & Francis, 1997), p. 100.

18. W. Fordyce et al., "Pain Complaint–Exercise Performance Relationship in Chronic Pain," *Pain* 10 (1981): 311–21.

19. W. Fordyce et al., "Operant Conditioning in the Treatment of Chronic Pain," *Archives of Physical Medicine and Rehabilitation* 54 (1973): 399–408.

20. Tkachuk and Martin, "Exercise Therapy for Patients with Psychiatric Disorders," pp. 275–82.

21. Fordyce et al., "Pain Complaint–Exercise Performance," pp. 311–21.

22. Tkachuk and Martin, "Exercise Therapy for Patients with Psychiatric Disorders," pp. 275–82.

Chapter 8

1. J. Morris et al., "Incidence and Prediction of Ischemic Heart Disease in London Busmen," *Lancet* 1 (1966): 552–59.

2. J. Morris et al., "Vigorous Exercise in Leisure Time and the Incidence of Coronary Heart Disease," *Lancet* 1 (1973): 333–39.

3. R. Paffenbarger et al., "Energy Expenditure, Cigarette Smoking, and Blood Pressure Level as Related to Death from Specific Diseases," *American Journal of Epidemiology* 108 (1978): 12–18.

4. I.-M. Lee and R. Paffenbarger, "Exercise Intensity and Longevity in Men: The Harvard Alumni Health Study," *Journal of the American Medical Association* 273, no. 15 (1995).

5. J. Brody, "Vigorous Workouts, Longer Life," *New York Times* (April 19, 1995).

6. S. Blair et al., "Physical Fitness and All-Cause Mortality: A Prospective Study of Healthy Men and Women," *Journal of the American Medical Association* 262 (1989): 2395–401.

7. S. Blair et al., "Influences of Cardiorespiratory Fitness and Other Precursors on Cardiovascular Disease and All-Cause Mortality in Men and Women," *Journal of the American Medical Association* 276 (1996): 205–10.

8. J. Manson et al., "A Prospective Study of Walking as Compared to Vigorous Exercise in the Prevention of Coronary Heart Disease in Women," *New England Journal of Medicine* 341 (1999): 650–58.

9. M. Tanasescu et al., "Exercise Type and Intensity in Relation to Coronary Heart Disease in Men," *Journal of the American Medical Association* 288 (2000): 1994–2000.

10. U. Kujala et al., "The Relationship of Leisure-Time Physical Activity and Mortality," *Journal of the American Medical Association* 279 (1998): 440–44.

11. Department of Health and Human Services, *Physical Activity and Health: A Report of the Surgeon General* (Atlanta: U.S. Department of Health and Human Services, 1996), pp. 1–8, 85–172, 175–207; NIH Consensus Panel, "Physical Activity and Cardiovascular Health: NIH Consensus Development Panel on Physical Activity and Cardiovascular Health," *Journal of the American Medical Association* 276 (1996): 241–46.

12. I.-M. Lee and R. Paffenbarger, "Physical Activity and Stroke Incidence: The Harvard Alumni Health Study," *Stroke* 29 (1998): 2049–54.

13. F. Hu et al., "Physical Activity and Risk of Stroke in Women," *Journal of the American Medical Association* 283 (2000): 2961–67.

14. J. Fries, "Aging, Cumulative Disability, and the Compression of Morbidity," *COMP THER* 27 (2001): 322–29.

15. S. Blair and M. Wei, "Sedentary Habits, Health, and Function in Older Women and Men," *American Journal of Health Promotion* 15 (2000): 1–8.

16. E. Nadel, "Physiological Adaptations to Aerobic Training," *American Scientist* 73 (1985): 334–43.

17. W. Haskell et al., "Coronary Artery Size and Dilating Capacity in Ultradistance Runners," *Circulation* 87 (1993): 1076–82.

18. Ibid.

19. H. Hartung and J. Foreyt, "Effect of Alcohol Intake on High Density Lipoprotein Cholesterol Levels in Runners and Inactive Men," *Journal of the American Medical Association* 249 (1983): 747–50; H. Higdon, "In with the Good," *Runner's World* (December 1987): 50–54.

20. P. Wood, W. Haskell, and H. Klein, "The Distribution of Plasma Lipids in Middle-Aged Male Runners," *Metabolism* 25 (1976): 1249–57.

21. P. Wood et al., "Changes in Plasma Lipids and Lipoproteins in Overweight Men During Weight Loss Through Dieting as Compared with Exercise," *New England Journal of Medicine* 319 (1988): 1173–79.

22. P. Williams et al., "The Effects of Running Mileage and Duration on Plasma Lipoprotein Levels," *Journal of the American Medical Association* 247 (1982): 2674–79; P. Wood, "Running Away from Heart Disease: Becoming Familiar with Your Lipoproteins Could Save Your Life," *Runner's World* (June 1979): 78–81; P. Wood, "Does Running Help Prevent Heart Attacks?" *Runner's World* (December 1979): 85–91; P. Wood, "The Eat-More, Weigh-Less Diet," *Runner's World* (September 1980): 42–44; P. Wood, *California Diet and Exercise Program* (Mountain View, CA: Anderson World Books, 1983); Wood, Haskell, and Klein, "Distribution of Plasma Lipids," pp. 1249–57; Wood et al., "Changes in Plasma Lipids," pp. 1173–79.

23. R. McCunney, "Fitness, Heart Disease, and High-Density Lipoproteins: A Look at the Relationships," *Physician and Sportsmedicine* 15 (1987): 67–79.

24. Wood et al., "Changes in Plasma Lipids," pp. 1173–79.

25. Hartung and Foreyt, "Effect of Alcohol Intake," pp. 747–50; Higdon, "In with the Good," pp. 50–54; Williams et al., "Effects of Running Mileage," pp. 2674–79; P. Wood and W. Haskell, "The Effect of Exercise on Plasma High Density Lipoproteins," *Lipids* 14 (1979): 417–27.

26. J. Hanna, "Physical Activity and Cancer," *Fifty-Plus Bulletin* (December 2000): 1–9.

27. D. Batty and I. Thune, "Does Physical Activity Prevent Cancer?" [online], bmj.com/cgi/content/full/321/7274/1424 [December 9, 2000].

28. B. Rockhill et al., "A Prospective Study of Recreational Physical Activity and Breast Cancer Risk," *Archives of Internal Medicine* 159 (1999): 2290–96.

29. I. Thune et al., "Physical Activity and the Risk of Breast Cancer," *New England Journal of Medicine* 336 (1997): 1269–75.

30. L. Bernstein et al., "Physical Exercise and Reduced Risk of Breast Cancer in Young Women," *Journal of the National Cancer Institute* 86 (1995): 1403–408.

31. C. Friedenreich, K. Courney, and H. Bryant, "Relation Between Intensity of Physical Activity and Breast Cancer Risk Reduction," *Medicine and Science in Sports and Exercise* 33 (2001): 1538–45.

32. Bernstein et al., "Physical Exercise and Reduced Risk," pp. 1403–408.

33. Ibid.

34. G. Wyshak and R. Frisch, "Breast Cancer among Former College Athletes Compared to Non-Athletes: A 15-Year Follow-Up," *British Journal of Cancer* 82 (2000): 726–30.

35. "Runner's World Survey," *Runner's World* (May 1989).

36. F. Behling, "Health Survey: 2002 Results," *Fifty-Plus Bulletin* (May 2003).

37. M. Cimons, "Experts Give More Weight to Exercise in Preventing Cancer," *Los Angeles Times* [online], www.beezodogsplace.com/Pages/Articles/ExerciseCancer/.

38. C. Tymchuk et al., "Evidence of an Inhibitory Effect of Diet and Exercise on Prostate Cancer Cell Growth," *Journal of Urology* 166 (2001): 1185–89.

39. K. Schmitz, "Cancer Risk Reduction: Exercise and Cancer" [online], www.cancer.umn.edu/page/patients/riskred3.html [June 18, 2002].

40. Diabetes Prevention Program Research Group, "Reduction in the Incidence of Type 2 Diabetes with Lifestyle Intervention or Metformin," *New England Journal of Medicine* 346 (2002): 393–403.

41. E. Gregg et al., "Relationship of Walking to Mortality among US Adults with Diabetes," *Archives of Internal Medicine* 163 (2003): 1440–47.

42. N. Lane and J. Buckwalter, "Exercise: A Cause of Osteoarthritis?" *Rheumatic Disease Clinics of North America* 19 (1993): 617–33.

43. N. Lane et al., "Aging, Long-Distance Running, and the Development of Musculoskeletal Disability," *Journal of the American Medical Association* 82 (1987): 772–80.

44. Osteoarthritis Information Center, "The Latest Research on the Role of Exercise in Osteoarthritis Treatment," American Federation for Aging Research [online], www.onfaging.org/d-8-r-exerc.html [March 28, 2003].

45. J. Francisco, "At 95, She's Still Dancing: Maintaining Activity Key to Health in Later Years," *San Jose Mercury News* (September 2, 2003).

46. N. Lane et al., "Long-Distance Running, Bone Density, and Osteoarthritis," *Journal of the American Medical Association* 255 (1986): 1147–51.

47. D. Feskanich et al., "Walking and Leisure-Time Activity and Risk of Hip Fracture in Postmenopausal Women," *Journal of the American Medical Association* 288 (2002): 2300–306.

48. R. Sapolsky, *Why Zebras Don't Get Ulcers* (New York: W. H. Freeman, 2000), pp. 103–104.

49. American College of Sports Medicine, "ACSM Position Stand on Osteoporosis and Exercise," *Medicine and Science in Sport and Exercise* 27 (1995): i–vii.

50. D. Nieman, "Exercise, Upper Respiratory Tract Infection, and the Immune System," *Medicine and Science in Sport and Exercise* 26 (1994): 128–39.

51. D. Nieman et al., "Infectious Episodes in Runners Before and after the Los Angeles Marathon," *Journal of Sports Medicine and Physical Fitness* 30 (1990): 316–28; E. Peters and E. Bateman, "Respiratory Tract Infections: An Epidemiological Survey," *South African Medical Journal* 64 (1983): 582–84; 50. D. Nieman et al., "The Effects of Long Endurance Running on Immune System Parameters and Lymphocyte Function in Experienced Marathoners," *International Journal of Sports Medicine* 10 (1989): 317–23.

52. D. Nieman et al., "The Effects of Moderate Exercise Training on Natural Killer Cells and Acute Upper Respiratory Tract Infections," *International Journal of Sports Medicine* 11 (1990): 467–73.

53. D. Nieman et al., "Physical Activity and Immune Function in Elderly Women," *Medicine and Science in Sports and Exercise* 25 (1993): 823–31.

54. Nieman, "Exercise, Upper Respiratory Tract Infection," pp. 132–34.

55. Y. Kasuka, H. Kondou, and K. Morimoto, "Healthy Lifestyles Are Associated with Higher Natural Killer Cell Activity," *Preventive Medicine* 21 (1992): 602–15.

56. Nieman, "Exercise, Upper Respiratory Tract Infection," p. 135.

Chapter 9

1. M. Lean, T. Hans, and J. Seidell, "Impairment of Health and Quality of Life in People with Large Waist Circumference," *Lancet* 351 (1998): 853.

2. A. Peeters et al., "Obesity in Adulthood and Its Consequences for Life Expectancy: A Life-Table Analysis," *Annals of Internal Medicine* 138 (2003): 24–32.

3. K. Fontaine et al., "Years of Life Lost Due to Obesity," *Journal of the American Medical Association* 289 (2003): 187–93.

4. E. Calle et al., "Overweight, Obesity, and Mortality from Cancer in a Prospectively Studied Cohort of U.S. Adults," *New England Journal of Medicine* 348 (2003): 1625–38.

5. I. Hajjar and T. Kotchen, "Trends in Prevalence, Awareness, Treatment, and Control of Hypertension in the United States, 1988–2000," *Journal of the American Medical Association* 290 (2003): 199–206.

6. S. Kenchaiah et al., "Obesity and the Risk of Heart Failure," *New England Journal of Medicine* 347 (2002): 305–13.

7. G. Roth et al., "Biomarkers of Caloric Restriction May Predict Longevity in Humans," *Science* 297 (2002): 297–311.

8. C.-K. Lee et al., "Gene Expression Profile of Aging and Its Retardation by Caloric Restriction," *Science* 285 (1999): 1390–93.

9. A. Stunkard et al., "The Body-Mass Index of Twins Who Have Been Reared Apart," *New England Journal of Medicine* 322 (1990): 1483–87.

10. C. Bouchard et al., "The Reponse to Long-Term Overfeeding in Identical Twins," *New England Journal of Medicine* 322 (1990): 1477–82.

11. K. Brownell, "Obesity: Understanding and Treating a Serious, Prevalent, and Refractory Disorder," *Journal of Consulting and Clinical Psychology* 50 (1982): 820–40.

12. R. Leibel, M. Rosenbaum, and J. Hirsch, "Changes in Energy Expenditure Resulting from Altered Body Weight," *New England Journal of Medicine* 332 (1995): 621–28.

13. P. Pacy, J. Webster, and J. Garrow, "Exercise and Obesity," *Sports Medicine* 3 (1986): 89–113.

14. G. Kolata, "Metabolic Catch-22 of Exercise Regimens," *Science* 236 (1987): 146–47.

15. Ibid.

16. C. Barlow et al., "Physical Fitness, Mortality, and Obesity," *International Journal of Obesity* 19 (supplement 1995).

17. D. Costill, *A Scientific Approach to Distance Running* (Los Altos, CA: Track and Field News, 1979).

18. D. Beir and V. Young, "Exercise and Blood Pressure: Nutritional Considerations," *Annals of Internal Medicine* 98 (1983): 864–69.

19. D. Costill, "Coffee Makes Running Easier," *Runner's World* (July 1978).

20. Costill, *Scientific Approach to Distance Running*.

21. S. Bortz, "Hold the Bun! Hold the Meat! Hold the . . ." *Fifty-Plus Bulletin* (May 2002).

22. Ibid.

23. American College of Sports Medicine, "Position Stand: The Recommended Quantity and Quality of Exercise for Developing and Maintaining Cardiorespiratory and Muscular Fitness, and Flexibility in Healthy Adults," *Medicine and Science in Sports and Exercise* 30, no. 6 (1998): 975–91.

24. American College of Sports Medicine, "Position Stand: Proper and Improper Weight Loss Programs," *Medicine and Science in Sports and Exercise* 15 (1983): ix–xiii.

25. M. Skender et al., "Comparison of 2-Year Weight Loss Trends in Behavioral Treatments of Obesity: Diet, Exercise, and Combination Interventions," *Journal of the American Dietetic Association* 96 (1996): 342–46.

Chapter 10

1. K. Cooper, "Running Without Fear," *Runner's World* (August 1985).

2. M. Ragosta et al., "Death During Recreational Exercise in the State of Rhode Island," *Medicine and Science in Sports and Exercise* 16 (1983): 339–42.

3. M. Freidman et al., "Instantaneous and Sudden Deaths, Clinical and Pathological Differentiation in Coronary Artery Disease," *Journal of the American Medical Association* 225 (1973): 1319–28; L. Opie, "Sudden Death and Sport," *Lancet* 1 (1975): 263–65.

4. L. Krieger, "No One Is Immune to Heart Problems," *San Jose Mercury News* (September 22, 1998).

5. D. Siscovik et al., "Physical Activity and Primary Cardiac Arrest," *Journal of the American Medical Association* 248 (1982): 3113–17.

6. N. Lane et al., "Aging, Long-Distance Running, and the Development of Musculoskeletal Disability," *American Journal of Medicine* 82 (1987): 772–80.

7. American College of Sports Medicine, "Position Stand: The Recommended Quantity and Quality of Exercise for Developing and Maintaining Cardiorespiratory and Muscular Fitness, and Flexibility in Healthy Adults," *Medicine and Science in Sports and Exercise* 30, no. 6 (1998): 975–91.

8. W. Glasser, *Positive Addiction* (New York: Harper and Row, 1976).

9. W. Morgan, "Negative Addiction in Runners," *Physician and Sportsmedicine* 7 (1979): 57–70.

10. W. Morgan, "Selected Psychological Factors Limiting Performance: A Mental Health Model," *Medicine and Science in Sports and Exercise* 17 (1985): 94–100.

11. F. Baekeland, "Exercise Deprivation," *Archives of General Psychiatry* 22 (1970): 365–69.

12. L. Thaxton, "Physiological and Psychological Effects of Short-Term Exercise Addiction on Habitual Runners," *Journal of Sports Psychology* 4 (1982): 73–80.

13. M. Sacks, "Running Addiction," in *Psychology of Running*, ed. M. L. Sacks and M. H. Sacks (Champaign, IL: Human Kinetics, 1981); J. Williams and W. Straub, "Sport Psychology: Past, Present, and Future," in *Applied Sport Psychology: Personal Growth to Peak Performance*, 3d ed., ed. R. Singer, M. Murphy, and L. Tennant (Mountain View, CA: Mayfield, 1992).

14. R. Dishman, "Medical Psychology in Exercise and Sport," *Medical Clinics of North America* 69 (1985): 123–43.

Chapter 12

1. J. Pocari et al., "Is Fast Walking an Adequate Aerobic Training Stimulus for 30- to 69-Year-Old Men and Women?" *Physician and Sportsmedicine* 15 (1987): 119–29.

2. R. Dishman, "Exercise Adherence and Habitual Physical Activity," in *Exercise and Mental Health*, ed. W. Morgan and S. Goldston (Washington, DC: Hemisphere, 1987).

Epilogue

1. "The Nietzsche Channel: Poems/Gedichte" [online], www.geocites.com/the-nietzschechannel/ poems.htm [October 17, 2003].

2. P. Seraganian, ed., "Current Status and Future Directions in the Field of Exercise Psychology," in *Exercise Psychology: The Influence of Physical Exercise on Psychological Processes* (New York: Wiley, 1993), pp. 383–90.

INDEX